7/2018 lw

The Surface Designer's Handbook

Dyeing, Printing, Painting, and Creating Resists on Fabric

Holly Brackmann

INTERWEAVE PRESS

OCM 64084787

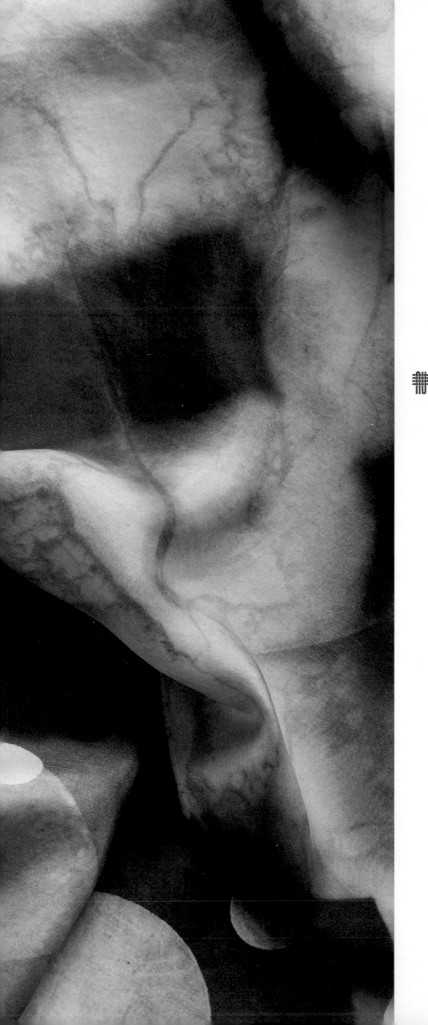

This book is dedicated with love to Roger Foote, my husband, who encourages my creative endeavors, and helped with this project in innumerable ways.

Design, Amy Thornton and Paulette Livers

Text © 2006 Holly Brackman
Photography © Interweave Press LLC

INTERWEAVE PRESS
201 East Fourth Street
Loveland, CO 80537-5655 USA
www.interweave.com

Printed and bound in China by Codra Enterprises Inc.

Library of Congress Cataloging-in-Publication Data

Brackman, Holly, 1947-
  The surface designer's handbook : dyeing, printing, painting,
and creating resists on fabric / Holly Brackman, author.
      p. cm.
  Includes bibliographical references and index.
  ISBN 13: 978-1-931499-90-3 (hardcover)
  ISBN 10: 1-931499-90-X (hardcover)
  1. Dyes and dyeing, Domestic. I. Title.
  TT854.5.B73 2006
  746.6'2--dc22
                                              2006005288

10 9 8 7 6 5 4 3 2 1

Acknowledgments

When *Handwoven* magazine editor, Madelyn van der Hoogt, and I first talked about my writing a book on surface design, I had no idea what a richly rewarding experience it would be, one that would bring together many people and many ideas.

Interweave Press employees have been especially helpful. Betsy Armstrong assisted in organizing my ideas and developing the book title. Rebecca Campbell kept me on track and made sure details were carried out. Amy Thornton and Paulette Livers, book designers, took a multitude of words, photos, and tables and organized them into beautiful form. Two photographers, Tom Liden and Joe Coca took stunning, aesthetic images.

The text of the book went through many modifications. Lolli Jacobsen, Carol Larson, and Jason Pollen were early readers who made excellent suggestions. Editor Judith Durant has been with me through the entire process, offering valuable advice and guidance. Technical editors Cheryl Kamera, Vicki Jensen of PRO Chemical & Dye, and Betsy Strauch asked difficult questions and made sure the recipes were correct. Stephanie Hoppe read through a late version of the manuscript and gave pertinent recommendations. Doug Wilson gave technical advice and allowed me to use portions of his dye glossary.

Over the years, many artists have introduced me to dye and surface design techniques. I would especially like to thank the Surface Design Association for their stimulating conferences and the extraordinary guidance of Jason Pollen, President. A few of the artists who have shared their discoveries and knowledge include Jane Dunnewold, whose concept of complex cloth encouraged me to layer surface design; Yoshiko Wada introduced me to indigo and shibori; Joy Boutrup showed me dévoré and dye transfer printing; Catharine Ellis introduced me to vat dyes and woven shibori; Ana Lisa Hedstrom taught me silk scouring and furthered my knowledge of shibori. Thanks also to the many other fiber artists who shared their photographs and ideas for this book.

Many friends and colleagues have assisted me in making this book a reality. Lolli Jacobsen, Lynn Harris, Anita Sison, Lelia Kazimi, Cassie Gibson, and Jane Spanbauer made samples and helped as stylists for a two-day photo shoot. Roxy Wells listened to daily descriptions of the book process during our walks, and gave valuable advice. Meridith Randall, Dean of Instruction/Acting Chief Instructional Officer at Mendocino College, lent her support and allowed us to use the art department for a photo shoot.

Thanks to the students I've met during my thirty years of teaching at Mendocino College who have continually asked, "What if?" They have stretched my knowledge, inspired me to learn new techniques, and provided me with answers. Several of the artists in this book are former students who have gone on to develop their own textile voices.

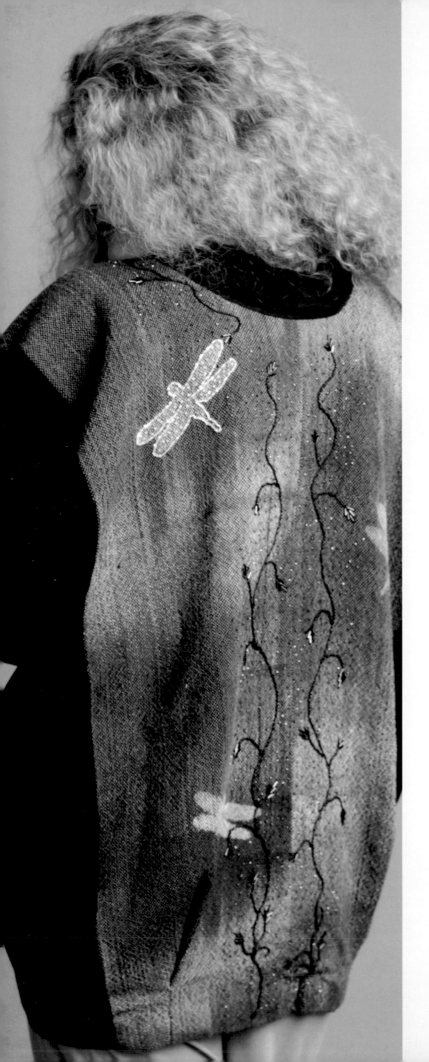

Contents

Foreword

When Holly Brackmann asked me to look over and comment on her "in progress" book on surface design, focusing primarily on dyes and dye processes, I was enthusiastic and grateful. After reading it in one sitting, I was euphoric! This is the textbook we need. A recent survey of members of the Surface Design Association reveals, not surprisingly, that dye techniques are by far their area of greatest interest. We have all been waiting for the definitive "dyer's manual" to turn to, to unravel the mysteries of accurately getting color into and out of cloth, and now we have it. I have been a professional fiber artist, textile designer, and educator for more than forty remarkable years, and feel qualified to say that no other book in print in the United States covers so thoroughly as many key approaches to surface design.

Holly Brackmann has written a superb, well-researched, user-friendly textbook that will serve our community well for many years. Artists, designers, students, and hobbyists will welcome it. Holly has put together dye, resist, discharge, and special technique recipes that are easy to follow and provide reliable, repeatable results. In addition, the sections on screen and monoprinting will be particularly useful in the classroom. Sections on safety issues are invaluable to both serious and casual dyers.

The significant increase in the number of new surface designers in the last few years is, in part, due to the great variety of extraordinary processes and techniques available to us. This book lays out a step-by-step approach to their mastery. We are all fortunate indeed that Holly Brackmann has given us just the right tool!

—Jason Pollen, President
Surface Design Association
Chair, Fiber Department
Kansas City Art Institute

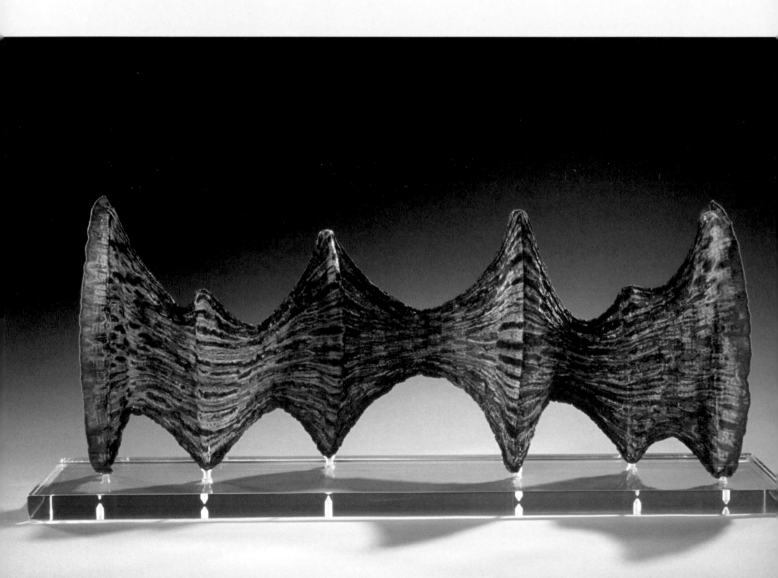

Introduction

Dyeing and applying surface design to fabric are expressive, exciting, and richly rewarding activities. That is why I began exploring the topic. A plethora of techniques allows you to create unique colors and effects, transforming fabric by adding depth and complexity. While making a woven wall hanging as part of a graduate seminar at UCLA, I needed specific colors of unspun mohair, which I prepared on the family stove. In retrospect, I handled the fibers entirely wrong and ignored safe dye practices besides. I've come a long way since then.

The following pages lay the groundwork for inspirational surface design by first discussing the basics of studio practices, safety, fibers, and color. I cover the foundations of surface design techniques by introducing the major dye groups: fiber-reactive, acid, vat, and disperse. Next, I show how to alter and change surfaces using discharging, screen printing, monoprinting, stamping, stenciling, resists, dévoré, and textile paints. Embellishments—foiling, embroidery, beadwork, collage—provide a final touch. I have included many hints that have helped my students as well as illustrations of techniques and fabrics by many artists for clarity and inspiration. Vignettes of dye and technical history explain the evolution of synthetic dyes.

Synthetic dyes were a revelation to me. They promise reproducible colors, are relatively safe, and are also easy to use. They can be used on many types of fabrics and adapted to a wide variety of techniques. These dyes have been a part of my college and workshop teaching for more than thirty years.

Like many other artists, I began dyeing with Procion MX fiber-reactive dyes, the most widely used studio dye. Eager to learn other dye and surface techniques I began my exploration of acid, vat, and disperse dyes. As I began to understand each dye's characteristics and how it interacts with other dyes, I found that I could combine dyes to produce effects far beyond my original goal of producing a single color. As an example, consider *Shrouded Shibori* (at left and right), which I wove from white polyester/cotton yarn. First, I applied fiber-reactive dye, which I subsequently discharged in certain areas with vat dye. Next, I mixed disperse dyes with dévoré solution to burn out parts of the surface and add color in a single step. Finally, I heat-set the polyester pleats and applied foil. I had used a total of three dyes and three surface design techniques on this one textile. As you can see, dyeing is much more than plunging yarn or fabric into a dyepot.

Use this book as a starting point or to enhance your knowledge, whether you are a student, educator, hobbyist, beginner learning independently, or knowledgeable surface design artist. Use it as a guide to dyes and surface techniques and as inspiration for experimentation. The processes may be used with commercial and handwoven fabric, yarn, handmade paper, wood, and leather.

Inspiration for surface design is all around us; it may come from a picture in a magazine, a pattern of fallen leaves on the sidewalk, a shadow pattern across the kitchen floor, or a piece of beautiful cloth. Find your own voice. Experiment, try different dyes and techniques to discover your personal style, and let your creativity flow into glorious textiles. Happy dyeing!

Facing page: Shrouded Shibori *by Holly Brackmann, 11½" h × 27" w × 6" d (29 cm × 68.5 cm × 15 cm) mounted. Handwoven polyester/cotton with dévoré and woven shibori; fiber-reactive, vat, and disperse dyes; metallic foil; permanently pleated. Above: Detail. Photos by Hap Sakwa.*

Chapter One
Studio Practices and Safety

Location and Physical Space Requirements

The ideal dye studio space is isolated from any living space. To keep you and your family safe, do not use your home kitchen or bathroom. If you don't have the luxury of a separate building, try the basement, laundry room, patio, or garage. You do not need to begin with a large, fully equipped studio. Start small with a few techniques on small pieces of fabric and a single type of dye. Increase equipment and studio area as your knowledge and understanding of the materials and techniques develop.

Good natural light or color-corrected bulbs are essential for matching colors. Studio floors should be easy to clean; painted concrete or vinyl are the best surfaces, but you may also cover the floor with plastic sheeting. It is important to be able to mop and wipe up any spilled materials.

Electrical outlets for plugging in a mixer, clip-on lamps, a hair dryer, or a fan are helpful. Hot and cold running water in a large sink are ideal but not absolutely necessary. An outside garden hose can be used as a water source.

Solutions that must be heated require a stove or hotplate. Commercial natural-gas stockpot stoves are costly but excellent—the heating surface is low, limiting undue back strain when you're lifting heavy pots. A good outdoor heat source is a propane camp stove or crab cooker.

A top-loading washing machine is useful for preparing fabric for dyeing and for extracting water after dyeing. It can also be used for dyeing large quantities of fabric. The family washer may be used if you clean it after each dye process. A dryer is optional. An iron and ironing board, to be used only in your studio, are essential for pressing fabric and for techniques such as foiling and dévoré.

Because minerals in hard water can adversely affect solutions used in dyeing, have your household water tested for hardness. Many water retailers and water-conditioning specialists will do the test free of charge.

Tools and Equipment
Dyeing Containers

Dyepot materials must not react with dyes and other chemicals. Therefore, do not use aluminum or cast iron containers as they react with these substances. Plastic containers work well for cool and warm dyeing. For hot dyeing, stainless steel pots are long lasting and durable. Unchipped enamel pots are satisfactory, but the rust that develops in chipped spots will interfere with the processes. Stirring rods can be stainless steel or plastic spoons, plastic chopsticks, or dowels coated with several layers of polyurethane.

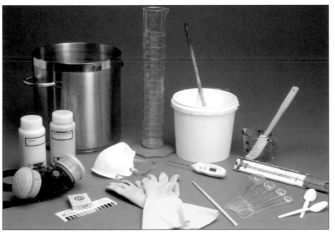

1.1 A variety of dye tools including stirring stick, chopstick, measuring spoons, graduated cylinder, measuring cup, plastic bucket, stainless steel pot, labeled storage containers, pH paper, thermometer, scraper, dust mask, respirator, rubber gloves, and plastic spoons. Photo by Tom Liden.

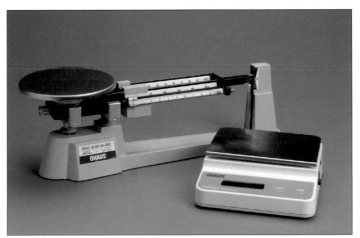

1.2 Metric weighing devices: a triple-beam balance and an electronic scale with tare. Photo by Tom Liden.

Opposite: Shibori dévoré scarf by Holly Brackmann. 69"l × 8"w (175 cm × 20.5 cm). Photo by Joe Coca.

Measuring Tools

Careful measurement of ingredients is essential for creating reproducible dye colors. A scale or balance is especially helpful for accurate measurements of dyes and chemicals. You can begin with a diet or postal scale. More costly, but also much more accurate, are a triple-beam balance or a digital electronic scale accurate to 0.1 g. The latter should have a capacity of at least 500 g and a tare feature (resets to zero to account for the weight of the container). When using a triple-beam balance to measure dry dye, weigh the empty container and record its weight. Set the sliding block to the total of the weight of the container plus the desired amount of dye and then add the dye until the pointer is at the balance point. If using an electronic scale with a tare, place the container on the scale, press the tare button, and then add dye to the correct weight. Liquid measuring tools include U.S./metric cups (available in grocery and kitchen stores), graduated metric cylinders and beakers (glass or plastic), plastic or stainless steel measuring spoons, and syringes (available from farm or pet suppliers) marked in cubic centimeters (cc) or milliliters (ml) for measuring small amounts of liquids.

Storage Containers

Dyes and chemicals should be stored in glass or plastic jars. You may also use wide mouth glass canning jars, plastic yogurt containers, recycled restaurant jars, or buckets with lids. Always label and date each container as you fill it.

Miscellaneous Tools

Miscellaneous tools include a color wheel; scissors; needle and thread; electronic calculator; timer; pH paper strips or rolls; immersion thermometer; stainless steel T-pins; natural bristle and foam brushes; plastic funnel; plastic wrap; hair dryer; electric blender; electric fan; electric mixer or stainless whisk; newspapers to place under dye buckets and in the mixing box; and rags, sponges, and paper towels for cleanup.

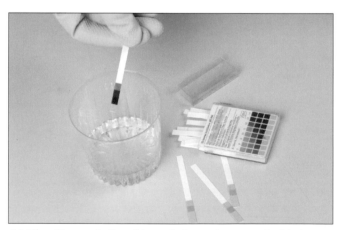

1.3 The pH paper is dipped in a solution and compared with the chart on the packaging. Some dyes require monitoring of the pH level. Photo by Tom Liden.

Record Keeping

Record keeping is essential. Why create an amazing piece of fabric if you can't later figure out how you got a specific color or effect because you have no notes? Make copies of the "Dye Worksheet" on page 119 and use one with each dye project to record all dye and chemical calculations. Keep your dye worksheets in a binder or manila folders. Your records will allow you to reproduce the colors you desire, which is especially important if you plan on going into business and taking orders for dyed fabrics.

Dye Disposal

Occasional dyebaths (several per month) from an artist's studio are not considered hazardous when poured down the drain into city sewage systems. The large quantities of water used in rinsing greatly dilute the concentration of dyebath chemicals that go down the drain. Such diluted dyebaths similarly are not harmful to septic systems. When in doubt, consult with your local sewage district or environmental health department. It is better for the environment to adjust the dyebath's pH level to neutral (pH 7) before disposing. Neutralize an acid dyebath with soda ash. Neutralize fiber-reactive or other alkaline dyebath with a weak acid such as vinegar. Do not dump used dyebaths on the ground or into storm drains, which flow to streams or rivers.

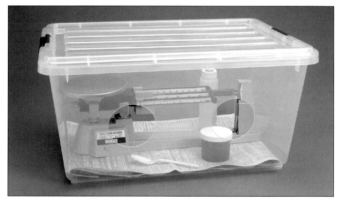

1.4 A mixing box helps to keep dye particles and other powders from escaping into your breathing environment. To make a mixing box, cut holes for arms in the side of a plastic container large enough to hold a scale and other containers. Cut or fold a stack of newspapers to fit in the bottom of the box. Before measuring dry chemicals or pasting dye, mist the top sheet of newspaper and replace the clear plastic lid. The damp paper will attract dry dye powder or chemicals, keeping them from wafting through the air. Discard the damp top sheet after each process. Idea for using a plastic box by Jane Spanbauer. Photo by Tom Liden.

Studio Safety

Some of the materials and chemicals used in dyeing and decorating fabrics are potentially harmful. Before beginning any process, learn how to safely handle the supplies for that process. Maintain clean work habits and dispose of materials in an environmentally safe manner.

- Do not eat, drink, or smoke in the area where dyes and chemicals are used as you will be ingesting minute amounts of those substances, which could be harmful.
- Wear protective coverings for your nose, mouth, eyes, hands, and clothing.
- Work in a well-ventilated but draft-free room. If spraying dyes, use an exhaust system such as a spray booth or laboratory hood or work outdoors away from living areas and vegetable gardens. When heating dyes, use an exhaust fan in front of an open window to direct vapors away from yourself.
- Weigh and mix dry dyes and chemicals on a surface covered with a dampened newspaper and near a local exhaust fan, or use a mixing box (see illustration 1.4). Some dye powders are extremely fine and easily inhaled. Some airborne particles can even spot fabrics across the room.
- Never mingle dye equipment with eating or regular kitchen utensils.
- Keep dyes and chemicals in tightly covered containers away from children and pets. You should have a refrigerator dedicated to storage of studio materials.
- Label and date all dyes, stock solutions, and chemicals. Some have only a short shelf life and should be discarded when that period has expired.
- All work surfaces should have a plastic covering or otherwise be easily cleaned with damp towels or sponges.
- Wipe up spills immediately. Do not sweep up dry spills with a broom; instead, use a damp paper towel or wet mop.
- Have a fire extinguisher and first-aid kit containing bandages and burn and cut medications in the dye area.
- Know your materials. For each product, ask for a Material Safety Data Sheet (MSDS) from the manufacturer or dye supplier to learn its hazards, proper handling techniques, and emergency first-aid measures. Dye and chemical suppliers are legally required to provide safety sheets for every product that they sell. Keep MSDS sheets in a binder for easy reference.
- Do not use toxic chemicals, dyes, or paints if you are pregnant or lactating.

Personal Protective Coverings

The lungs and skin are especially susceptible to toxins from dyes and chemicals.

- Wear old clothes when dyeing and wash them separately when soiled.
- Wear a full-length smock or apron. Plastic aprons are easy to wash. Use these garments only in the studio to avoid introducing chemicals into living spaces.
- Wear waterproof gloves to protect your hands. For many dye recipes, thin disposable or household gloves are sufficient, but when working with hot chemicals or lye, which becomes hot when mixed with water, wear heavier gloves and glove liners for added protection. Never clean dye-stained hands with bleach; instead, use a hand cleaner such as Reduran.
- A disposable dust mask (available at hardware stores) may be sufficient to protect you from occasional exposure to dye powders and dry chemicals, but it will not protect you from vapors.
- For processes involving vapors, such as vat dyes or dévoré, wear a well-fitting respirator with the appropriate cartridge. The most common type of respirator covers the mouth, nose, and chin and can be used with a variety of cartridges. One type of cartridge protects you from organic vapor, dust, and mist while another protects you from acid gas. Have a safety supplier fit you for the respirator; people with a small face and/or a beard can be difficult to fit. Replace respirator cartridges as needed: if you smell a contaminant while wearing the respirator, it is past time to replace the cartridge. The service life of a cartridge depends upon many factors, including environmental conditions, breathing rate, cartridge filtering capacity, and the amount of contaminants in the air. Check with your safety supplier or the manufacturer for more details. Store respirators in resealable plastic bags. Some doctors advise against a pregnant woman's wearing a respirator because doing so reduces her supply of oxygen to the fetus—one reason pregnant women should not use toxic chemicals, dyes, or paints. Wearing a respirator does not take the place of good ventilation.
- Wear eye protection. Goggles will prevent splashes from dyes, chemicals, and spray mists getting into your eyes. Wearers of contact lenses should wear unvented goggles because contacts can absorb dye powders and chemicals. Don't wear contacts when using lye: a drop of lye can weld a contact lens to the eyeball.

1.5 The Safe Dyer. Although not all dye processes require this much covering, be safe and wear proper protective equipment when working with dyes and chemicals. Photo by Tom Liden.

Chapter Two
Dyes, Fibers, and Fabrics

Dyes

Dyes are colorants that are dissolved in water and through a chemical reaction impart a particular hue to the fabric while not changing the hand (feel) of the textile. The best ones are lightfast and washfast—they resist fading and remain in the fabric when it is laundered. Most dyes work better on some fabrics than on others. It is important to know which dyes to use with which fibers. See "Dyes and Fibers," Chart A, below.

Synthetic dye was discovered by accident in 1856 by William Perkin, who was trying to make quinine (a drug to control fever) from coal tar. Instead, he produced aniline purple (mauveine) when the compound was dissolved in alcohol. Conditions were ripe for Perkin's discovery. The

2.1 An assortment of synthetic dyes including union (Rit), Cibacron F, WashFast acid, Lanaset, vat, disperse, Procion H, and Procion MX. Photo by Tom Liden.

Chart A Dyes and Fibers

Dye group	Fiber	Types and brands	Advantages	Disadvantages	Washfastness	Lightfastness
Fiber-reactive	Cellulose (cotton, viscose rayon, linen, hemp, ramie, Tencel), silk, wool	Procion MX (Dylon, Aljo Cold Process), Cibacron F (Sabracron F), Procion H	Bright colors mix readily to create many hues, easy to use, many techniques possible. Procion H and Cibacron F less reactive, so easier to rinse out, and stock solutions possible	Inhaling dye powder may cause allergies. Procion MX has short life after mixing with water, is hard to wash out. Cibacron F and Procion H have fewer colors	Excellent	Excellent
Acid	Proteins (wool, cashmere, alpaca, mohair, angora, silk), nylon, some acrylics	Kiton, 1:2 Metal Complex (Lanaset, Telana, Sabraset), WashFast (Nylomine)	Bright colors (except 1:2 Metal Complex), easy to apply, exhaust well for less waste	Some not level or streak easily. Some powders harder to dissolve	Varies	Varies
Vat	Cellulose, silk, nylon, acetate, wool	Zymo Fast, Pro Chem Vat, Inkodye	Strike quickly, will discharge some fiber-reactive and acid dyes (can discharge and dye in one process), resistant to chlorine bleaching	Lye needed for alkaline solution necessitates wearing goggles, gloves, respirator, protective clothing. May damage wool.	Excellent	Excellent
Disperse	Synthetics (polyester, acetate rayon, acrylic, Mylar, nylon, Lycra, plastics, Polar Fleece)	PROsperse, Dispersol, Aljo Disperse for Acetate-Nylon, Aljo Disperse for Polyester	Bright colors, easy to use, dyes water-repelling polyesters. Used for transfer printing	May irritate skin. Gas fading to adjacent fabrics with high temperatures	Good to excellent	Good to excellent

Opposite: Fabric dyed with Procion MX, screen printed with textile paints and red foil dots applied. Photo by Joe Coca.

industrial revolution had greatly increased the quantities of fabrics being manufactured, but dyeing them all required the harvesting and use of more and more natural dyestuffs. Subsequent discoveries made in the field of synthetic dyes led to a flourishing industry. Today, many companies throughout the world produce dyes for use in food, cosmetics, paint, and paper, as well as textiles.

Fibers and Fabrics

Fibers may be natural or synthetic. Natural fibers include cellulose (derived from plants) and protein (from animals). Synthetics include regenerated natural fibers such as rayon. A fiber or fabric can be identified by appearance, feel, and the way it reacts when burned (see Chart B, below). For instance, reeled silk fabric appears lustrous, feels supple, smooth, and slippery, and smells like burning feathers or hair when held over a flame.

To perform a burn test, hold one end of a small strip of fabric with sturdy metal tweezers or forceps over a bowl of water. Place the other end of the strip in the flame. Remove it from the flame after it ignites and observe how it burns, how it smells, and what the remaining ash looks like.

Cellulose Fibers and Fabrics

Cellulose fibers include cotton, hemp, flax (linen), jute, ramie, sisal, lyocell (Tencel), viscose rayon, and some basketry materials such as wicker and dried grass. The most effective dyes for plant fibers are fiber-reactive and vat dyes.

Cotton is the fibrous covering of cotton seeds; these fibers vary widely in length (staple). Sea Island, Pima, and Egyptian cottons, which have the longest staple of any cotton, 1½" (3.8 cm), produce the highest-quality fabrics. Most cotton fabrics in the United States are made from fibers of intermediate staple, ¹³⁄₁₆" to 1¼" (2.1 cm to 3.2 cm). Cotton is generally off-white to tan in color, but is usually bleached white. In recent years, Sally Fox has developed natural brown, tan, and green colors through selective breeding, marketed under the name FoxFibre. Cotton is very absorbent but dries slowly, can withstand high temperatures and vigorous agitation, and dyes easily. It is the most widely used fiber in the world; cotton fabrics range from coarse canvas to the finest batiste. Mercerized cotton has been put through a caustic soda bath to make it more lustrous and more receptive to dye.

Linen is the oldest known fabric, with examples dating back to 6000 B.C.E.; its fiber, called flax, comes from the stem of the flax plant. Individual fibers range from 4 to 40 inches (10.2 to 101.6 cm) in length, are very straight and smooth, and are stronger than cotton. Linen is naturally light cream to gray and very durable. It absorbs water readily and dries faster than cotton. It is stronger when wet than when dry, but it has little resilience and therefore wrinkles easily. Linen can be machine-washed and –dried; in fact, repeated washing and ironing makes it lustrous. But because it is subject to abrasion, stored fabrics should be refolded periodically to even out wear.

Viscose rayon, invented in 1892 as a substitute for silk, was the first manufactured fiber. It is made by breaking down wood pulp or linters (the shortest cotton fibers) with a strong alkali, then extruding the mixture through tiny holes to make thread. It is weaker when wet than when dry and stretches easily, and so it should be laundered carefully. Because it has a low resilience and recovery, it wrinkles easily but drapes beautifully. Rayon absorbs dye extremely well, producing intense colors. A newer version of rayon, lyocell (Tencel is a trade name), is produced in an environmentally sound process from wood pulp. It has the same dyeing characteristics as rayon.

Opposite: 2.2 Fabrics appropriate for dyes discussed in this book include (from top to bottom) bleached cotton, unbleached cotton muslin, bleached linen, viscose rayon, viscose rayon challis, lyocell (Tencel), hemp, silk habotai, silk organza, silk noil, wool flannel, sheer polyester, polyester satin, and nylon. Photo by Joe Coca.

Chart B Burn Test

Fiber	Burning/melting	Removed from flame	Ash	Smell
Cotton, ramie	Burns quickly, yellow flame	Continues to burn with afterglow	Small amount, feathery, gray; (black for mercerized cotton)	Burning paper
Linen	Burns quickly, yellow flame	Continues to burn with afterglow	Small amount, feathery, gray	Burning paper
Viscose rayon	Burns quickly, yellow flame	Continues to burn with afterglow	Small amount, feathery, gray	Burning paper
Wool	Curls away from flame, burns slowly	Self-extinguishes	Dark, brittle, small black bead, easily crushed	Burning hair
Silk	Curls away from flame, burns slowly	Self-extinguishes	Round, shiny black bead, easily crushed	Burning hair
Nylon	Melts and burns slowly, yellow flame	Self-extinguishes	Round, hard, gray or brown bead, won't crush	Celery
Polyester	Melts and burns slowly, yellow flame	Self-extinguishes	Hard, tough black bead	Chemical, sweetish

Ramie, naturally white, comes from the stem of a plant in the nettle family. It is the strongest of the cellulose fibers and dyes easily. Like those of linen, the fibers are not resilient or elastic, and so the fabric wrinkles easily, but it is absorbent and dries quickly.

Hemp comes from the stem of the marijuana plant, a member of the mulberry family. It is very strong, naturally dark tan or brown, and difficult to bleach, thus is better dyed to dark colors.

Protein Fibers and Fabric

Protein fibers include wool, angora goat (mohair), cashmere goat, alpaca, camel, angora (rabbit), and the cocoons of silkworms. They are dyed mainly with acid dyes but will take fiber-reactive and vat dyes as well.

Wool is obtained from the fleece of domesticated sheep. The fibers have a natural crimp or wave that makes wool fabric wrinkle resistant with good insulating qualities. The outer layer of the wool fiber comprises scales that overlap like roof tiles. The scales swell and open with heat, moisture, and agitation, and they close in cool water. If the water temperature is drastically lowered when washing wool, the scales can interlock with those on adjacent fibers, the fabric can shrink, and the result is felt. Once wool has been felted, it is felted for good. To prevent felting, wool should be washed in cool water with little agitation. It is very absorbent and will hold 30 percent of its weight in water without feeling damp, but it dries slowly. Wool is yellowed by exposure to the sun, damaged by alkaline solutions and chlorine bleach, and attacked by moths and carpet beetles.

Mohair, alpaca, cashmere, and angora are hair fibers from the coats of other animals. Because they lack the crimp found in wool fibers, they are often blended with wool.

The caterpillar of the cultivated moth Bombyx mori produces *white silk* fiber; these caterpillars, which today are raised mainly in China, are fed a diet of mulberry leaves. Wild silkworms, many species of which eat oak leaves, produce a creamy brown fiber called *tussah silk,* which is coarser and less lustrous than white silk. Silk caterpillars spin a single continuous filament, usually more than 300 yards (274.3 m) long, into a cocoon that is held together by a gum called sericin. *Silk organza,* used in the resist-scouring process (see "Resist-Scouring Silk" page 98), is stiff because the fabric still contains sericin. The highest quality, most lustrous silk is obtained by killing the silk moth in the cocoon and reeling, or unwinding the filament and degumming it. If the moth is allowed to emerge from the cocoon, it will cut the filament as it exits; the resulting short fibers are used to make noil (raw silk), which has less luster than reeled silk. Silk fibers are very fine, strong, absorbent, and resilient. Like wool, silk is damaged by exposure to the sun and chlorine bleach.

Synthetic Fibers and Fabric

Nylon (polyamide), developed in 1935, was the first synthetic fiber. Although first used for women's stockings, its major uses today, because of its lightness and strength, include carpeting, tents, and backpacks. Nylon has good abrasion resistance and flexibility. It is more absorbent than other synthetic fibers but is damaged by sunlight. Nylon can be dyed with acid, disperse, and vat dyes. Pleats and other folds can be permanently set with heat.

Polyester was developed in 1941 and today is second to cotton in usage. It is often blended with cotton, linen, or wool, but is also used alone either as fiber or as fiberfill for insulation. It is a very strong fabric, resistant to abrasion, wrinkling, and frequent washing. As with nylon, pleats and other shapes can be permanently set with heat. Polyester microfiber produces fabrics with improved hand, drape, and texture that more closely resemble silk than do regular polyester fabrics. Low absorbency means that polyester dries quickly. Trade names include Dacron, Mylar, Trevira, Polar Fleece, and Polartec. Some of the latter two fabrics are sometimes made of recycled plastic bottles. Polyester can be dyed only with disperse dyes.

Treated Fabric

Permanent-press, stain-resistant, water-repellent, and flame-retardant finishes interfere with dyeing. Most commercially available textiles have a coating, or sizing, that makes them look crisper than their untreated counterparts but also interferes with dyeing. See "Preparing Fabric for Dyeing" on page 120 to learn how to remove sizing and other impurities. Fabrics available from dye suppliers labeled as "PFD" (prepared for dyeing) are free of sizing, other finishes, and optical brighteners but still need some preparation for dyeing. Check a fabric's readiness for dyeing by performing a simple water-drop test (see illustration 2.3).

2.3 Water-drop test. All fabric should be tested to ensure that it is ready to accept liquids, whether labeled PFD (prepared for dyeing) or not. Place a drop of water on the fabric. If the water is immediately absorbed, the fabric will take dye, chemicals, or textile paint. If the drop "beads" (sits) on the surface, the fabric has a finish, which can be removed by scouring. See "Preparing Fabric for Dyeing" on page 120. Photo by Tom Liden.

Chapter Three
Color

Knowledge of the basic principles of color is essential to producing colors and combinations that work. Many color theories and color wheels have been developed to guide you. Below is a brief overview to get you started.

When we perceive an object of a particular color, we are really seeing the light waves that are being reflected by that object. A piece of fabric that we perceive as blue is actually absorbing all the other colors in the spectrum and reflecting only blue. All colors of dyes or textile paints exhibit this reflective principle.

Colors have hue, value, and intensity. The easiest way to understand color relationships is by looking at the twelve-spoke color wheel (see illustration 3.1). *Hue* is the name we give to a color, such as red or purple, which in dyeing comes from a specific dye or combination of dyes. *Value* is the lightness or darkness of a color. In dyeing, this refers to the depth of shade (DOS), usually expressed as a percentage, which is the ratio of the weight of dye to the weight of fabric (WOF) being dyed. Visualize the range of red from the light value pink to the dark value maroon. Preparing a series of samples using increasing concentrations of a particular dye and color to achieve a gradation from light to dark will familiarize you with the nature of that color and dye type. *Intensity,* or *chroma,* is the brightness, dullness, or saturation of a color. Mixing it with its complement (opposite on the color wheel) or black will decrease the saturation of a color. Compare a bright, pure

yellow with a dulled yellow to which black or purple has been added.

The three primary hues are red, yellow, and blue. Mixing pairs of two primary colors produces the secondary colors: green, orange, and purple. Mixing a primary and an adjacent secondary color results in the intermediate, or tertiary, colors of red-orange, yellow-orange, yellow-green, blue-green, blue-purple, and red-purple. Complementary colors are those pairs lying opposite each other on the color wheel (red and green, blue and orange, yellow and purple). When complementary colors are mixed, they neutralize each other—adding a small amount of blue to orange will lessen the intensity, making it duller (less saturated). Colors next to each other on the color wheel are called analogous. Dyers often stick to analogous color schemes because they are easy to use and require only a few colors.

Mixing Colors

Since dye colors are transparent, mixing colors or overdyeing one color with a second will result in new colors or new values or hues. Light colors are produced by using white fabric and less dye than for darker colors. Some colors within a particular dye group are much stronger and more intense than others, and different kinds of fiber take a given color in a dye group differently (see dévoré examples from the same dyebath in illustration

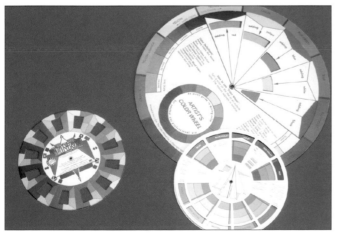

3.1 *A variety of color wheels. Photo by Tom Liden.*

3.2 *Dévoré samples were all put in the same Procion MX long dyebath. Note how the dye reacts differently on (from left to right) polyester/cotton (Azeta), silk/rayon velvet, polyester/rayon, and silk/rayon charmeuse. Photo by Tom Liden.*

3.2). Also, the quality of a color, such as red, will vary from one dye group to another. Each dye group has what is considered a medium depth of shade or color strength. For fiber-reactive dyes on cotton, it is 2%. Acid dyes on wool use a 1% DOS.

To explore color mixing, start with primary or pure colors. Check with your dye supplier to find out which are pure and which are mixed colors or test a particular dye using the "Mixed or Pure Color Test," illustration 3.3. Paula Burch's website, listed in the "Bibliography," offers charts showing which Procion MX, WashFast acid, and Lanaset colors are pure and which are mixtures.

Premixed dyes are combinations prepared by the supplier. While these are convenient, you'll learn more about the nature of color by preparing your own. To learn about the basic dye colors associated with a particular dye group, make up stock solutions from pure colors (see "Calculating Stock Solutions, Dye Quantities, and Color Mixing" on page 124) and combine them in different proportions to make a color chart. This exercise will show you how many hues can be mixed from a few basic colors and can be an invaluable reference for future dyeing. As "Procion MX and Cibacron F Color Mixtures on Paper," illustration 3.4, shows, mixing only a few colors will yield many combinations. As you get to know the colors within a particular dye group, you will gain confidence, control, and mastery in predicting how they will interact.

Color Inspiration

Which colors to choose? Color choice is very personal, and our preferences are influenced by culture, society, age, and where we live. Begin dyeing with colors you like. For inspiration, look at pictorial magazines, colorful calendars, picture books, and nature. Note the range of colors in a flower, rock wall, favorite piece of clothing, or tide pool. Don't be afraid to plunge in and experiment!

3.4 Procion MX and Cibacron F Color Mixtures on Paper. The color charts show 1% DOS. The charts were made using 140 pound cold press 100% rag (cellulose) watercolor paper, which reacts with the dye to produce the same colors found on cotton fabric. Because the charts will never be washed, only water and dye were mixed together. Two approaches are shown for using the charts. Procion MX colors were mounted on a ring, to be fanned out for color matching. Cibacron F used single pieces of paper, which can be placed in a notebook or on the wall. Photo by Tom Liden.

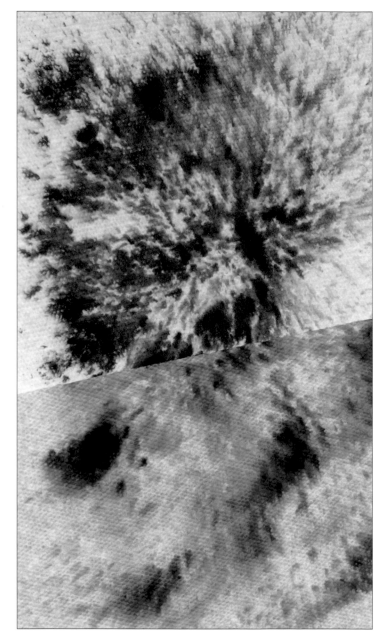

3.3 Mixed or pure color test. Spray a coffee filter or paper towel with water. Wearing a dust mask and gloves, sprinkle on a small amount of dye. A mixed color, such as the purple on the top, will contain particles of many colors. A pure color, like the blue on the bottom, will have particles of a single color. Photo by Tom Liden.

Chapter Four
Fiber-Reactive Dyes

Fiber-reactive dyes are the best choice for cellulose fibers. They will also work on silk and, by modifying the recipe, on wool. This dye class is suitable for a wide range of surface design techniques, including tie-dye, shibori, dip dyeing, resist dyeing, handpainting, and screen printing.

Choose the type of dye based on the availability of desired colors, shelf life of the form you want to use (powder, stock solutions, thickened dye, etc.), and special requirements (see Chart C, below).

Chemistry

The molecules of fiber-reactive dyes share electrons with fiber molecules to form covalent bonds, strong chemical bonds that are insoluble in water. The result is fast colors. The various fiber-reactive dyes differ in their chemical structure. The most common of these are dichlorotriazine (Procion MX), monofluorotriazine (Cibacron F), and monochlorotriazine (Procion H).

Procion MX

The two chlorine atoms in dichlorotriazine (Procion MX) not only bind with fiber but also react with water in a process known as hydrolysis. The effect of this reaction is to tie up some of the dye so that it is no longer available to react with the fiber; at the end of an MX dyebath, therefore, some dye goes down the drain. Procion MX dyes must be used within 4 to 5 days after mixing with water (refrigerated solutions may be used for several days, but colors will be paler); thickened dyes must be used within 4 hours.

Imperial Chemical Industries (ICI) of England first marketed fiber-reactive dyes in 1956 under the brand name Procion (now called Procion MX). The original Procion was offered in a full range of bright hues that were easily mixed, economical, and safe to use. The one disadvantage was the extra care needed to thoroughly wash the unfixed dye out of the material. Now that the patent on Procion MX has expired, several companies, including PRO Chemical & Dye, Dharma Trading Company, Aljo Manufacturing Company, and Rupert, Gibbon and Spider (Jacquard Products) are offering generic versions to studio dyers under various names. But although many mixed colors are available, they have few pure colors. For a chart showing which colors are pure and which are mixes, see Paula Burch's website, listed in the "Bibliography."

Cibacron F

Monofluorotriazine dye (Cibacron F) was introduced by CIBA-Geigy (now Novartis) of Switzerland in 1979. (Cibacron F dyes are also sold under the name Sabracron F). Its single fluorine atom makes it is less reactive than Procion MX dyes; stock solutions therefore are more stable, and the unfixed dye is more easily washed out at the end of processing. However, low reactivity requires a higher temperature during dyeing to promote chemical bonding.

Chart C Fiber-Reactive Dye Comparison

Dye	Temperature	Colors	Shelf life	Other
Procion MX (highly reactive)	Low, 85° to 105° F (29° to 41° C); turquoise, 130° to 140° F (54° to 60° C); minimum, 70° F (21° C) for batch curing	Wide range	Powder, 2 years; solutions with water 4–5 days; thickened with alkali, 4 hours	Requires extra rinsing and washing
Cibacron F (very reactive)	Warm, 113° to 150° F (45° to 66° C)	Less dye needed for deep colors; fewer colors, no true red	Powder, 2 years; stock solutions, 2 weeks; thickened with alkali, 4 hours	Under 105° F (41° C) requires more time for batch curing or up to 48 hours at 70° F (21° C)
Procion H (less reactive)	175° to 185° F (79° to 85° C)	High color yield; fewer premixed colors	Powder, 2 years; stock solutions, 2 months; thickened with alkali, 1 month	Requires heat or steam to fix

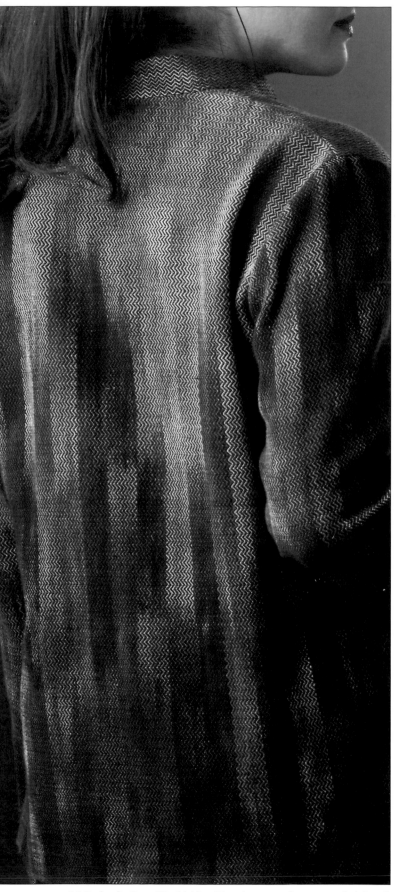

Less Cibacron F than Procion MX dye is required for deeper colors, and Cibacron F produces a true black on cotton and rayon, which is very difficult to achieve with Procion MX. Cibacron F colors attach to the fiber at nearly the same rate, which can't be said for Procion MX. Cibacron F dyes can be mixed in the same dyebath with Procion MX dyes. Color combinations are shown on page 12, illustration 3.4, "Procion MX and Cibacron F Color Mixtures on Paper."

Procion H

Monochlorotriazine dye (Procion H) was developed by ICI to remedy MX's shortcoming of hydrolyzing too rapidly when mixed with water. Its single chlorine atom is less reactive than MX's two, resulting in stock solutions that can be stored for at least 2 months and unfixed dyes that wash out easily. However, lower reactivity requires a higher temperature during dyeing to promote chemical bonding.

 Safety Alert
Inhaling fiber-reactive dye powders over long periods may result in a respiratory allergy. Cibacron F dye powders, whose particles are more crystalline and thus heavier than those of Procion MX, are safer for long-term use and for anyone susceptible to respiratory problems. Always wear a dust mask while working with dry dye and alkali.

4.2 Untitled *by Patricia Littlefield. 8" h × 12" w × ¼" d (20 cm × 30.5 cm × .65 cm). Muslin and paper handmade from abaca linters and process flax dyed with Procion MX. Pulp dyed before paper was made. Manipulated digital images and tampico grass inserted between layers of fabric and paper. Photo by Patricia Littlefield.*

4.1 *Jacket by Suza Wooldridge. Tencel warp and cotton weft painted with Procion MX. Warp dye colors overlap to create a third color. Photo by Shevaun Williams.*

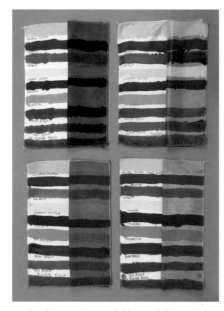

4.3 Effects of overdyeing and color mixing on different fabrics. Fabrics on the top are rayon challis (left) and silk habotai (right). The bottom row shows mercerized cotton (left) and silk noil (right). Pieces of fabric were painted with thickened stripes of the same Procion MX dyes and the fabric cut into two pieces. The left half of each fabric sample shows color stripes on the fabric before overdyeing, while the right half shows the effects of color mixing by overdyeing in blue (upper two samples) or pink (lower two samples). Photo by Tom Liden.

4.4 Peaceful Garden Jacket by Mollie Freeman. Cotton and rayon warp painted with Cibacron F, handwoven, discharged with Thiox, stamped and stenciled with textile paints, kumihimo embellishments, polymer clay buttons. Photo by Mollie Freeman.

Factors in Dyeing with Procion MX and Cibacron F

Coloring cellulose fibers with fiber-reactive dyes requires salt, alkali, water, and relatively low heat. When dyeing wool, replace the alkali with acid (see page 26). Silk can be dyed with either alkali or acid.

The addition of ordinary table salt (sodium chloride) to a dyebath reduces the solubility of the dye, thus promoting dye absorption by the fiber for even color. When salt is added in increments, the dye migrates into the fiber at an even rate, producing level color. Dyeing darker colors, which have more dye molecules than lighter ones, requires more salt than dyeing lighter colors. Buy table salt at the grocery store or look for fine feed salt at a farm supplier.

Alkali raises the pH of the dyebath and acts as an activator, that is, causing the dye to attach to fiber molecules. For permanent fixation on cellulose fiber, a pH of 10.5 to 11 is necessary. Sodium carbonate, also known as soda ash, is the most common alkali used in dyeing. As soon as an alkali has been added to a fiber-reactive dyebath or thickened print paste, the rate of hydrolysis increases rapidly to the extent of rendering an immersion dyebath ineffective even though some color remains in the solution. Mixed or thickened dyes prepared for direct application must be used within 4 hours after the addition of soda ash. Refrigeration of the dye mixture will slow down hydrolysis. Soda ash can be purchased from chemical, dye, or swimming pool suppliers. Washing soda, marketed for laundry use and available at the grocery store, is mostly hydrated soda ash (weaker than pure sodium carbonate) and may also contain ingredients that interfere with dyeing.

The amount of water in a fiber-reactive dyebath is critical. Using too much water results in more hydrolysis (bonding of the dye with water) and less dye available to bond with the fiber. Using too little water will produce splotchy color (this result can be used creatively). So use only enough water for the fabric to move freely in the dye solution. For an immersion dyebath, use a ratio of 20 parts water to 1 part dry fiber by weight (20:1).

Temperature is also crucial with fiber-reactive dyes. If it is too high, the dye will react mainly with the water and not with the fabric. If it is too low, the colors will not be fast. The optimum temperature range for Procion MX is 85° to 105° F (29° to 41° C), except for turquoise, which you must heat to 130° to 140° F (54° to 60° C). Optimum temperatures for all colors of Cibacron F are 113° to 150° F (45° to 66° C). During batch curing—a technique for fixing the color of fibers dyed by direct application of thickened dyes—the temperature must not go below 70° F (21° C) or the colors will not be permanent.

Rinsing and Washing Out Unfixed Dye

No matter which fiber-reactive dye you choose or how you process it, some dye will not be fixed to either the fabric or the water. Illustration 4.5, "Unfixed Dye Test," shows how unfixed dye can be transferred to other fabrics. To prevent bleeding, rubbing off, or back-staining of fabric during laundering, unfixed dye must be removed from the dyed fabric. See "Rinsing, Washing, and Drying Fabric" on page 122.

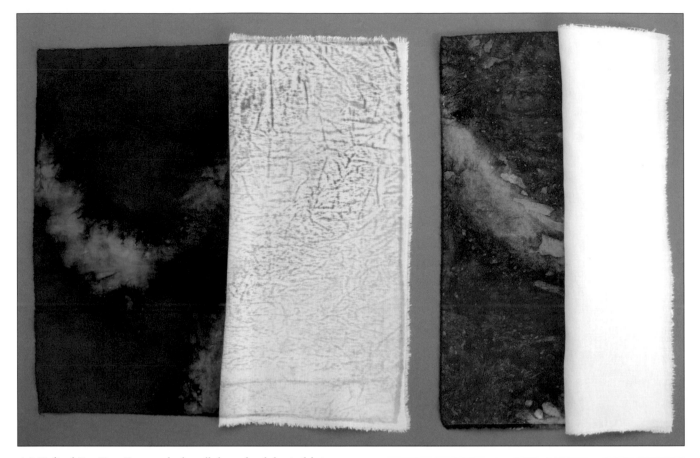

4.5 *Unfixed Dye Test. To test whether all the unfixed dye in fabric dyed with Procion MX has been removed in rinsing and washing, lay a piece of damp, undyed cotton fabric on top of a dry, dyed piece. Press for several seconds with a dry iron set on "cotton." The fabric on the left was rinsed in cold running water but not washed with Synthrapol. The staining on the pressing cloth shows that not all of the unfixed dye was removed. The fabric on the right was rinsed in cold running water, washed with Synthrapol in hot water, and rinsed in hot water; no dye was transferred to the pressing cloth. Photo by Tom Liden.*

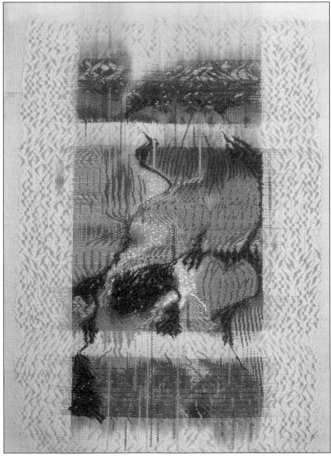

4.6 Murmurings *detail. Photo by George Waters.*

4.7 Murmurings *by Cecilia Christensen. 39" h × 20" w (99 cm × 51 cm). Procion MX painted on cotton warp and used for handwoven brocade; weft of linen, cotton, rayon, Swiss straw, and tussah silk. Photo by George Waters.*

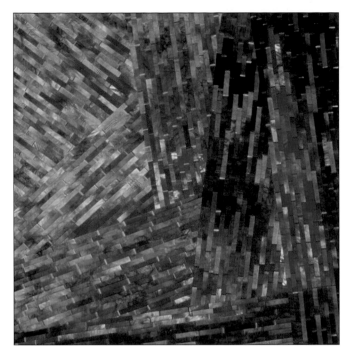

4.8 Flaring Red on Blue *by Judith Larzelere. 54" h × 65" w (137 cm × 165 cm). Machine strip piecing and strip quilting on cotton. Fabric dyed by Heide Stoll-Weber. Photo by David Caras.*

Procion MX and Cibacron F Immersion Dyeing

This procedure requires care and constant stirring but produces the most even colors on cellulose and silk. As soon as the fabric is placed in the dyebath, the dye molecules begin to migrate into the fabric. After the alkali is added, bonding takes place. Deeper colors, which have more dye molecules than lighter colors, take longer to bond with the fabric. Careful calculations and measurement of ingredients are essential for producing even, reproducible colors. Sample calculations are shown in Chart D, page 18.

1. Weigh dry fabric and record weight of fiber or fabric (WOF) on "Dye Worksheet" on page 119. *All dye and auxiliary chemical calculations are based on this weight.*

2. Scour the fabric, referring to "Preparing Fabric for Dyeing" on page 120. If the fabric is already clean and dry, place in warm water and add ¼ teaspoon (1.25 ml) Synthrapol. Soak for an hour or longer. Thoroughly wetting the fabric will produce the most even colors.

3. Calculate the following amounts:

Dye, amount according to desired depth of shade (DOS):

pale value = 0.5% to 1% WOF

medium value = 1% to 2% WOF

dark value = 2% to 4% WOF

navy = 6% WOF

deep black = 6% to 10% WOF

Water/fiber ratio, 20:1 is preferred; use 40:1 for pieces weighing less than 3.5 ounces (100 g).

4.9 Dialogue with African Patterns, Kuba Series #3 *by Candace Crockett. 58" h × 36" w (147.5 cm × 91.5 cm). China silk with image created by printing, painting, and immersion dyeing with Procion MX and discharging. Candace was inspired by the strong geometric, graphic images of Kuba patterns, but instead of the handwoven, coarse cotton traditionally used by native artists, she used fine, transparent silk with layered repeats and pattern variations, adding and subtracting color.*

Sodium hexametaphosphate (water softener), if the water is hard, use 1% WOF.

Salt, amount is based on the DOS and WOF

pale value (less than 1% DOS), use 50% WOF

medium value (1% to 2% DOS), use 100% WOF

dark value (2% to 4% DOS), use 150% WOF

very dark values, including navy and black (greater than 4% DOS), use 200% WOF

Soda ash, amount is based on the WOF

pale to medium values, add at 10% WOF

dark and very dark values, add at 15% WOF

4. Measure dye powder or liquid dye stock solution, salt, and soda ash in separate containers (see "Stock Solutions" on page 124).

5. Measure water into a nonreactive container. Reserve about 1 cup (237 ml) to mix with soda ash (see "Fiber-Reactive Dye Comparison," Chart C, page 13, for temperatures).

6. For hard water, add sodium hexametaphosphate and stir to dissolve.

7. In a separate container, place a small amount of dyebath water and paste dry dye into it. Stir until no dye particles are visible in the container.

8. Pour the soda ash slowly into the reserved water, stirring continuously until dissolved to prevent a hard crust from forming on the bottom of the container. Set aside.

9. Pour the dye paste or stock solution into the dyebath and stir well until all the dye particles are in solution.

10. Add clean, wet fabric to dyebath and stir for 10 minutes.

11. Lift the fabric out of the dyebath, letting the water drip back into the dyepot.

12. Add about ⅓ of the salt to the dyebath and stir to dissolve.

13. Return the fabric to the dyepot and stir 5 minutes.

14. Remove the fabric as above and add ½ of the remaining salt; stir to dissolve.

15. Return the fabric to the dyepot and stir 5 minutes.

16. Remove the fabric again and add the remaining salt; stir to dissolve.

17. Return the fabric to the dyepot and stir 20 minutes.

18. Remove the fabric and add the dissolved soda.

19. Return the fabric to the dyepot and stir constantly for 10 minutes. The addition of the soda ash starts the bonding of the dye to the fiber; most of the reaction occurs in the first 10 minutes after the soda ash is added.

20. How long to stir after the soda ash is added depends on the depth of the color desired. Darker colors have more dye molecules and you need to allow time for as many as possible to bond with the fiber.

Procion MX and Cibacron F Immersion Dyeing Hints

■ The dyebath may change color during dyeing, especially after the addition of soda ash to a Procion MX dyebath; this will not affect the final results.

■ Colors are always darker when wet than when dry. Wait until the fabric is dry before judging a color.

■ Run every dyebath for as long as specified for the depth of color you chose. Taking the fabric out early will result in poor light- and washfastness.

■ Work with a basic set of colors and the same fiber-reactive dye to build a base of knowledge and skill in obtaining predictable results.

■ Viscose rayon and mercerized cotton will dye darker than other cellulose fabrics. Silk will dye pastel to medium colors using soda ash.

■ Overdyeing can add variations and depth to dyed fabric as dyes are transparent and one color will affect another color; however, a fabric can take up dye only as long as dye sites are available on the fiber molecules.

■ Unexpectedly pale colors may be caused by using too little salt or dye, incomplete scouring before dyeing, or choosing the wrong fabric, such as polyester or a blend of cellulose and synthetic fibers or one with a permanent-press or other finish.

Less than 1% DOS, stir for 30 minutes
1% to 2% DOS, stir for 45 minutes
Greater than 2% DOS, stir for 60 minutes

21. Remove the fabric from the dyebath and wring out excess liquid. Place fabric in a bucket of cool water to rinse.

22. Follow instructions for "Rinsing, Washing, and Drying" on page 122.

23. Add small amounts of vinegar to the dyebath in increments, testing with pH paper until you reach neutrality (pH 7). Pour the dyebath down the drain (see Chapter 1, "Studio Practices and Safety," for information on dyebath disposal).

Chart D   Procion MX and Cibacron F Immersion Dyeing Sample Measurements

The following recipe will dye about 7 ounces (200 g) of cloth, or about 5 yards (4.6 m) of medium-weight silk or 1 to 2 yards (1 to 2 m) of light- to medium-weight cotton. Follow the immersion dyeing procedure.

1% pale value	2% medium value	4% dark value
Powdered dye		
200 g WOF x 0.01 = 2 g dye	200 g WOF x 0.02 = 4 g dye	200 g WOF x 0.04 = 8 g dye
Water at water/fiber ratio of 20:1		
200 g WOF x 20 = 4000 g = 4000 ml = 4 l water	200 g WOF x 20 = 4000 g = 4000 ml = 4 l water	200 g WOF x 20 = 4000 g = 4000 ml = 4 l water
Water softener 1% WOF		
200 g WOF x 0.01 = 2 g	200 g WOF x 0.01 = 2 g	200 g WOF x 0.01 = 2 g
Salt		
200 g WOF x 0.50 = 100 g	200 g WOF x 1.0 = 200 g	200 g WOF x 1.50 = 300 g
Soda ash		
200 g WOF x 0.10 = 20 g	200 g WOF x 0.10 = 20 g	200 g WOF x 0.15 = 30g

Procion MX and Cibacron F Immersion Dyeing in a Washing Machine

Use an automatic washer to produce even colors on large amounts of fabric. A standard top-loading washer holds about 20 gallons (76 l) of water at full capacity (refer to your owner's manual) and will dye 5 pounds (2.3 kg) or about 20 yards (18.2 m) of light- to medium-weight cotton. Top loaders are better than front loaders for dyeing because they can be opened during processing.

Cut the fabric into lengths no longer than 4 yards (3.7 m) and untangle it frequently during dyeing to promote even color.

These instructions are for dyeing a medium DOS with maximum water. If dyeing less fabric, use less water, dye, and chemicals. Use a timer to track progress of dyeing.

1. Scour fabric in the washer (see "Preparing Fabric for Dyeing" on page 120). After the last rinse, remove the fabric and set it aside.

2. Fill the washer with *water* (see "Fiber-Reactive Dye Comparison," on page 13, Chart C, for temperatures). If the temperature of household water is not hot enough, boil some water on the stove and add to obtain the desired temperature.

3. Remove about 2 quarts (2 l) of water and set aside for later mixing.

4. Add 1 tablespoon (14.8 g) *sodium hexametaphosphate* (for hard water) to the washer and agitate to dissolve.

5. Add 10 cups (3.3 kg) of *salt* to the washer. Agitate until the salt is dissolved.

6. Thoroughly paste and dissolve ⅓ cup (46 g) *Procion MX* or *Cibacron F* in 2 cups (474 ml) of the reserved water. Pour into the washer and agitate for 5 minutes.

7. Put the wet fabric in the washer, distributing it evenly around the agitator. Set the machine for a regular cycle and agitate for 15 minutes. If the wash cycle is shorter than 15 minutes, stop the machine and restart the agitation. Make sure that the washer does not drain. Untwist fabric as necessary.

8. Dissolve 1¾ cups (427 g) of *soda ash* in the remaining reserved water (see #3 above). Restart the agitation. Either pour the soda ash solution into the liquid bleach dispenser or pour it slowly into the machine but not directly onto the fabric because it will cause streaks. Alternately, remove the fabric, place it in a large bucket, add the soda ash, and replace the fabric. Agitate for 15 minutes, restarting agitation if necessary. Don't let the machine drain.

9. Stop the washer and let the fabric sit for 5 minutes. Agitate for 5 to 10 minutes longer. Repeat these steps for 60 minutes. Finally, let the washer complete the wash, rinse, and spin cycles.

10. Reset the washer to "cold wash/cold rinse" and run an entire wash, rinse, and spin cycle with water alone.

11. Reset the washer to "hot wash/warm rinse." Add 1 to 2 tablespoons (15 to 30 ml) Synthrapol and repeat the entire wash, rinse, and spin cycle.

12. Check the water for color during the last rinse. If necessary, rinse again until the water is clear. Dark colors may require additional hot wash/warm rinse cycles to remove excess dye.

13. Dry the fabric on a clothesline or in a dryer. If streaks appear at the edges of the fabric, unfixed dye was not completely removed. Rewash with Synthrapol and rinse again.

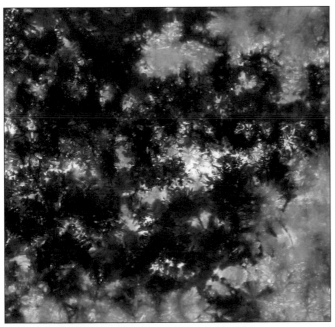

4.10 Opus 2 *by Carlene Keller and Judy Bianchi. Random dyeing with Procion MX on cotton. Detail of fabric 36" l × 45" w (91.5 cm × 114.5 cm). Photo by Andrea Orvik.*

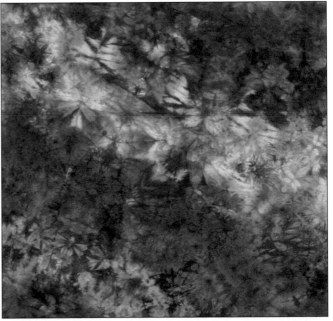

4.11 Opus 14 *by Carlene Keller and Judy Bianchi. Random dyeing with Procion MX on cotton. Detail of fabric 36" l × 45" w (91.5 cm × 114.5 cm). Photo by Andrea Orvik.*

Direct Application Techniques

Instead of dyeing entire lengths of cloth, color may be applied to specific areas of the fabric surface. Dyes can be thin for dipping, shibori, and painting or thickened for painting, stamping, stenciling, and screen printing. All must be cured to fix the dye before washing out any unfixed dye and chemicals.

Procion MX and Cibacron F Random Dyebath

This is a quick-and-easy recipe that produces varied and random colors. Use the immersion dyeing measurements based on WOF.

1. Scour fabric, referring to "Preparing Fabric for Dyeing" on page 120.
2. Measure the *water* and *sodium hexametaphosphate* (if water is hard) into a plastic bucket. Stir to dissolve.
3. Add *salt*. Stir to dissolve.
4. Measure the *dye powder*.
5. Stuff dry fabric into a nylon stocking or mesh laundry bag. The tighter the fabric is bunched together, the less surface will be exposed to the dye, resulting in more white or original color in the finished fabric.
6. Place the fabric bunch in the dye bucket with the water and chemicals.
7. Sprinkle the dye powder on top of the fabric bunch. Do not stir. Let sit for ½ hour.
8. Sprinkle the *soda ash* into the bucket without removing the fabric and stir very lightly.
9. Let the dye bucket sit for 1 hour.
10. Follow the instructions for "Rinsing, Washing, and Drying Fabric" on page 122. It's done!

4.12 *Soda soak painting with Procion MX on wet fabric. Photo by Tom Liden.*

4.13 *Purple Chair by Daphne Gillen. 18" h × 21" w × 1/16" d (46 cm × 53.5 cm × .16 cm). Soda-soaked and painted with Procion MX. Stitched and quilted. Photo by Joe Coca.*

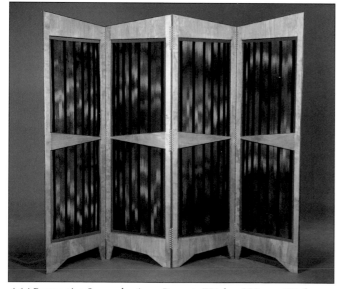

4.14 Perspective Screen *by Anne Bossert. 75" h × 92" w × ¾" d (190.5 cm × 234 cm × 2 cm). Procion MX painted on cotton warp and Baltic birch plywood with brass fittings. Dyeing, weaving, and woodworking by the artist. Photo by Joe Mendoza.*

4.15 Perspective Screen *detail. Photo by Joe Mendoza.*

Options for Random Dyebath

- Sprinkle Procion MX or Cibacron F dye powder on the fabric before bunching it and placing it in the nylon stocking. More dye can be added to the dye bucket as described above. The dye in the bunched fabric will produce splotches of color.

- For information on other low-water immersion techniques to produce color gradations by bunching, folding, or manipulating fabric, see *Color by Accident* by Ann Johnston, listed in the "Bibliography."

Procion MX and Cibacron F Soda Soak Technique

Soda soak is a fast and simple way to achieve varied results by painting or dipping or using resists. After soaking the fabric in a solution of soda ash and water, immediately apply one or more colors to the wet fabric. Fabric can alternatively be soaked in soda ash solution, air-dried, and dyed up to several months later, but the fabric will turn yellow if it sits too long. Dye silk within 2 weeks if it has been soaked and dried. Treated fabric scorches very easily when ironed. Dyes applied to adjacent areas of wet fabric immediately after soaking will blend together, but colors applied to dry fabric will remain more separate. Wear a dust mask when working with dried soda soak fabric to prevent inhalation of particles.

Dissolving the dye in a solution of urea instead of plain water not only speeds dissolution but slows drying of the fabric while it is curing. It is especially useful in dry climates. To make *urea water:* mix 1 quart (946 ml) hot water with 1 cup (180 g) urea and 1 teaspoon (5 g) sodium hexametaphosphate (optional, with hard water) in a blender. The urea absorbs heat as it dissolves, cooling the water. Wait until the temperature of the solution is below 95° F (35° C) before mixing with dye. The urea water can be stored at room temperature in a closed container almost indefinitely. Discard if it smells like ammonia.

1. *Soaking Solution.* Mix ½ cup (122 g) *soda ash* and 1 gallon (3.8 l) hot *water.* Soak clean wet or dry fabric for at least 15 minutes. The soda soak solution can be stored at room temperature in a bucket with a tight-fitting lid for several months.

2. *Dye Solution.* Mix 1 teaspoon (3 g) *dye powder* with 1 cup (237 ml) *plain or urea water.* Vary the amount of dye depending on the intensity desired. This quantity will produce a medium value. Optional: add 3 teaspoons (19 g) *salt* and stir well. If using salt, maintain a ratio of 1 part dye to 3 parts salt. Some artists believe salt promotes dye migration into the fiber, resulting in more vibrant colors.

3. *Application.* Lay wet, soaked fabric on a plastic-covered table. Paint dye on the cloth with a bristle or foam brush, making sure that the dye penetrates the fabric. You can also apply the dye with a syringe or squeeze or spray bottle. If spraying, wear a mask or respirator with dust/mist cartridges. The fabric can be folded, tied with

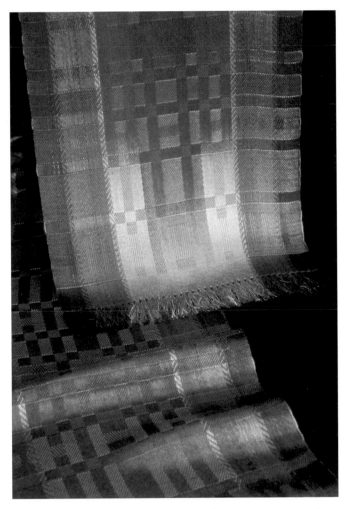

4.16 Scarf by Susan Neal. Silk warp painted with Cibacron F and silk weft immersion-dyed in Lanaset. Five-end satin, handwoven on 15 shafts at 50 ends per inch. Photo by Margot Geist.

4.17 Black is very difficult to achieve with any dye and is not possible on silk with Procion MX dye. Shown are the effects of a 10% DOS black (several blacks were mixed together) with immersion dyeing on (from bottom to top) cotton muslin, mercerized cotton, viscose rayon, silk noil, silk habotai, and silk/hemp. Photo by Tom Liden.

rubber bands, or wrapped on a pole and dipped in the dye. See "Resists" chapter beginning on page 89.

4. *Batch Curing (Fixing the Color).* Place wet fabric in a plastic bag or between layers of plastic, maintaining 70° F (21° C) or higher. Procion MX dyed areas must remain damp for 24 hours, while Cibacron F requires 48 hours. Remove the fabric from the plastic and dry.

5. Follow the instructions for "Rinsing, Washing, and Drying Fabric" on page 122.

Procion MX and Cibacron F Dyes on Silk

Procion MX and Cibacron F dyes yield good results on silk. If used with the same recipes as for cellulose, the colors will be different and not as bright because silk has fewer sites available to accept fiber-reactive dyes than cel-

4.19 Chartreuse Duster *being painted by Mark Thomas with thickened Procion MX. Photo by Leslie Hirsh.*

4.18 Chartreuse Duster and Scarf *by Mark Thomas. Solid dyed background and handpainted silk/rayon velvet with Procion MX. Photo by Leslie Hirsh.*

4.20 Overview of Chartreuse Duster *by Mark Thomas in his studio. Photo by Leslie Hirsh.*

Chart E Print Paste Measurements

	To make 1 cup (237 ml) paste	To make 1 quart (946 ml) paste	To make 1 gallon (3.8 l) paste
Water (hot)	1 cup (237 ml)	1 quart (946 ml)	1 gallon (3.8 l)
Sodium hexametaphosphate (for hard water)	¼ teaspoon (1.25 g)	1 teaspoon (5 g)	4 teaspoons (20 g)
Urea	3 tablespoons plus 2 teaspoons (40 g)	¾ cup plus 2 tablespoons (157 g)	3½ cups (630 g)
Sodium alginate, high-viscosity, low-solids	1¾ teaspoon (6.7 g)	2 tablespoons plus 1 teaspoon (26.6 g)	½ cup (91.2 g)

lulose fibers. It is impossible to dye it a deep black with fiber-reactive dye (see illustration 4.17). Use any of the preceding fiber-reactive dye recipes for silk. After rinsing and washing, neutralize the soda ash with vinegar to prevent degradation of the silk by the alkali. Prepare a solution of ¼ cup (59 ml) vinegar in 1 gallon (3.8 l) of water and soak the fabric for 10 minutes. Rinsing in plain water is optional, however unrinsed fabric will smell of vinegar.

Hints for Batch Curing

- To maintain a temperature of 70° F (21° C) in cool weather, place the plastic-wrapped fabric on top of a refrigerator, in a small room warmed by a space heater, or in a tent made from an electric blanket or water-bed heater.
- For solar heating, place the fabric in a black plastic bag and put outdoors or inside a car in the sun, maintaining 70° F (21° C) or higher.

Immersion Dyeing Silk Using Procion MX or Cibacron F as an Acid Dye

Using an acid solution of fiber-reactive dyes will prevent damage to the silk that an alkali can cause if not properly rinsed or neutralized. Use a water/fabric ratio of 30:1 to 40:1 and a dyebath temperature of 185° F (85° C). A medium DOS is 2%. Replace the soda ash with vinegar at 100% of the dry WOF and heat to 185° F (85° C). The following recipe will dye a 2% DOS solid color on about 7 ounces (200 g) or 5 yards (4.6 m) medium-weight silk.

1. Scour fabric, referring to "Preparing Fabric for Dyeing" on page 120. If the fabric is already clean and dry, soak it for at least an hour or overnight (preferred).
2. Measure a scant 1½ teaspoons (4 g) *dye.* Paste dye with a small amount of warm water and stir until no dye particles are visible in the container.
3. Measure 1½ to 2 gallons (5.7 to 7.6 l) of *water* into a nonreactive pot. This should be enough water to cover the fabric.
4. Add 3 tablespoons (61.5 g) plain *salt* and stir to dissolve. Salt is optional: some artists think that salt makes the dye more level while others omit it.
5. Add the dye mixture and 7 tablespoons (104 ml) *vinegar* to the water. Stir to mix evenly.
6. Add the wet silk to the dyepot and stir.
7. Heat slowly over 30 minutes to 185° F (85° C). Do not boil. Stir every 5 minutes to prevent streaks.
8. Move the silk to one side and stir in another 7 tablespoons (104) ml *vinegar.*
9. Hold at 185° F (85° C) and stir every 5 minutes for 30 minutes longer.
10. Turn off heat and allow dyebath to cool to room temperature.
11. Follow the instructions for "Rinsing, Washing, and Drying Fabric" on page 122.

Thickened Procion MX or Cibacron F on Cellulose and Silk

Dyes must be thickened to the right consistency for painting, stamping, stenciling, or screen printing. The most popular thickener is sodium alginate, which is made from seaweed (see "Thickeners and Printing" on page 125). The following recipes are for "regular" (high-viscosity, low-solids) sodium alginate. Sodium bicarbonate (baking soda), a weak alkali at room temperature, is used with thickened fiber-reactive dyes that are fixed by steaming, during which the baking soda is converted to sodium carbonate (soda ash). A mixture of sodium carbonate and sodium bicarbonate is used when batch-curing thickened dyes at room temperature and on silk. The addition of urea prevents the fabric from drying during batch curing while promoting penetration of the dye into the fiber. One cup of thickened dye will cover 1 square yard (about 1 square meter) printed with a design that covers 50% of the area. Scour or wash and then dry the fabric before applying thickened dye.

1. Nearly fill a blender with hot water and add sodium hexametaphosphate. Put on the lid and turn to "blend."
2. While the blender is running, add the urea through the center opening.
3. Add the sodium alginate slowly through the center opening to avoid lumps. Replace the center cap. The mixture will begin to thicken immediately.
4. Pour the mixture into a nonreactive container and whisk in any remaining water called for in the recipe.

More water can be added later if the mixture is too thick. The mixture will look grainy, but after at least 1 hour it will become clear and thick. Letting it sit overnight will yield a smoother print paste.

Print paste thickness is a personal preference and technique. The above recipe is based on Holly's recommended amounts. For a thinner recipe, use 1 teaspoon (3.8 g) and for a thicker recipe use 3 teaspoons (11.4 g) sodium alginate for one cup of paste.

Unused print paste can be stored in a closed container for 6 months or more in the refrigerator. Return it to room temperature before using, skimming off any mold that may have formed on it before using. The print paste will become thinner when stored for a long time, but it is still good unless it smells strongly of ammonia.

Fixing Thickened Procion MX and Cibacron F Dyes

Fabrics dyed with print paste must be treated to ensure successful fixing of the dye with the fiber. Batch curing is the only suitable fixing treatment for silk as heated alkali will damage the fabric. Allow other fabrics to dry before heating and steaming (see "Steaming," page 126).

- *Batch curing.* Cover the fabric or roll between layers of plastic. Set aside for 12 to 48 hours in a room whose temperature is *at least 70° F (21° C).* Turquoise and dark colors need at least 24 hours to cure. Dry before washing.
- *Canning kettle with rack.* Steam for 15 to 30 minutes.
- *Steam iron.* Iron small pieces for 5 to 10 minutes in a well-ventilated space.
- *Pressure cooker.* Steam for 5 to 10 minutes under pressure.
- *Professional steamer,* such as a bullet or horizontal steamer. Steam for at least 15 to 30 minutes after steam is seen escaping from the vent. The length of time required depends on the amount of fabric in the steamer. Increase the steaming time for larger rolls of fabric, based on personal experience.

After fixing the dye, rinse and wash (see "Rinsing, Washing, and Drying Fabric" on page 122).

Hints for Fixing Thickened Procion MX and Cibacron F Dyes

- If colors run during steaming, decrease the amount of urea.
- Some artists use ¼ teaspoon (0.5 g) Ludigol (an oxidizing agent) per cup of thickened dye when steaming to produce bright, vibrant colors.

Chart F Thickened Procion MX and Cibacron F Dye Paste Measurements for 1 cup (237 ml)

Dye (dry powder or stock solution)	Light: ½ to 1 teaspoon (1.5 to 3 g) Medium: 2 to 3 teaspoons (6 to 9 g) Dark: 4 to 6 teaspoons (12 to 18 g) Black: 8 to 10 teaspoons (24 to 30 g)
Thin applications, handpainting, monoprinting, stamping	1 to 2 teaspoons (5 to 10 ml) mixed print paste plus water to make 1 cup (237 ml)
Thick applications, monoprinting, screen printing, stamping	1 cup (237 ml) mixed print paste with no added water
Alkali fixed with heat (not for silk)	1 teaspoon (5.3 g) baking soda
Alkali for batch curing	1 teaspoon (5.3 g) mixed alkali (see note below)

Note: Mixed alkali is used with batch curing and with silk. Mix 4 tablespoons (63.6 g) baking soda with 1 tablespoon (15 g) soda ash. Label, date, and store in a closed container for up to 6 months.

1. Mix *dye* with 2 tablespoons (30 ml) water to a lump-free paste.

2. *For thin dye paste,* mix 1 to 2 teaspoons (5 to 10 ml) *print paste* with the dye paste that you just made in Step 1 above or an equal amount of stock solution or liquid dye. Add water to make 1 cup (237 ml). Stir thoroughly.

For thick dye paste, mix 1 cup (237 ml) prepared print paste with the dye paste from Step 1 or an equal amount of stock solution or liquid dye. Stir thoroughly.

3. Add *baking soda or mixed alkali* to the thick or thin dye paste that you just made and mix thoroughly. Use the dye paste within 4 hours; otherwise the color will not be fixed and will wash out.

4. Handpaint, monoprint, stamp, stencil, or screen-print fabric on a padded surface (see "Printing Surfaces and Printing Tables" on page 70).

5. Fix dye by batch curing or steaming.

4.21 Vegetables *by Sally Jones. 64" l × 7" w (162.5 cm × 18 cm). Cassava-paste resist printed on white silk. Vegetable shapes printed with Procion H dyes. Pattern is from a heavy cord glued onto a block and transformed into a repeating pattern in Photoshop. Border attached separately. Photo by Jeff Baird.*

4.22 Horses *by Sally Jones. 70" l × 10" w (178 cm × 25.5 cm). Procion H dyes printed on silk charmeuse. Four designs pieced to make one scarf. Photo by Jeff Baird.*

Left: 4.23 Water 4 Life *by Iren Rothenberger. 72" l × 15" w (183 cm × 38 cm). Screen-printed with thickened Procion H. Also gutta resist, Tinfix and DuPont dyes. Designs from manhole cover rubbings and metal print plate letters. Right:* 4.24 Water 4 Life *detail. Photos by Iren Rothenberger.*

Procion MX and Cibacron F Dyes on Wool

Wool can be dyed with Procion MX or Cibacron F fiber-reactive dyes using an acid process. Even when outdated and no longer viable for cellulose fabrics, these dyes can be used on wool although the colors will not be the same as on cellulose fabrics. In general, however, genuine acid dyes are preferred for dyeing wool (and in some instances, silk). When using fiber-reactive dyes on wool, acid is used in place of the alkali and a hot dyebath is required. Change temperatures gradually to prevent felting.

Use a water/fiber ratio of 30:1 to 40:1. A medium DOS is 2%. Acid and salt are the dye assistants. You may use vinegar at 100% of the dry WOF or citric acid crystals at 8% to bring the dyebath to pH 5. Add salt at 10% WOF. For best results, use a high-quality white virgin wool that is free of excess lanolin, which feels greasy to the touch. See "Preparing Fabric for Dyeing" on page 120 for removal of excess lanolin. The following recipe will dye a solid color on about 7 ounces (200 g) of wool, about 2 yards (2 m) of lightweight wool such as challis.

1. Soak the clean wool 30 minutes to overnight in 2 gallons (7.6 l) warm water plus ½ teaspoon (2.5 ml) Synthrapol. Squeeze out the excess water. Rinsing is not necessary.
2. Measure a scant 1½ teaspoons (4 g) *dye* for a medium color, 2% DOS, and up to 5 teaspoons (15 g) for dark colors. Add it to a small amount of warm water and stir until no dye particles are visible in the container.
3. Measure 1½ to 2 gallons (5.7 to 7.6 l) *water* into a non-reactive pot and add water softener (hexametaphosphate) if water is hard.
4. Add 1 tablespoon (20.5 g) *salt* and stir until dissolved.
5. Add the dye to the dyepot. Stir well.
6. Add ½ cup (118 ml) *vinegar* or 2 teaspoons (8 g) *citric acid crystals*. Stir well.
7. Add the wet wool to the dyepot and stir.
8. Heat slowly for 30 to 45 minutes, stirring gently but continuously so that the wool will take up the dye evenly. After 45 minutes, the bath should reach a simmer (not a rolling boil).
9. Push the fabric to one side and add another ½ cup (118 ml) *vinegar* or 2 teaspoons (8 g) *citric acid crystals*. Stir to mix.
10. Simmer the fabric at 200° F (93° C) (not a rolling boil) for 30 minutes; little color should remain in the bath.
11. Allow the fabric to cool to room temperature in the dyebath. Rinse well in room-temperature water.
12. Aftersoak. Mix 2 tablespoons (30 ml) household ammonia and 1 gallon (3.8 l) room-temperature water. Move the wool gently in the solution for 3 to 5 minutes. Rinse in room-temperature water.
13. Neutralize the ammonia in a solution of ¼ cup (59 ml) vinegar in 1 gallon (3.8 l) room-temperature water, moving the wool gently in the solution. Squeeze out excess water.
14. Air-dry the wool, avoiding direct sunlight, which yellows wool.

Procion H Dyes

Don't mix Procion H and MX dyes. (Think of "H" standing for "heat" as a way to remember that Procion H dyes need heat to react.) Because of their stability, Procion H dyes are sold in both powder and liquid forms—4 teaspoons (20 ml) liquid dye is equivalent to about 1 teaspoon (3 g) dry dye powder. Procion H liquid is a good choice of fiber-reactive dye if you are allergic to dye powders. Dye powder can be made into a stock solution (see "Calculating Stock Solutions" on page 124). Ludigol (sodium salt of m-nitrobenzene sulfonic acid, also sold as PRO Chem Flakes) is an oxidizing agent that is added to thickened dyes to maximize colors during steam fixing, especially dark colors and with silk fabric. Procion H can be used for thin or thick applications. Because these dyes are not as popular with artists as other fiber-reactive dyes, fewer mixed colors are sold.

Thin and Thickened Procion H Dye

Thin applications are used to paint on cotton, silk, linen, and rayon with watercolor effects or with resists (gutta, Presist, or water-based resist) for traditional silk painting. If using a resist on thin fabric or silk, stretch the fabric on a frame or stretcher bars. The resist must penetrate to the back of denser fabrics. Check the back of the fabric to make sure the resist has penetrated the fabric. If the resist has not penetrated, apply the resist to the back of the fabric, following the same pattern as on the front. Allow the resist to dry before proceeding. The thickened recipe is for screen printing, stamping, stenciling, monoprinting, or handpainting on cotton, linen, rayon, or silk.

1. Scour fabric, referring to "Preparing Fabric for Dyeing" on page 120.
2. Make 1 quart (946 ml) urea water.
   Measure 2 cups (474 ml) hot *water* in a glass jar.
   Add 1 teaspoon (5 g) *sodium hexametaphosphate* (optional); use if the water is hard, stir to dissolve.
   Add 10 tablespoons (110 g) *urea* and 1 tablespoon *Ludigol* (6 g), stir to dissolve.
   Add 2 cups (474 ml) warm *water* to make 1 quart (946 ml) of urea water and cool to room temperature. The urea water can be stored almost indefinitely in a closed container at room temperature. Discard if it smells like ammonia.
3. Thin application for painting, watercolor effects, and for use with resists.
A. *Dye powder.* Dissolve ½ to 4 teaspoons (1.5 to 12 g) dye, 8 teaspoons (24 g) for black, in ¼ cup (59 ml) of

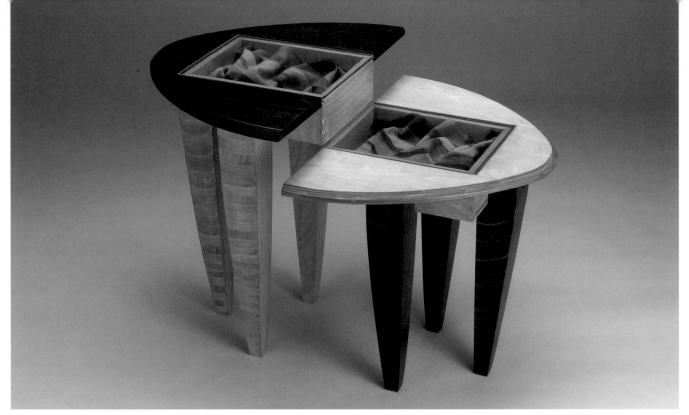

4.25 Kimono Side Table *by Anne Bossert. 21½" h × 30" w × 22" d (54.5 cm × 76 cm × 56 cm). Procion MX used on cotton painted warp and Baltic birch plywood. Dyeing, weaving, and woodworking by the artist. The colors were inspired by an antique kimono. Photo by Joe Mendoza.*

urea water. Add urea water to make 1 cup (237 ml), stirring thoroughly. Store for up to 2 months in a cool, dark place. Discard if it smells like ammonia.

B. *Liquid dye.* Measure 1 to 20 teaspoons (5 to 100 ml) into a measuring cup and add urea water to make one cup (237 ml). This solution can be stored for up to a year in a cool, dark place. Discard if it smells like ammonia.

C. Just before painting, dissolve *alkali* in 1 cup (237 ml) dye mixture.
   Cotton, linen, or rayon: 1 teaspoon (5 g) *soda ash*
   Silk: 1 teaspoon (5.3 g) *baking soda*
   The dye mixture will keep for 3 weeks if activated with soda ash or 2 months if activated with baking soda. Discard expired mixtures.

D. Apply the mixture to the fabric with a brush. Let the dye spread, or try overlapping brushstrokes of different colors. Salt can be sprinkled on the wet areas for starburst effects. Brush off the salt when the fabric is dry.

4. Thickened applications (printing, stamping, stenciling, monoprinting).

A. Print paste. Measure 1 cup (237 ml) of *urea water* in a blender or nonreactive bowl. Add ¾ teaspoon (1.4 g) *Ludigol* and stir to dissolve. Add high-viscosity, low-solids *sodium alginate* according to the thickness of paste desired.
   thin (handpainting), 1 teaspoon (3.8 g)
   medium (monoprinting, stamping), 2 teaspoons (7.6 g)
   thick (monoprinting, screen printing, stamping), 3 teaspoons (11.4 g)
   Stir the sodium alginate rapidly into the liquid with

a whisk or a blender until the sodium alginate particles are evenly distributed. Let stand for 1 hour or overnight for smoothest printing. Print paste can be stored in a refrigerator in a closed container for up to 6 months. Return to room temperature before using.

B. Dye paste. Mix 1 cup (237 ml) of the print paste with Procion H. *Dye powder:* Dissolve ½ to 4 teaspoons (1.5 to 12 g), 8 teaspoons (24 g) for black, in just enough water to make a lump-free paste, then add to print paste. *Liquid Procion H:* Use 1 to 20 teaspoons (5 to 100 ml) thin with urea water if necessary (see Step 2).

C. Add soda ash or baking soda fixative to the dye paste just before applying it to the fabric.

Soda Ash (cotton, linen, rayon). Add 1 teaspoon (5 g) soda ash per cup (237 ml) of dye paste. Stir until thoroughly dissolved.

Baking soda (silk). Add 1 teaspoon (5.3 g) bicarbonate of soda per cup (237 ml) of dye paste. Stir until thoroughly dissolved.

The dye mixture will keep for 3 weeks if activated with soda ash or 2 months if activated with baking soda.

D. Screen-print, stamp, stencil, monoprint or handpaint the fabric.

5. Air-dry fabric thoroughly.

6. Fix the dye (see "Steaming" on page 126).
   Bake in an oven at 300° F (149° C) for 5 to 30 minutes.
   Steam-iron small pieces for 10 minutes.
   Steam for 30 to 45 minutes. Steaming produces the most brilliant colors.

7. See "Rinsing, Washing, and Drying Fabric" on page 122.

Chapter Five
Acid Dyes

Acid dyes, first manufactured in 1862, are used on protein (animal) fibers and can also be used on nylon and some acrylics. These dyes contain acidic groups in their molecular structure; some require additional acid in the dyebath to promote chemical bonding with the fiber. Common studio dyes are Kiton, 1:2 Metal Complex, and Wash-Fast. Because they are stable and do not react with water (hydrolyze), stock solutions have a long shelf life. Most of an acid dye goes into the fabric during dyeing. At a 1%

Safety Alert
Wear an apron, gloves, eye protection and an acid gas respirator when handling acids. Glacial (undiluted) acetic acid is very corrosive to the skin and respiratory system. Vinegar (usually standardized to 5% acetic acid) is safer and less irritating to the skin, but continuous inhalation can cause bronchitis, so work outdoors or provide good ventilation.

5.1 Chainlink *by Carolyn and Vincent Carleton. 11' h × 13' w (3.5 m × 4 m). Acid dye on worsted wool weft and Belgian linen warp. Handwoven summer and winter block doubleweave. Photo by John Birchard.*
Opposite: Fabric clamp-resisted and immersion-dyed in WashFast acid dyes, then painted, stamped, and resisted with thickened WashFast acid dye. Photo by Joe Coca.

DOS, the dyebath should be clear at the end of processing. Food colorings are acid dyes. Their relative innocuousness makes Kool-Aid, Easter egg, or cake-decorating colors popular as dyes for children's art projects; however, they are expensive, color control is difficult, and the results may not be lightfast or washfast. Acid dyes are also a component of all-purpose household (union) dyes such as Rit.

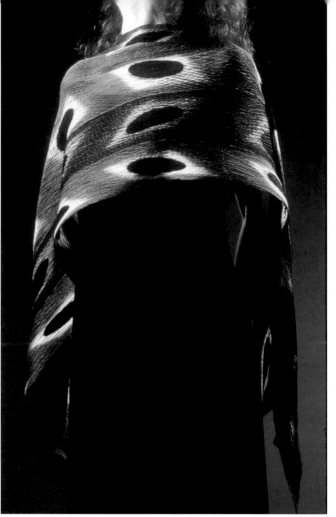

Clockwise from left:
5.2 Red Sea Orange Feathers by Jean Cacicedo. Immersion and resist-dyed shibori with acid dyes on fulled and felted wool. Stitched polyester, pieced and quilted. Photo by Kate Cameron.
5.3 China Silk Scarf by Laura Hunter. 75" l × 18" w (190.5 cm × 46 cm). Silk was immersion-dyed with acid dyes, folded and clamped with a circular shape, and discharged with thiourea dioxide. Then the circle was replaced with a square, clamped, and dyed purple. Finally, the scarf was put through an arashi shibori or pole-wrapping process and dried to set the pleats. Photo by Doug Yaple.
5.4 Fantasy Flower Jacquard by Jacquelyn Rice and Uosis Juod-valkis. Digital image printed on a wide-bed inkjet printer with acid dyes on silk. Photo by Uosis Juodvalkis.

Top left: 5.5 Chinese Butterfly Wool Jacket *by Jacquelyn Rice and Uosis Juodvalkis. Digital image printed on a wide-bed inkjet printer with acid dyes on wool. Photo by Uosis Juodvalkis.*

Top right: 5.6 Blue Butterfly Silk Georgette Jacket Swish *by Jacquelyn Rice and Uosis Juodvalkis. Digital image printed on a wide-bed inkjet printer with acid dyes on silk. Photo by Uosis Juodvalkis.*

Bottom left: 5.7 Watercolors *by Judith Content. 52" h × 65" w × ¼" d (132 cm × 165 cm × .63 cm). Shibori-dyed Thai silk with acid dyes, discharged, pieced, and collaged. Inspired by the infinite colors of water as reflected from the earth, sky, and fire.*

Bottom right: 5.8 Watercolors *detail. Photos by James Dewrance.*

Kiton Acid Dyes

Kiton acid dyes, also called leveling acid dyes, produce rich shades and even (level) colors. They are lightfast but are only moderately washfast; keep wash water at less than 105° F (41° C) to minimize fading. Although the original brand name was changed to Erio when the manufacturer, Ciba, Ltd., merged with Geigy in the 1970s, many people still refer to these as Kiton dyes. When stored in a cool, dark, dry place, the dye powders have a shelf life of 4 years or longer.

Factors in Dyeing with Kiton Acid Dyes

Multiple bright colors can be mixed from the basic colors of red, yellow, blue, magenta, turquoise, and black. The dyes are so concentrated that 1 ounce (28.3 g) will dye 2 to 6 pounds (0.9 to 2.7 kg) of fabric. For coloring protein or nylon fibers, Kiton acid dyes require acid, salt, water, and heat, the amounts depending on the dry WOF. All fibers do not take up the dye to the same extent; for example, dyeing wool yarn plied with silk will not result in a yarn of a uniform color (see illustration 5.11). This characteristic could be used to advantage.

Acid promotes the reaction between the dye molecules and the fiber. Glacial (95% to 99%) acetic acid, sold by chemical suppliers, should be diluted by adding 1 part acid to 4 parts water. Wearing rubber gloves and eye protection, add *acid to water* (not the reverse). Another option is to purchase 28% strength acetic acid from a photographic darkroom supplier. White vinegar or citric acid crystals are other choices; the crystals are popular because they are odorless. The pH of the dyebath should be 3 to 5.5. With too little acid (that is, with a higher pH), the dye will not penetrate into the fiber but remain in the dyebath; with too much acid (that is, with a lower pH) the dye will bond rapidly, causing streaks; therefore add the acid in increments to avoid uneven color.

Salt slows the migration of dye molecules into the fiber molecules, resulting in a more evenly dyed fabric. Table salt is added in increments, but Glauber's salt (sodium sulfate), another alternative, is added all at once. Too much salt will prevent some dye from bonding with the fiber.

Water carries the dissolved dye chemicals to the fabric. If there is too little water, the fabric cannot circulate sufficiently, resulting in streaky color. Using a small, narrow pot ensures coverage of a small amount of fabric with the least amount of water.

Heat increases the rate of the chemical reaction and the permanence of the color. For even color, increase the temperature slowly and hold the bath at the maximum temperature for the time recommended for each kind of fiber. Most of the dye reaction occurs between 158° F (70° C) and 176° F (80° C).

Kiton Acid Dye Immersion Dyeing

Wear an acid gas respirator and have good ventilation while heating the dyebath. See the notes at the end of the recipe for variations based on fiber type. Prepare dye stock solutions (see page 124).

1. Weigh dry fabric and record WOF on "Dye Worksheet" (see page 119).
2. Scour the fabric (see "Preparing Fabric for Dyeing" on page 120). If the fabric is already clean and dry, place in warm water and add ¼ teaspoon (1.25 ml) Synthrapol and soak for at least an hour or overnight (preferred).
3. Calculate the following amounts (see sample calculation below):

Water/fiber ratio, 30:1 to 50:1 (40:1 preferred)

Dye stock solution based on DOS:
    pale value = less than 1% DOS
    medium value = 1% DOS, except 2% DOS for nylon
    dark value = over 3% DOS
    black = 6% DOS

Salt (choose one)
    table salt at 50% WOF
    Glauber's salt at 15% to 20% WOF

Acid (choose one)
    28% acetic acid at 16% WOF
    vinegar at 100% WOF
    citric acid crystals at 8% WOF

4. Measure water into a nonreactive pot.
5. Add dye stock solution and stir.
6. Add the salt and stir to dissolve.
7. Immerse the fabric, begin heating and timing. Add the acid a little at a time while very slowly raising the temperature as required by the fiber type (see below). Stir every 10 minutes.
    Silk: 104° to 185° F (40° to 85° C)
    Wool: 195° to 200° F (91° to 93° C)
    Nylon: 212° F (100° C)
8. Hold at the temperatures based on the fiber
    Silk: 45 minutes
    Wool: 60 to 90 minutes
    Nylon: 60 minutes

Facing page, clockwise from top left:
5.9 Bark and Leaves by Jeung-Hwa Park. Bark is 100" h × 75" w (254 cm × 190.5 cm), machine-knitted, stitched, and felted wool and rayon. Leaves are 50" h × 10" w (127 cm × 25.5 cm), machine-knitted, tied, and felted wool. Both were colored with acid dyes. Photo by Karen Philippi.
5.10 Spying on China by Jessica Smith. Digital print with acid dyes on Indian douppioni silk. Photo by Jessica Smith.
5.11 Handspun plied wool and silk yarn dyed with Kiton dyes, showing the different absorption rates of the same color on two fibers. Photo by Tom Liden.
5.12 Oceans Eleven by Rae Gold. 34" (86.5 cm) long. Machine-knitted merino wool was acid-dyed with three colors, then stitched, pleated, and tied, and finally immersed in a fourth color. Photo by Craig Thompson.
5.13 Pieced Coats by Ana Lisa Hedstrom. Acid dyes on silk with shibori and discharge. Photo by Elaine Keenan.

9. Remove dyepot from heat. Let stand, covered, overnight. More dye may be absorbed during cooling. Drying the fabric before rinsing may increase color retention. After the bath has cooled below 185° F (85° C) pour into a plastic bucket.

10. Follow instructions for "Rinsing, Washing, and Drying Fabric" on page 122.

Fiber Variations in Kiton Acid Dyeing

Silk Do not allow a silk dyebath to go above 185° F (85° C). Boiling will weaken the silk and reduce its luster. If dyeing shiny silk, use table salt as the leveler—Glauber's salt may reduce the luster. Silk is less washfast when dyed with Kiton acid dyes than with fiber-reactive dyes; use the latter on silk that will be washed frequently.

Wool The dyebath can be brought just to a simmer, but not a rolling boil. Temperature changes must be gradual and stirring limited to prevent felting. Use the same procedures with mohair, alpaca, and cashmere.

Nylon absorbs the dye less readily than either wool or silk and is more prone to streaking. Stir frequently to maximize leveling.

Kiton Dyeing Hints

■ Different colors penetrate the fibers at different rates. In a dyepot containing a mixture of three colors, the fabric may go through three color changes before it takes on its the final color.

■ If the desired color is reached before the dyebath time is up, transfer the fabric to another pot with the same amount of water, acid, and salt, but no dye. Process for the remaining time required by the recipe to allow the absorbed dye to bond completely with the fiber. Omitting this "stop bath" will result in a fabric that will not be wash- or lightfast.

Microwave Dyeing with Kiton Dyes

Using a microwave can save time when dyeing small (less than ¼ yard or ¼ meter) quantities of fabric, but penetration of the dye into the fiber is likely to be incomplete, possibly leading to fading through exposure to ultraviolet light or abrasion. Calculate dye, acid, table salt, and water amounts based on the immersion recipe.

1. Put *water* in microwave-safe container.
2. Add the *dye stock solution,* half the *acid,* and half the *table salt.*
3. Add wet fabric.
4. Cook on high power for about 5 minutes; the time will depend on the power of the microwave. Experiment with your microwave for the best amount of time.
5. Remove the container from the microwave. The fabric and container will be very hot, so use caution when handling. Lift the fabric and hold it above the dyebath so that excess liquid drips back into container. Stir in remaining acid and salt and replace fabric.
6. Cook on high power for about 5 minutes.
7. Remove the container from the microwave. Turn fabric and stir dye liquid.
8. Cook on high for about 5 minutes longer.
9. Allow the container and fabric to cool completely. More dye will be absorbed during cooling.
10. Follow instructions for "Rinsing, Washing, and Drying Fabric" on page 122.

1:2 Metal Complex Dyes (Lanaset, Telana, and Sabraset)

These dyes, which have one metal atom attached to two dye atoms, combine an acid dye with a wool-reactive dye. They are more complicated to use than other dyes but will dye wool and silk the same color and work well with shibori or bound resist techniques. Usually, all the dye goes

---

Chart G Sample Calculation for Kiton Acid Dye Bath

The following recipe will dye about 7 ounces (200 g) of cloth, about 5 yards (4.6 m) medium-weight silk, or 2 yards (2 m) of lightweight wool such as challis. Although there are two salt and three acid choices for dyeing with Kiton acid dyes, only one of each is shown.

0.5% pale value	1% medium value	3% dark value
1% stock solution 200 g WOF x 0.5 = 100 ml dye stock	200 g WOF x 1 = 200 ml dye stock	200 g WOF x 3 = 600 ml dye stock
Water at water/fiber ratio of 40:1 200 g WOF x 40 = 8000 g = 8000 ml = 8 l water	200 g WOF x 40 = 8000 g = 8000 ml = 8 l water	200 g WOF x 40 = 8000 g = 8000 ml = 8 l water
Salt (table) at 50% WOF 200 g WOF x 0.50 = 100 g salt	200 g WOF x 0.50 = 100 g salt	200 g WOF x 0.50 = 100 g salt
Citric acid crystals at 8% WOF 200 g WOF x 0.08 = 16 g citric acid	200 g WOF x 0.08 = 16 g citric acid	200 g WOF x 0.08 = 16 g citric acid

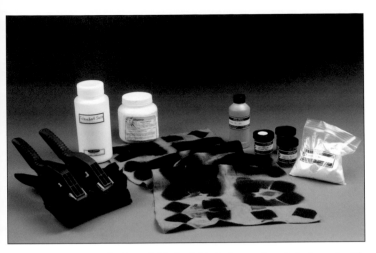

5.14 *Lanaset dyed wool fabric, folded, clamped, and discharged with Thiox (thiourea dioxide). Photo by Tom Liden.*

into the fiber for a clear dyebath at the end of processing. A 1% DOS is considered a medium color. They are light- and washfast. These dyes discharge with thiourea dioxide (see "Discharging" on page 57). Some colors discharge to an off-white while others become a different color. Dry dye powders will keep indefinitely, and stock solutions are good for 6 months when stored in a cool, dark place.

Factors in Dyeing with Lanaset Dyes

Lanaset dyes come in thirteen manufactured colors. Not all the colors are as bright as Kiton or WashFast acid dyes, and the red range is weak. The black is excellent, which is especially important as black is one of the hardest colors to achieve. They are economical to use, with 1 ounce (28 g) of dye powder coloring 6 pounds (2.7 kg) of wool to a medium shade. Stock solutions are recommended for ease and safety (see "Stock Solutions" on page 124). Lanaset dyes are used with acetic acid, sodium acetate, Glauber's salt, and Albegal SET.

Acid provides Lanaset dyes with the needed pH of 4.5 to 5.0.; the absorption of colors stops if the pH goes above 5.5 so careful monitoring is essential. Either 56% acetic acid or distilled white vinegar may be used. Glacial (95% to 99%) acetic acid, sold by chemical suppliers, should be diluted by adding 1 part acid to 1 part water. Wearing rubber gloves and eye protection, add *acid to water* (not the reverse). Another option is to purchase 56% strength acetic acid from a photographic darkroom supplier. Vinegar is safer, easier to get, and cheaper in small quantities, but not recommended for large-scale production. Because of its weak strength (around 5%), large amounts of vinegar would be required for big dye projects. The amount of acid needed in a given dyebath will vary according to the pH of the water.

Sodium acetate is used to buffer (stabilize) the pH of the dyebath. Even if the dyebath begins at pH 4.5, the pH may increase during dyeing. If the pH rises above 5.5, add a few drops of acid to lower it. If the pH goes below 4.5, add 1 tablespoon (13.2 g) of sodium acetate to raise it.

Glauber's salt (sodium sulfate) retards the rate of dye uptake to promote even color and improve dye exhaustion.

Albegal SET slows down the rate at which the dye migrates into the fiber to promote level dyeing, but too much will cause poor dye exhaustion.

Water provides the medium for the chemicals, dye, and fiber to come into contact. The water ratio is based on the fiber being dyed. The pH level of the water being used in the dyebath can affect dyeing, so check with pH paper. The amount of acid you need to add to the dyebath will be affected by the acidity of the water. If your water is hard, use sodium hexametaphosphate to soften it.

Heat must be increased slowly to prevent streaking. Most Lanaset dyes exhaust between 198° and 212° F (92° and 100° C). Cooling at least 30 minutes or overnight (preferred) will extract the maximum amount of color from the dyebath.

Lanaset Immersion Dyeing

See sample calculations below. Make stock solutions (see page 124). Wear an acid gas respirator and provide good ventilation while heating the dyebath.

1. Weigh dry fabric and record WOF on "Dye Worksheet" (see page 119).
2. Scour the fabric, referring to "Preparing Fabric for Dyeing" on page 120. If the fabric is already clean and dry, place in warm water, add ¼ teaspoon (1.25 ml) Synthrapol, and soak for at least an hour or overnight (preferred).
3. Calculate the following amounts:

Water/fiber ratio
   40:1 for silk
   20:1 to 30:1 for wool, other protein fibers, and nylon

Dye stock solution, amount according to DOS
   pale value = less than 1% DOS
   medium value = 1% DOS
   dark value = over 3% DOS
   black = 6% DOS

Acid (choose one)
   56% acetic acid at 2% to 4% WOF or
   vinegar at 100% WOF

Sodium acetate
   begin at 1% to 2% WOF, the amount depends on the pH of water

Glauber's salt
   2% to 5% WOF for silk
   10% WOF on wool, other protein fibers, and nylon

Albegal SET
   2% WOF for silk
   1% WOF for wool, other protein fibers, and nylon

4. Measure warm water and pour into nonreactive pot that is large enough for the fabric to move freely in. For hard water, add *sodium hexametaphosphate.*

5. Add Glauber's salt, Albegal SET, acid, and sodium acetate. Stir to dissolve.

6. Measure the pH; adjust with acid or sodium acetate to pH 4.5 to 5.0.

7. Add clean, wet fabric. Heat slowly to 120° F (49° C) and stir for 10 minutes.

8. Remove fabric from the dyepot.

9. Add dye stock solution and stir.

10. Return the fabric to the dyebath.

11. Keep the temperature at 120° F (49° C) for 10 minutes longer.

12. Increase the temperature slowly over 45 to 60 minutes to prevent streaking to
    Silk: 185° F (85° C)
    Wool: 200° F (93° C)
    Mohair and other hair fibers: 180° F (82° C)
    Nylon: 205° F (96° C)

13. Stir the fabric every 10 to 15 minutes.

14. Hold at the temperature specified for the fiber
    Silk: 20 to 30 minutes
    Wool: 30 to 45 minutes
    Hair fibers: 15 to 20 minutes
    Nylon: 30 to 45 minutes
    Black may require more time to exhaust.
    If dyeing a pale value, a colorless dyebath means that all the dye has combined with the fiber. Stop heating and skip to Step 17.

15. Cool fabric in the covered dyebath for at least 30 minutes or overnight (preferred). More dye will fix during cooling. Drying the fabric before rinsing may increase color retention.

16. Add soda ash to neutralize the dyebath to pH 7 before discarding.

17. Follow instructions for "Rinsing, Washing, and Drying Fabric" on page 122.

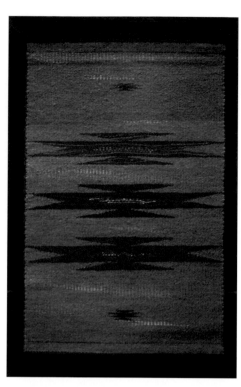

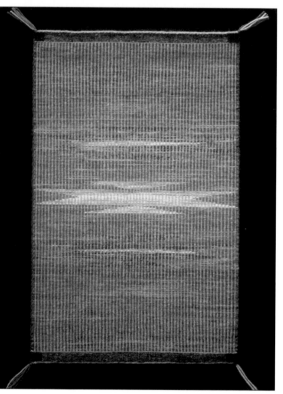

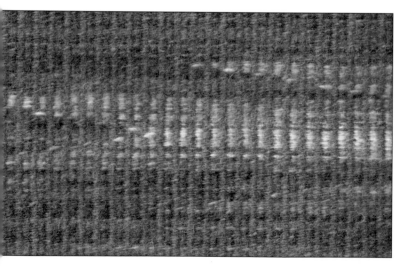

Top: 5.15 Snapdragons *by Stephanie Hoppe. 40" h × 25" w × ¼" d (101.5 cm × 63.5 cm × .63 cm). One-ply wool weft dyed with Lanaset and WashFast acid dyes. This rug began as an inquiry into red dyes. Because there was no suitable Lanaset cool red, a WashFast dye was used. A total of thirty-five different reds were used in the rug. Plain weave, twining, discontinuous eccentric wefts, and four selvedges woven on a Navajo-Hopi-style loom with 4-ply wool warp. Above: 5.16* Hibiscus *by Stephanie Hoppe. 40" h × 25" w × ¼" d (101.5 cm × 63.5 cm × .63 cm). One-ply wool and silk weft yarns dyed with Lanaset. Plain weave on a Navajo-Hopi-style loom with 4-ply wool warp, discontinuous wefts, and four selvedges. Left: 5.17* Hibiscus *detail. Photos by Stephanie Hoppe.*

Chart H Sample Calculation for Lanaset Immersion Bath

The following recipe will dye about 7 ounces (200 g) of cloth, about 5 yards (4.6 m) medium-weight silk. Lanaset calculations differ according to the fiber and type of acid used; this example is for silk using 1% sodium acetate and 3% Glauber's salt.

0.5% pale value	1% medium value	3% dark value
1% stock solution 200 g WOF x 0.5 = 100 ml dye stock	200 g WOF x 1 = 200 ml dye stock	200 g WOF x 3 = 600 ml dye stock
Water at water/fiber ratio of 40:1 for silk 200 g WOF x 40 = 8000 g = 8000 ml = 8 l water	200 g WOF x 40 = 8000 g = 8000 ml = 8 l water	200 g WOF x 40 = 8000 g = 8000 ml = 8 l water
Acid (vinegar) 100% WOF 200 g WOF x 1.00 = 200 ml vinegar	200 g WOF x 1.00 = 200 ml vinegar	200 g WOF x 1.00 = 200 ml vinegar
Sodium acetate, begin with 1% to 2% WOF depending on water pH (2% used here) 200 g WOF x 0.01 = 2 g	200 g WOF x 0.01 = 2 g	200 g WOF x 0.01 = 2 g
Glauber's salt 2% to 5% WOF for silk (3% used here) 200 g WOF x 0.03 = 6 g	200 g WOF x 0.03 = 6 g	200 g WOF x 0.03 = 6 g
Albegal SET 2% WOF for silk 200 g WOF x 0.02 = 4 ml	200 g WOF x 0.02 = 4 ml	200 g WOF x 0.02 = 4 ml

Neutral Acid Dyes (WashFast, Nylomine)

Neutral acid dyes are used in a slightly acid to neutral solution of pH 6.5 to 7.0. Also known as milling colors, they were originally used to dye wool in mills. Most are lightfast and washfast up to 120° F (49° C) but may be difficult to dissolve. A wide range of colors is available, including an excellent black. These dyes are sold under the names WashFast and Nylomine (the latter was originally developed to dye nylon). Dye powders stored in a cool dark place will keep at least 4 years.

Factors in Dyeing with WashFast Acid Dyes

WashFast acid dyes dye quickly, but level colors are harder to achieve with mixed colors because the component colors are absorbed by the fiber at different rates. They exhaust well. Acid and salt are the dye auxiliaries. Stock solutions are recommended for ease of use and safety (see "Stock Solutions" on page 124). WashFast acid dyes are economical: 1 ounce (28.3 g) of dye powder will color 6 pounds (2.7 kg) of wool a medium shade.

Use 56% acetic acid (from a photographic darkroom supplier), white distilled vinegar, or citric acid crystals to produce a dyebath of pH 6.5 to 7.0. Ammonium sulfate, a crystalline solid available from dye suppliers or as fertilizer from garden stores, is another choice. Heating dissolved ammonium sulfate results in the formation of small amounts of sulfuric acid, which lowers the pH of the dyebath. As the dyebath becomes more acidic, the dye molecules attach to the fiber more slowly for more level results.

Salt aids in leveling by slowing down molecular binding and also helps to exhaust the dyepot. Either Glauber's salt or table salt may be used. Use more salt with colors that are hard to level. If level colors are not an issue, such as shibori or tie-dye techniques, the salt can be omitted.

WashFast Acid Immersion Dyeing

Begin with stock solutions (see page 124). Sample calculations are below. Wear a respirator with acid gas cartridges and provide good ventilation while heating the dyebath.

1. Weigh dry fabric and record on the "Dye Worksheet" (see page 119) before scouring or soaking fabric in water.
2. Scour the fabric to be dyed, referring to "Preparing Fabric for Dyeing" on page 120. If the fabric is already clean and dry, place in warm water, add ¼ teaspoon (1.25 ml) Synthrapol, and soak for at least an hour or overnight (preferred) for maximum even color.
3. Calculate the following amounts:

Water/fiber ratio, 20:1 to 40:1
Dye stock solution, amount according to DOS
    pale value = less than 1% DOS
    medium value = 1% DOS
    dark value = over 3% DOS
    black = 6% DOS
Acid (choose one)
    56% acetic acid at 3% WOF
    vinegar at 36% WOF
    citric acid crystals at 3% WOF
    ammonium sulfate at 3% WOF for wool and nylon, 1% to 2% WOF for silk
Salt (choose one)
    Glauber's salt at 3% to 5% WOF
    table salt at 3% to 5% WOF

4. Measure warm water and pour into nonreactive pot large enough for the fabric to move freely in. Add *sodium hexametaphosphate* if the water is hard.

5. Add the acid and salt. Stir to dissolve.

6. Add clean, wet fabric. Stir gently for 10 minutes.

7. Remove the fabric from the dyepot.

8. Add the dye stock solution and stir.

9. Return the fabric to the dyebath.

10. Increase the temperature gradually over 45 minutes to prevent streaking to
    Silk: 185° F (85° C)
    Wool: 212° F (100° C)
    Nylon: 205° F (96° C)

11. Stir the fabric every 10 to 15 minutes for more even dyeing.

12. Hold at the specified temperature for a total of 60 minutes. Black or dark colors may require more time to exhaust. If the dyebath is not clear after an hour, add half the original quantity of ammonium sulfate, acetic acid, or vinegar to dyepot and simmer 10 to 30 minutes longer. Do not pour chemicals directly on the fabric.

13. Cool fabric in the dyebath for at least 30 minutes or overnight (preferred). More dye will fix during cooling. You may line-dry the fabric before rinsing to increase color retention.

14. Add soda ash to neutralize the dyebath to pH 7 before discarding.

15. Follow instructions for "Rinsing, Washing, and Drying Fabric" on page 122.

5.18 Duster and scarf by Mark Thomas. Lanaset and WashFast dyes used with arashi shibori and ombre dip dyeing.
5.19 Duster and scarf detail. Photos by Chia Wen.

WashFast Immersion Dyeing Hints

■ Some WashFast stock solutions (especially red and blue) thicken on sitting at room temperature. Heat slightly to thin.

■ Vinegar, acetic acid, and citric acid crystals yield darker colors and black than ammonium sulfate.

■ If a particular color is not washfast, consider not washing after dyeing. The acid will not harm either wool or silk fabric, and the piece can be dry-cleaned later if soiled.

■ Some artists mix Lanaset and WashFast dyes in the same dyebath, mainly red, because of Lanaset's weak range of reds.

Chart I   Sample Calculation for WashFast Immersion Dye Bath

The following calculations are for dyeing about 7 ounces (200 g) of cloth, about 5 yards (4.6 m) medium-weight silk. Although there are two salt and four acid choices, the sample shows only one of each, 1% ammonium sulfate and 4% Glauber's salt.

0.5% pale value	1% medium value	3% dark value
1% stock solution 200 g WOF x 0.5 = 100 ml dye stock	200 g WOF x 1 = 200 ml dye stock	200 g WOF x 3 = 600 ml dye stock
Water at water/fiber ratio of 30:1 200 g WOF x 30 = 6000 g = 6000 ml = 6 l water	200 g WOF x 30 = 6000 g = 6000 ml = 6 l water	200 g WOF x 30 = 6000 g = 6000 ml = 6 l water
Ammonium sulfate 1% to 2% WOF for silk 200 g WOF x 0.02 = 4 g	200 g WOF x 0.02 = 4 g	200 g WOF x 0.02 = 4 g
Glauber's salt 3% to 5% WOF (4% used here) 200 g WOF x 0.04 = 8 g	200 g WOF x 0.04 = 8 g	200 g WOF x 0.04 = 8 g

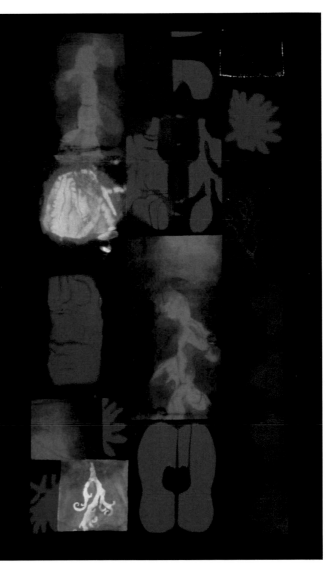

Above: 5.20 Losing Oxygen 2 *by Carol LeBaron.* 56" h × 30" w *(142 cm × 76 cm). Wooden shapes clamped to folded wool as a resist with WashFast acid dyes. Smaller pieces handstitched together. Photo by Cathy Carver.*

Left: 5.21 Wool Challis Scarf *by Holly Brackmann.* 78" l × 9 ½" w *(198 cm × 24 cm). Fabric clamp-resisted and immersion-dyed in WashFast acid dyes, then painted, stamped, and resisted with thick-ened WashFast acid dye. Photo by Joe Coca.*

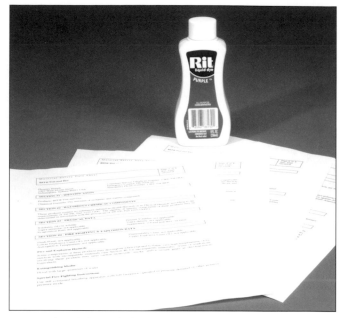

5.22 *Wool flannel resisted with masking tape. Thickened WashFast acid dye applied and steamed to set the color. Photo by Tom Liden.*

5.23 *Rit liquid dye with the Material Safety Data Sheet (MSDS) downloaded from the manufacturer's website. Photo by Tom Liden.*

Thickened WashFast Dyes

WashFast dyes can be applied thin or thick by varying the amount of sodium alginate: less for handpainting, more for stamping, stenciling, or screen printing. After drying, the fabric must be steamed to fix the color. The following recipe will make about 1 cup (237 ml) thickened dye.

1. Scour the fabric to be dyed, referring to "Preparing Fabric for Dyeing" on page 120.
2. Measure 1 cup (237 ml) of 1% to 4% *dye stock solution.*
3. Add 1½ teaspoons (9 g) *ammonium sulfate* for wool and silk OR 1 teaspoon (6 g) ammonium sulfate for nylon. Stir well.
4. Add ¼ teaspoon (1.25 ml) *Synthrapol.* Stir well
5. Add ½ to 2 teaspoons (1.9 g to 7.6 g) *sodium alginate,* depending on the thickness desired. Slowly pour the alginate into the stock solution, mixing in a blender or with a whisk. Let set for 10 to 15 minutes to thicken. Stored in a cool, dark place, thickened WashFast dyes will last for 5 months.
6. Handpaint, monoprint, stamp, stencil, or screen-print fabric on a padded surface (see "Printing Surfaces and Printing Tables" on page 70).
7. Allow the fabric to dry.
8. Fix the dye by steaming 30 minutes for pale values and 60 minutes for dark values or black. The time also will vary depending on the size, weight, and amount of fab-

ric—larger areas or heavier materials require more time. Allow the fabric to cool to room temperature. See "Steaming" on page 126.
9. Follow instructions for "Rinsing, Washing, and Drying Fabric" on page 122.

Union Dyes

Union dyes are a mixture of acid and direct dyes, making them usable on both animal and plant fibers; they are packaged with additives to make dyeing easier. Because each kind of fiber reacts with only one of the included dyes, unused dye and chemicals end up being washed down the drain and wasted. Though they are easy to use, union dyes are wasteful and expensive for dyeing large quantities of a single type of fabric; instead, purchase the appropriate dye for that particular fiber. Union dyes are useful when dyeing a fabric combining protein or nylon and cellulose, such as a garment made of cotton with nylon trim. Union dyes have good lightfastness but poor to fair washfastness, especially on cellulose, as the direct dyes tend to continually wash out and bleed. Colors are muted and dull. Follow the directions on the package: very hot or simmering water is necessary. Common brands of union dyes include Rit, Dylon Multi-Purpose, Tintex High Temperature (sold in the United States as Tintex Easy Fabric Dye), and Deka L Hot Water (available only in Europe).

Chapter Six
Vat Dyes

Vat dyes are some of the oldest known dyes, used as early as 2000 B.C.E. The most familiar vat dye is indigo, found worldwide in blue jeans and countless other textiles. "Vat" refers to the container used to ferment indigo leaves. Vat dyes are insoluble in water but can be trapped in fiber to produce color. Except for indigo, these dyes are light- and washfast and not affected by bleach. Coloring the fiber surface and striking (penetrating) very quickly, vat dyes are perfect for tie-dye, shibori, and other resists. The color range is narrower than in some other dyes, but the hues are intense.

Most fiber-reactive and many acid dyes are discharged by vat dyes (see illustration 6.1), that is, the original color is replaced with the vat dye color in a single step. If the vat dye does not discharge a particular color or one hue in a mixture, it will overdye it and combine with it. Vat dyes will scour (remove the sericin) and overdye black silk organza in one step. See "Resist-Scouring Silk" on page 98.

Factors in Vat Dyeing

Vat dyes work well on all cellulose and silk fibers, some nylons, and acetate. The strong alkalis can damage wool, silk, and other protein fibers. Damage to silk can be minimized by not leaving it in the dye for extended periods. Vat dye colors are slightly darker on cellulose than on silk.

Vat dye is not attracted to fiber and is insoluble in water, but once converted to a water-soluble form by adding a reducing agent (sodium hydrosulfite or thiourea dioxide),

Safety Alert

As vat dye powders may cause allergic reactions, use the liquid form of dye when available. Use sodium hydroxide (lye) with extreme caution. Wear a respirator with organic vapor cartridges, rubber gloves, and an apron when working with lye. Always add lye to cold water, never the other way around. If contact is made, flush the eyes or skin for 20 minutes with water and seek medical attention. In case of swallowing, rinse the mouth with cold water and drink one or two glasses of milk or water. Do not induce vomiting. Get medical help immediately. Sodium hydrosulfite, a reducing agent, is irritating to the respiratory tract and decomposes to sulfur dioxide gas; it can cause severe burns. Use a mixing box (see illustration 1.4) to distance yourself from these toxic chemicals.

6.1 *Dress by Roxy Wells. Black silk organza with arashi shibori pole-wrapping resist. Immersed in vat dye to discharge the black, scour the silk, and overdye in one step. Photo by Joe Coca.*

which removes the oxygen, and a caustic alkali (lye), the dye attaches to the fiber at a specific temperature, usually 120 to 160° F (49 to 71° C). The color of the reduced (leuco) dyebath is usually very different from the target color being dyed. When the fabric is removed from the dyebath, oxygen reacts with the dye to change it to the final color, which is insoluble and is now trapped in the fiber.

Vat dyes are sold as both powders and liquids under various brand names, including Zymo-Fast and PRO Vat. A 2-ounce (59-ml) bottle will dye 5 to 6 pounds (2.3 to 2.7 kg) of fiber a medium value. The dyes are usable for at least 4 years if kept cool and dark. Inkodye is a brand of vat dye that is sold in ready-to-use liquid leuco form.

Vat Immersion Dyeing

A vat dyebath is usable for 3 to 4 hours but must be brought back to temperature if allowed to cool during that period. Vat dyebaths made with thiourea dioxide can be reused later if stored in a tightly covered, nonreactive container. When ready to reuse, add thiourea dioxide equal to the original quantity and heat the dyebath until the vat is reduced to the leuco state.

Top left: 6.2 Dévoré Dida by Holly Brackmann. 10" h × 15" w × 4" d (25.5 cm × 38 cm × 10 cm). Dyed flat with Procion MX, drawn up for woven shibori, and immersed in vat dye to dye and discharge in one step. Disperse dye put in the burnout solution for dévoré. Metallic foil applied before opening up the fabric. Permanently pleated by putting in a pressure canner for 30 minutes. Handwoven cotton/polyester fabric. Bottom left: 6.3 Dévoré Dida detail. Photos by Hap Sakwa.
Above: 6.4 Ethno-shibori #3 by Pavlos Mayakis. 60" h × 30" w (12.5 cm × 76 cm). Handwoven cotton and metallic thread with woven shibori. Vat dye discharge on commercially dyed cotton. Photo by Joe Coca.

The following recipe will dye 1 pound (454 g) of fabric, or about 10 yards (9.1 m) of medium-weight silk or 2 to 4 yards (1.8 to 3.7 m) of light- to medium-weight cotton cloth.

1. Scour the fabric, referring to "Preparing Fabric for Dyeing" on page 120. If the fabric is already clean and dry, place in warm water, add ¼ teaspoon (1.25 ml) Synthrapol. Soak for at least an hour or overnight if the fiber is difficult to wet out.

2. Measure 1 gallon (3.8 l) of room-temperature *water* into a nonreactive pot that is large enough for the fabric to move freely.

3. Measure 1 to 2 tablespoons (14.5 to 29 g) dye powder or 1 to 2 tablespoons (15 to 30 ml) liquid, up to 4

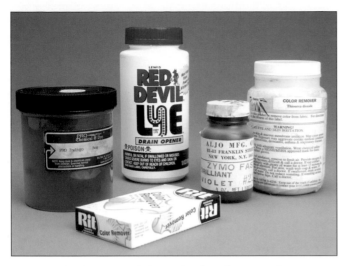

6.5 *Vat and indigo dye and chemicals. Photo by Tom Liden.*

tablespoons (58 g) *dye* powder or 4 tablespoons (59 ml) liquid for a dark color or black. Dissolve dye powder in a small amount of room-temperature water until all dye particles disappear. Set the dye aside.

4. Measure 1 cup (237 ml) *COLD water* into a nonreactive container. Carefully add 1 to 2 tablespoons (18 to 36 g) *lye to the water* and stir to dissolve. Use only 1 tablespoon lye if using sodium hydrosulfite (see Step 5).

5. Measure ½ to 1 teaspoon (1.7 to 3.4 g) *thiourea dioxide (Thiox)*, 2 teaspoons (7.4 g) for black, OR 1 tablespoon (15 g) *sodium hydrosulfite* and dissolve in the lye solution. Use Thiox on silk because it is less harsh.

6. Stir the dissolved dye and chemicals into the water in the pot and heat to 120° to 160° F (49° to 71° C). Different dye colors may require different temperatures: follow the supplier's directions. When the bath reaches the correct temperature, it should be in the reduced leuco state and a different color from the final color. To test the color, lower a white piece of paper or plastic spoon into the dyebath and remove. The dye on the paper or spoon should oxidize and change to the final color. Avoid vigorous mixing, which will introduce oxygen into the dyebath before the dye can enter the fibers.

7. Carefully add wet fabric to the bath and let stand for 1 to 5 minutes, moving the fabric gently under the surface for more even dyeing. Solid, dark colors may need to stand 15 to 30 minutes; however, shibori or tie-dye effects may be lost if fabric is left in the dyebath too long. Dye silk for the least amount of time possible to minimize exposure to the alkali.

8. Before removing fabric, place a bucket next to the dyebath to catch drips.

9. Squeeze the fabric below the surface of the dyebath and remove it without dripping or splashing liquid back into the dyebath. Drips will introduce oxygen, which will react with the leuco solution, thus shortening the life of the vat.

10. Place the fabric in a bucket of cool water or rinse in cool running water. The dye in the fabric will begin to oxidize.

11. Hang the fabric for 5 to 15 minutes; the remaining reduced dye will oxidize back to the original insoluble state and permanent color. Dye in yarn takes longer to oxidize than dye in fabric because oxygen takes longer to reach the center of the skein than it does to penetrate the fabric.

12. Repeat Steps 8 through 11 to obtain darker, more intense colors.

13. Neutralize silk. Mix 2 tablespoons (30 ml) plain distilled vinegar in 1 gallon (3.8 l) of room-temperature water. Soak for 5 to 10 minutes. Rinse in clear water. Orvus Paste in the final washing will give the fabric a softer hand.

14. Although vat dyes don't wash out very much, vat-dyed fabrics need to be washed to prevent crocking (rubbing off) of unfixed dyes. Follow instructions for "Rinsing, Washing, and Drying Fabric" on page 122.

Indigo

Indigo is one of the oldest dyes and magical when it works properly. Fabrics dyed with indigo have been found dating as early as 2500 B.C.E. in Egypt, Anatolia, China, and the Indus Valley. At one time, because the color was associated with power and divinity in those areas, only exalted persons in Africa, the Middle East, South America, China, Japan, and Indonesia could wear blue garments. Indigo gained world trade status when it was cultivated on a large scale in the seventeenth and eighteenth centuries. Originally derived from plant materials obtained from several genera of plants in various parts of the world, synthetic indigo was produced in 1880 by the German chemist Adolph von Bayer. Badische Anilin Soda Fabrik (BASF) marketed the first synthetic indigo in 1897. Within a few years, synthetic indigo, which has fewer impurities and more consistent color than natural indigo, became the industrial standard. Some commercial dyers, especially in Asia and Africa, still use natural indigo, as do some artists in Japan, Europe, and the United States.

The blue color of indigo is not washfast, and it crocks. Removing an indigo outfit made in Thailand one day, I was horrified to see that my armpits and thighs were blue. After a few washings, however, the indigo in the fabric no longer rubbed off.

Indigo will dye cellulose and silk, and it is the only vat dye that will dye protein fibers without damaging them irreparably. As with other vat dyes, the fiber does not turn blue until after oxidation occurs. If the blue is not dark enough, the fabric can be dipped again and reoxidized.

There are dozens of recipes for dyeing with indigo. The easiest and most popular call for lye and Thiox or lye and sodium hydrosulfite with variations for cellulose and protein fibers. A recipe using lye and Thiox is given below. Because cellulose fibers absorb indigo more slowly than protein fibers, several dips are more effective than one long one. Wool absorbs indigo rapidly and is harmed by prolonged exposure to alkali so that multiple immersions and long exposure may be both detrimental and unnecessary. The zinc/lime indigo vat, which some artists favor, is easy to maintain, but because zinc metal dust is toxic, I have not included it here. Historically, indigo was often converted to the leuco state by natural fermentation of organic matter, but this is a long and involved process. Other indigo variations include "instant indigo" (freeze-dried crystals combined with a reducing agent and an alkali) and prereduced indigo. See "Resources" on page 136 for suppliers of these two products.

Indigo with Lye and Thiourea Dioxide (Thiox)

This is a two-step process. First, prepare a reduced indigo stock solution with Thiox and lye. The Thiox reduces the indigo to its leuco form while the lye increases the solubility of the dye in water. Then prepare a container with Thiox alone, which keeps the reduced indigo from reoxidizing. Next, add the stock solution to the vat. The dyebath and fabric in it will be yellowish-green. The oxidation of the dye in the fabric produces the final blue.

The following recipe, for use on cellulose and silk or wool (based on instructions from PRO Chemical & Dye), makes 4 gallons (15.1 l).

1. Indigo stock solution (see "Vat Dye Safety Alert on page 41).
A. Dissolve *lye*. Measure 1½ cups (355 ml) **COLD water** in a plastic container. Slowly add 5 teaspoons (28 g) lye.

Above: 6.6 Indigo dyeing. Dipping a silk scarf into an indigo vat with oxidation beginning on the right and the resulting fabric on the left. Photo by Tom Liden.
Top right: 6.7 Fabrics dyed with indigo, including African paste resist fabric, Thai batik fabric, and Japanese shibori fabric. Photo by Joe Coca.
Right: 6.8 Shibori Strip Weaving #2 by Bren Ahearn. 116" h × 49" w (294.5 cm × 124.5 cm), including fringe. Dyed with indigo using various resist techniques. Handwoven plain-weave rayon strips sewn together with overhand stitches in red. This is part of Bren's continuing exploration of the integration of Japanese shibori techniques with the strip-weaving traditions of Ghana and Mali. Photo by Joe Coca.

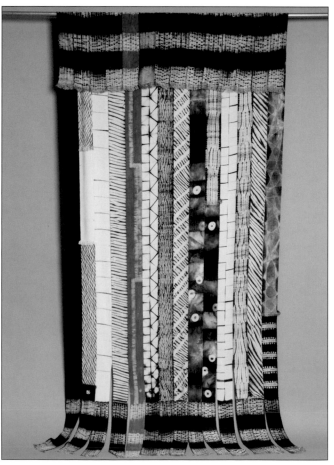

The solution will get warm. Set aside to cool.

B. Dissolve *indigo.* In a container, measure 3 tablespoons (18 g) synthetic indigo. Add enough water to make a lump-free paste.

C. Carefully stir the lye solution into the pasted indigo until smooth.

D. In another container, stir 1 teaspoon (3.4 g) *Thiox* into ½ cup (118 ml) of *warm water.* Stir until dissolved.

E. Add the Thiox solution to the indigo/lye solution. Stir very slowly to avoid creating air bubbles.

F. Let stand for 1 hour or longer. The solution should turn yellow except on the surface, where oxygen reacting with the dye will turn it blue. A drop of the solution allowed to run down a light-colored plate should turn blue in 20 to 30 seconds.

G. The attainment of the yellow color can be speeded up by placing the container holding the indigo, lye, and Thiox in a pan of hot water and heating the solution to 120° F (49° C). Do not allow the temperature to go above 140° F (60° C). Hold at temperature for 15 to 30 minutes or until the solution turns yellow.

H. If the solution remains greenish and not yellow, add more Thiox, ¼ teaspoon (0.9 g) at a time, and wait ½ hour to see if it turns yellow.

2. Dye vat. For cellulose or silk, prepare the dye vat in a plastic bucket with a lid. For wool, use a stainless steel or enamel pot with a lid. Deep, narrow dye containers are best because there is less surface area to react with oxygen. Use the lid to protect the vat when not in use and exclude oxygen.

A. Measure 3 gallons (11.4 l) *warm water* into the dyepot.

B. Add 1 teaspoon (5 g) *sodium hexametaphosphate* for hard water and stir to dissolve.

Cellulose and silk

    i. Add ¼ cup (82.5 g) plain *salt* and stir to dissolve.

    ii. Dissolve ½ teaspoon (1.7 g) *Thiox* in a small amount of warm water and stir in thoroughly. This will remove oxygen from the water. Let the bath sit for 30 minutes.

Wool

    i. Stir in 1 teaspoon (3 g) unflavored gelatin powder.

    ii. Stir in 1 teaspoon (5 ml) *Synthrapol.*

    iii. Stir in 2 tablespoons (30 ml) clear household *ammonia.*

    iv. Stir in 1 teaspoon (3.4 g) *Thiox* to remove oxygen.

C. Carefully and slowly, to avoid adding oxygen, pour the indigo stock solution from Step 1 above into the dyepot. Stir very gently.

D. If, after 30 to 60 minutes, the vat is a clear greenish-yellow with a shiny, dark blue metallic surface, the vat is ready to use. If the vat is not the proper color, wait 30 to 60 minutes longer and check again. It can take as long as 6 hours for the dye solution to reduce properly.

3. Vat temperatures

Cellulose and silk: use at room temperature.

Wool: maintain 120° F (49° C) during the dyeing.

4. See "Immersion Dyeing with Indigo" below.

5. If the vat needs correcting, see "Hints" on page 46.

Immersion Dyeing with Indigo

1. Scour the fabric, referring to "Preparing Fabric for Dyeing" on page 120. If the fabric is already clean and dry, place in warm water mixed with 1 teaspoon (5 ml) Synthrapol. Soak for at least an hour or overnight (preferred). Wool that is not thoroughly wet contains a lot of oxygen, which will destroy the indigo vat. Squeeze excess moisture from the fabric and avoid air pockets in the folds.

2. Skim the dark blue "flower" from the vat with a piece of paper and set it aside (do not discard). The dye will not penetrate fabric that has scum clinging to it. Replace the scum when the dyeing session is complete to help prevent further oxidation at the surface.

3. Introduce fabric.
Cellulose and silk: Carefully lower the fabric into the vat without splashing. Move the fabric slowly below the surface of the liquid for 1 to 10 minutes to help the dye penetrate but don't let the fabric touch the sediment at the bottom of the vat.
Wool: Immerse wool in the vat and heat to 122° F (50° C). Maintain a temperature of between 113° and 131° F (45° and 55° C) for 10 to 30 minutes. Gently move the wool below the surface of the liquid.

4. Squeeze out excess dye below the surface of the vat. Carefully remove the fabric to a separate container. Do not allow the fabric to drip into the vat, which will introduce oxygen. The fabric should look yellow-green.

5. Oxidize the color to blue; this should take about 15 to 30 minutes for wool, overnight for cellulose and silk. Placing wool in a bucket of water at the same temperature of the vat, which contains oxygen, will begin oxidation while removing excess indigo. This is not a substitute for washing. Hang the fabric on a line to continue oxidizing.

6. Redip the fabric as many times as needed for the desired shade of blue, remembering that fabric always appears darker when wet than when dry. However, more than five dips strains wool by repeated exposure to alkali.

7. Fabric variations after oxidation:

A. Allow cellulose fabric to dry for 24 hours to 1 month before washing. With bound or shibori techniques, dry the fabric and untie or cut the threads before washing to allow the water to penetrate all of the fabric.

B. Wash wool with soap and warm water as soon as it is fully oxidized; don't let it dry first. Repeated exposure to strong alkali can make the wool fiber stiff and brittle.

C. Neutralize wool or silk after washing by soaking in a

Hints for Dyeing with Indigo and Maintaining the Vat

■ The iridescent "bloom" or "flower" on the surface of the dyebath indicates that the indigo vat is alive and well.

■ Larger quantities of indigo stock solution can be mixed and stored indefinitely in a cool dark place. Label and date the container. Cover tightly to exclude oxygen. As the stock solution is used, replace the used portion with glass marbles to raise the liquid level and thus reduce the volume of air in the container.

■ If fabric does not turn blue and the vat looks gray or light-colored, more indigo is needed. Add indigo stock solution, 1 tablespoon (15 ml) at a time. If it still does not dye properly, it may also need more Thiox.

■ If the vat looks blue, it may have too much oxygen or need more alkali. Test by placing a small amount of dyebath in two white containers. Carefully add a small amount of lye to one and a little Thiox to the other. If the liquid in one container turns yellow-green, add that substance to the indigo vat. If neither liquid turns yellow-green, the vat needs both. Add small amounts of each.

■ If the vat looks blue or there are blue specks on dyed fabric, it has too much oxygen and needs to be reduced ("sharpened"). Dissolve ¼ teaspoon (0.9 g) Thiox in a small amount of water and add to the vat. Stir very gently. Wait 15 minutes; the vat should turn yellow. To test, dip in a piece of paper; it should turn blue when withdrawn.

■ If the vat looks milky or there are white specks on the dyed fabric, the vat is too acidic for the indigo to be reduced. The wool vat should have a pH of 8 to 10 and the cellulose vat, 9 to 12. Dissolve ¼ teaspoon (1.4 g) lye in ½ cup (118 ml) of cold water, add to the vat, and stir gently. Wait 15 minutes and check the vat with paper as above before dyeing. To test with pH paper, touch a strip to the surface so that water wicks up into the paper and its color is not masked by the indigo.

■ If the vat is very yellow beneath the blue surface, the vat is too alkaline. Add a drop or two of lemon juice or vinegar and test the pH as directed above.

■ If the fabric turns a lighter color with each successive dip, the vat contains too much reducing agent (Thiox), and indigo is being stripped out. Introduce a little oxygen by vigorously but carefully stirring the vat for 15 to 30 seconds.

■ If the vat sits for several days, it will oxidize and need to be reduced by refreshing with ¼ teaspoon (1 g) Thiox dissolved in water. Stir carefully.

■ Always dissolve Thiox and lye in water before adding them to the vat. Do not add dry chemicals.

■ Wait 15 to 20 minutes after each addition of chemical for the vat to stabilize, then test with a piece of fabric or paper. It may take more than one chemical to rebalance the vat. Be patient and add only small amounts of chemicals and stock solution at a time.

■ An indigo dye vat can last many months with proper adjustments.

■ Crocking can occur when too little alkali is used or the dye is insufficiently oxidized between indigo dips. For very dark colors, dip the fabric, oxidize, and wash before dipping again. If the fabric is not washed after each oxidation, a proper final washing with hot water and Synthrapol is needed to remove the unfixed dye.

■ If the fabric is dipped only once, the color will fade dramatically when washed. Successive dips serve to stabilize the color besides deepening it.

■ Oxidize fabric by placing it on plastic outdoors in the shade or hanging it on a clothesline. Turn fabric often so that the air can penetrate it completely.

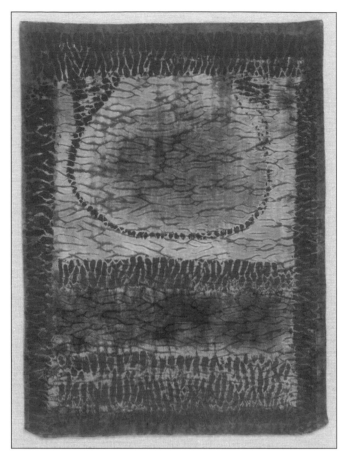

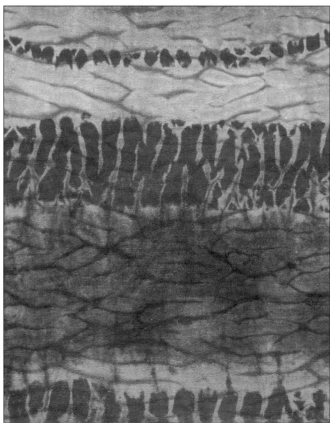

6.9 Mantle of Peace *by Barbara Shapiro. 39" h × 30" w × 1" d (99 cm × 76 cm × 2.5 cm). Handwoven stitch resist shibori with Procion MX dyes, discharged with Thiox, dyed in indigo, and textile paint applied.*
6.10 Mantle of Peace *detail. Photos by Sharon Risedorph.*

vinegar solution for 10 minutes. Mix 2 tablespoons (30 ml) plain distilled vinegar in 1 gallon (3.8 l) warm water. Rinse in warm water.

8. Follow instructions for "Rinsing, Washing, and Drying Fabric" on page 122.

Inkodye

Inkodye is a brand of liquid vat dye sold in a colorless, leuco form that is developed and rendered insoluble when exposed to sunlight or artificial light, ironed between layers of paper, or put in a clothes dryer. Inkodye works on cellulose, silk, and some synthetic fabrics. Like other vat dyes, Inkodye colors are very wash- and lightfast and unaffected by bleach. Unlike other vat dyes, they do not discharge fiber-reactive or acid dyes. They must be stored in opaque glass or plastic containers in a cool, dark place and used within 2 years of purchase.

Inkodye's slightly thick consistency makes it suitable for painting, sponging, dipping, stenciling, or screen printing. It is available in a full range of hues as well as black and brown. A clear extender can be used to make paler shades from the colors as they come from the bottle. Inkodye colors can be mixed together, but because the dye solutions are colorless, test by applying to a small piece of fabric and develop with ironing. To thin, dilute with water in an opaque, nonreactive container. To thicken for screen printing, stamping or stenciling, blend or whisk in a small amount of sodium alginate and wait at least 10 minutes for the alginate to thicken. Work in subdued light when mixing or using these dyes. Because Inkodye must be handled differently from other types of dye, instructions for their use with several techniques are presented here rather than in the chapters devoted to those techniques.

Tie-Dye

Create a design by bunching, folding, stitching, or tying the fabric (see "Resists" on page 89). Dilute Inkodye with 2 parts water for a vivid color or 5 parts water for a pastel color. Pour diluted dye into a small container. Dip the tie-dyed fabric or brush it on the edges of the fabric. Place in sunlight, turning every few minutes to develop the colors. Rinse in room-temperature water, then wash in warm water with Synthrapol.

Painting

Paint Inkodye on wet or dry fabric, then place in sunlight to develop. The colors can be premixed, blended by painting new colors on top of old ones while wet, applied with a dry brush, or applied over a resist.

Developing Inkodye Color

1. Sunlight (preferred). Expose damp fabric outside in warm, direct sunlight for ½ hour or less. More exposure

6.11 Inkodye techniques. Cotton fabric stamped with Inkodye and the colors developed by ironing on the left. Heliographic technique used on the right. Cotton was coated with three colors, covered with a plastic mesh and cardboard shapes, and placed in the sun to develop the color. Photo by Tom Liden.

time is needed for light shining through a window, overcast skies, or artificial light.

2. Iron the fabric slowly on "cotton" while it is damp until the piece is dry and no more steam is evident. If the fabric has dried, use a steam iron and iron slowly. Work in a well-ventilated room or outdoors. Ironing is not recommended for raw silk.

3. Place the fabric on a cookie sheet and bake at 280° F (138° C)—higher temperatures will darken yellow. The color will develop in about 5 minutes in small pieces of fabric, 15 minutes to 1 hour in larger ones. Check whether the dye is fully developed while the fabric is in the oven. Do not use the same oven for preparing food.

4. Steam in a canning kettle, pressure cooker, or professional steamer for 20 minutes (see "Steaming" on page 126).

5. Wash the fabric after the color is developed (see "Rinsing, Washing, and Drying Fabric" on page 122).

Heliographic or Sun Printing

1. Scour the fabric, referring to "Preparing Fabric for Dyeing" on page 120. Dry and iron.

2. Place fabric on a piece of stiff cardboard covered with plastic.

3. Brush dye on the fabric in subdued light.

4. While fabric is still wet, place objects such as leaves, stencils, keys, tools, doilies, etc., on it. For the clearest images, choose smaller objects that will lie in close contact with the fabric.

5. Move the fabric with objects on it into direct sunlight.

6. Leave the fabric in direct sunlight for 30 minutes or less. The angle of the sun and cloud cover will affect how fast the color develops.

7. To check the development of the color, lift a corner of an object and compare the fabric color under it with the exposed background color.

8. Wash the fabric after the color is fully developed (see "Rinsing, Washing, and Drying Fabric" on page 122).

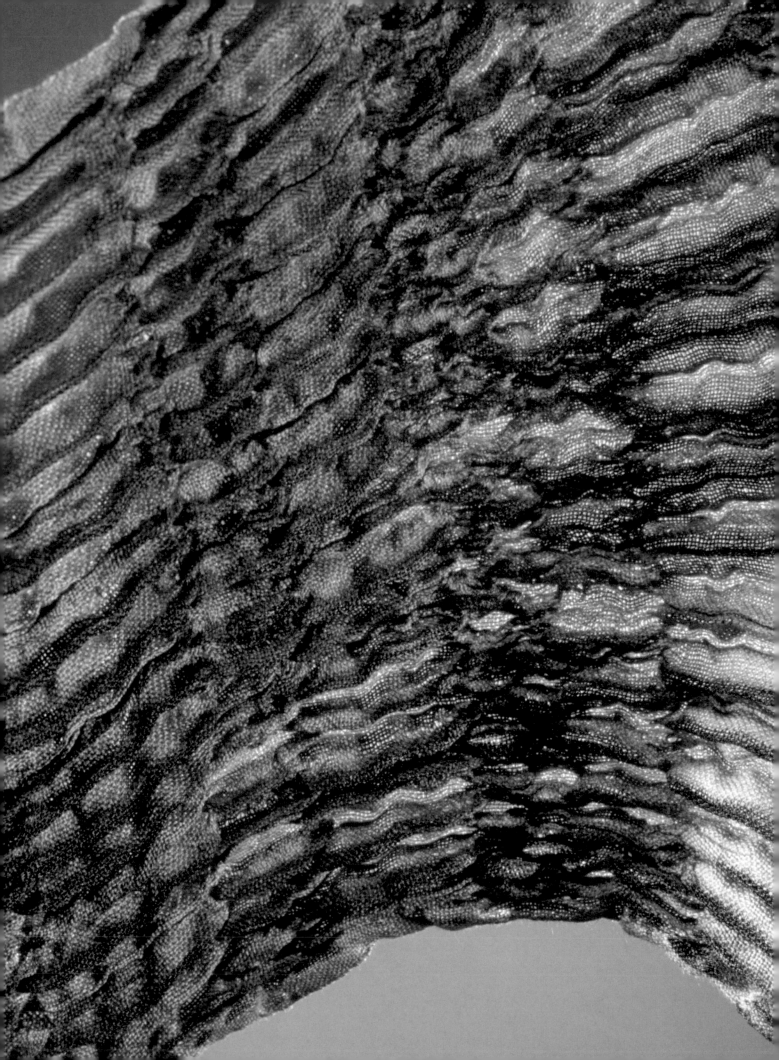

Chapter Seven
Disperse Dyes

A. G. Green and K. H. Saunders in England developed disperse dyes for acetate rayon in 1922. Today, disperse dyes are used to dye hydrophobic (water-repelling) polyester, nylon, acrylic, and acetate rayon. They are sold under the brand names Dispersol, PROsperse, and Aljo Disperse (Acetate-Nylon and Polyester versions).

Disperse dyes don't dissolve in water but are suspended as fine particles. The dye migrates to the fiber surface and then penetrates into it at elevated temperatures during boiling, direct application, or transfer printing. In industrial immersion dyeing of polyester, carrier chemicals together with extremely high temperatures under pressure swell the fiber and promote dye migration. But because these carriers give off strong, usually toxic vapors, using them requires excellent ventilation and great caution. You may be able to get away without using a carrier, see recipes below.

Disperse dyes are lightfast, washfast, and produce strong hues on synthetics. One ounce (28.3 g) of dye can color as much as 25 yards (about 23 m) of fabric. How-

Safety Alert
Some disperse dyes can cause dermatitis through direct contact or when disperse-dyed fabric is worn next to the skin. Even minute amounts of these dyes rubbing off onto the skin can cause an allergic reaction, so disperse-dyed fabrics are better used on outer garments, jackets, shawls, art fabrics, wall hangings, or theatrical textiles.

ever, a given dye may affect different fabrics differently, and it is often not possible in a studio to achieve the very high temperature and pressure necessary to produce dark colors and black. Fabrics dyed in some colors may undergo "gas fading" after long storage in an enclosed space and exposure to high temperatures. Dry dye powders are stable and have a shelf life of several years.

Direct application can be done with thin or thickened dye. A process unique to disperse dyes is dye transfer print-

7.1 *Undulation by Holly Brackmann. 22" h × 44" w × 16" d (56 cm × 112 cm × 40.5 cm). Handwoven polyester/cotton fabric. Dyed flat in Procion MX dyes, then drawn up for woven shibori and dyed in indigo. While gathered, disperse dyes mixed in the dévoré solution for burnout to dye and permanently pleat in one step. Opposite: 7.2 Undulation detail. Photos by Hap Sakwa.*

Chart J Sample Disperse Dye Immersion Calculation

The following recipe will dye about 7 ounces (200 g) nylon fabric.

0.5% pale value	1% medium value	3% dark value
1% stock solution 200 g WOF x 0.5 = 100 ml dye stock	200 g WOF x 1 = 200 ml dye stock	200 g WOF x 3 = 600 ml dye stock
Water at water/fiber ratio of 30:1 200 g WOF x 30 = 6000 g = 6000 ml = 6 l water	200 g WOF x 30 = 6000 g = 6000 ml = 6 l water	200 g WOF x 30 = 6000 g = 6000 ml = 6 l water
Synthrapol 1 teaspoon (5 ml)	1 teaspoon (5 ml)	1 teaspoon (5 ml)
Vinegar 30% WOF 200 g WOF x 0.30 = 60 ml vinegar	200 g WOF x 0.30 = 60 ml vinegar	200 g WOF x 0.30 = 60 ml vinegar

ing—you apply the dye to paper, allow it to dry, and then transfer the image to the fabric with heat and pressure. Wax transfer fabric crayons made from disperse dye and wax can also be used for transfer printing (see illustration 7.12).

Factors in Immersion Dyeing of Disperse Dyes

Coloring synthetic fibers with disperse dyes requires water, detergent, and heat. The amount of water should be sufficient to allow the submerged fabric to move freely in the dye solution. Too much water will dilute the dye particles, resulting in pale color. Too little water may prevent total fabric immersion, causing uneven color. Using a tall, narrow pot will permit a lower ratio of water to fiber. A nonionic detergent, such as Synthrapol, will keep the dye particles in suspension, helping them move uniformly into the fabric for a more level color.

Heat causes the dye molecules to move quickly into the fabric. The optimal temperature varies with the dye, the color, and the fiber.

Disperse dyes mix readily to produce many shades, tones, and diluted tints. Stock solutions are stable for 6 months or longer (see "Stock Solutions" on page 124). Experimentation is the key to mixing colors as some, especially red, are much stronger than others. For example, less red than blue is needed when blending dyes to obtain purple.

Disperse Immersion Dyeing of Nylon, Acetate, and Acrylic

Nylon and acetate are dyed at lower temperatures than acrylic. Expect pale to medium shades with acrylic, as dark colors are difficult to achieve in the studio without extremely high temperature and pressure. Test small samples before dyeing large quantities of fabric.

1. Weigh dry fabric and record WOF on "Dye Worksheet" on page 119. All dye and chemical calculations are based on this weight.
2. Scour fabric, referring to "Preparing Fabric for Dyeing" on page 120. If the fabric is already clean and dry, place in warm water and add ¼ teaspoon (1.25 ml) Synthrapol, soaking at least an hour or overnight (preferred).
3. Calculate the following amounts (see sample calculation above):
   Water/fiber ratio of 20:1 to 40:1 (30:1 preferred)
   Dye amount based on DOS
   pale value = less than 1% DOS
   medium value = 1% DOS
   dark value = over 3% DOS (nylon and acetate)
   black = 6% DOS (nylon and acetate)
   Synthrapol 1 teaspoon (5 ml) OR 1% WOF for large dyebaths
   Vinegar
   3% WOF for acrylic
   30% WOF for nylon and acetate
   Sodium hexametaphosphate for hard water
4. Measure warm water and pour into a nonreactive pot.
5. Measure liquid dye stock solution and add to pot. Stir well.
6. Measure and add Synthrapol. Stir well.
7. Measure and add vinegar. Stir well.
8. Enter the damp fabric. Begin heating and timing.
A. For acrylic, slowly increase the heat while stirring constantly. Raise the temperature to a boil, 212° F (100° C), over 30 to 40 minutes. Stir periodically for 40 to 60 minutes longer to prevent creasing.
B. For nylon and acetate, slowly increase the temperature to 205° F (96° C) and stir constantly. Hold at 205° F (96° C) for 30 to 45 minutes while stirring periodically.
9. Remove the dyepot from the heat. Let dyebath cool to below 150° F (66° C).
10. Run cool water into the dyepot to further cool the fabric.
11. Follow instructions for "Rinsing, Washing, and Drying Fabric" on page 122.

Disperse Immersion Dyeing of Polyester

Without a carrier, which is a potential health hazard, polyester will dye pale to medium shades but not dark colors. Try dyeing a sample of polyester with more dye than called for and Synthrapol to see if color results are satisfactory. Colors used for transfer printing and labeled as "transfer colors" by suppliers will produce the darkest values for immersion dyeing.

1. Follow Steps 1 and 2 above.
2. Calculate the following amounts
   Water/fiber ratio of 30:1
   Dye amount according to depth of shade (DOS). The following amounts are to be used as a starting point, and more dye may be needed for intense colors.
   pale value = less than 1% DOS
   medium value = 2% to 3% DOS
   dark value = over 4% to 5% DOS
   black = 6% DOS
   Sodium hexametaphosphate for hard water
   Synthrapol 1 teaspoon (5 ml)
   Vinegar as needed to bring the dyebath to pH 6
3. Follow Steps 4, 5, and 6 above.
4. Add vinegar as needed to bring the dyebath to pH 6. Stir well.
5. Enter the damp fabric. Begin heating and timing.
6. Raise the temperature to a boil, 212° F (100° C). Boil 20 to 30 minutes longer for pale shades, as long as 60 minutes for dark colors. Stir often to prevent creasing.
7. Rinse the fabric in water at 160° F (71° C).
8. Wash the fabric in water at 160° F (71° C) water with ½ teaspoon (2.5 ml) Synthrapol. Stir for 5 to 10 minutes.
9. Rinse in hot water.
10. Line-dry.

Direct Application of Disperse Dyes on Nylon, Rayon Acetate, and Polyester

Disperse dyes can be thickened to apply directly to nylon, rayon acetate, and polyester by painting, stenciling, monoprinting, or screen printing. Without a carrier, polyester will dye pale to medium shades but not dark colors. Try dyeing a sample of polyester without the carrier, add more dye ("transfer colors") and Synthrapol. The following recipe, based on one from PRO Chemical & Dye, makes 1 cup (237 ml).

1. Scour and dry the fabric, referring to "Preparing Fabric for Dyeing" on page 120.
2. Iron fabric to remove wrinkles as these will interfere with even dye application.
3. Pin or tape the fabric to a padded surface (see "Printing Surfaces" on page 70).
4. *Dye* amount based on value
   pale value = 1 teaspoon (2.5 g)
   medium value = 2 teaspoons (5 g)
   dark value = 3 teaspoons (7.5 g)
   black = 5 teaspoons (12.5 g)
5. Mix the dye with ¾ cup (177 ml) *water* at 90° F (32° C). Stir to dissolve. Strain through two layers of old nylons to remove any large particles of dye.

6. Add the following and stir to dissolve:
   ½ teaspoon (2.5 ml) *Synthrapol*
   ¼ teaspoon (0.5 g) *Ludigol* (an oxidizing agent used only for dark colors and black)
   ½ teaspoon (2.5 g) *sodium hexametaphosphate* for hard water
   1 teaspoon (4.4 g) *citric acid crystals* (only for polyester)
7. Sprinkle 2 to 3 teaspoons (7.6 g to 11.4 g) low-viscosity, high-solids *sodium alginate* on top of the mixture and stir.
8. Add *water* to make 1 cup (237 ml). Stir well to disperse any lumps. Let sit at least 1 hour for the sodium alginate to dissolve. Store unused dye in a covered container in the refrigerator.
9. Apply the thickened dye to the fabric.
10. Air-dry.
11. Fix the dye.

Nylon and rayon acetate
A. Steam for 30 minutes (see "Steaming" on page 126).
B. Rinse the fabric in warm water until the water runs clear.
C. Wash the fabric.
   i. Wash by hand in a bucket of hot water with ½ teaspoon (2.5 ml) Synthrapol per yard (meter) of fabric. Rinse in warm water. The last rinse should be clear.
   ii. Wash by machine. Set the washing machine on "hot wash/warm rinse." Add 1 teaspoon (5 ml) Synthrapol for a small load, up to 2 tablespoons (30 ml) Synthrapol for a large wash load. Run the fabric through a complete cycle.
D. Dry on a clothesline or in a dryer.

Polyester
A. Small amounts of dye can be ironed for 3 to 5 minutes with the iron set on "polyester." Place a press cloth on top of the fabric to keep the iron from touching the dye. Wear a respirator and provide good ventilation while ironing. Steam larger amounts of fabric for 30 to 60 minutes (see "Steaming" on page 126).
B. Rinse the fabric in water at 140° F (60° C).
C. Wash the fabric in water at 140° F (60° C) with ½ teaspoon (2.5 ml) Synthrapol.
D. Rinse in hot water.
E. Line-dry.

Transfer Printing

An observation made in the 1920s, that newly dyed fabrics in drying chambers transferred colors onto each other, ultimately led to the development in 1957 of transfer printing. Commercial use of the technique began in 1968 when transfer paper began being manufactured. Today, many commercial textiles are printed with this technique. The process is considered environmentally friendly because it produces little waste (besides the transfer paper) and no toxic effluents.

In transfer printing, disperse dyes (those labeled by suppliers as "transfer colors" yield the most intense colors) are

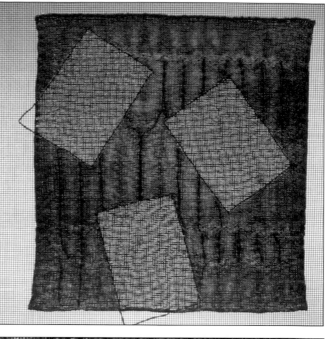

Clockwise from top left:

7.3 *Polyester Fabric* by Anita Sison. 118" *l* × 45" *w* (299.5 cm × 114 cm). *Disperse dyes painted and Thermofax-screened on paper, then transfer-printed on sheer fabric. Foil images applied last. Photo by Amy Melious.*

7.4 *Tumbling Rectangles* by Holly Brackmann. 9" *h* × 8¼" *w* (23 cm × 21 cm) fabric, 17⅛" *h* × 14¼" *w* × ¼" *d* (43.5 cm × 37.5 cm × 6 mm) mounted. *Handwoven polyester/cotton dyed flat with Procion MX dyes, then gathered for woven shibori. Disperse dyes applied in the dévoré solution to dye and burn out in one step. Stitched with cotton and nylon thread to mount on fiberglass screening.*

7.5 *Tumbling Rectangles detail. Photos by Hap Sakwa.*

7.6 *Origami Scarf* by Nuno Corporation, Japan. 60" *l* × 3" *w* (152.5 cm × 7.5 cm) closed, 76" *l* × 17" *w* (193 cm × 43 cm) open. *Polyester folded and then heated in a press to transfer-print with disperse dyes and permanently pleat in one step. The sheer fabric allows the colors to visually blend and merge. Photo by Tom Liden.*

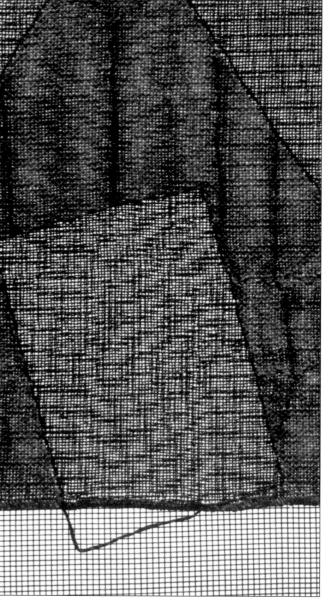

first painted, screened, stamped, or stenciled on plain paper and dried. The paper is then placed face down against synthetic fabric and dry heat is applied. The dye becomes a vapor, moves from the paper into the fabric, and then resolidifies. The print is deposited on only one side of the fabric, leaving the other side the original color. Transfer printing does not affect the hand of the fabric and is washfast.

This technique can be used on polyester (fiberfill, interfacing, woven fabric), nylon, Mylar, polyvinyl chloride, Ultrasuede, Naugahyde, and Lycra spandex, as well as objects made of ceramic, metal, wood, or glass covered with a superhard polymer coating. Polyester/cotton fabric blends containing at least 50% polyester can also be dyed, but the colors will be less brilliant.

For the most intense colors, use white or light-colored finely woven, smooth fabrics such as satin. Of all the synthetics, polyester yields the brightest colors. Sheer fabrics can be printed on both sides for a layered effect.

Make designs with thin or thickened disperse dye on smooth, nonabsorbent, plain paper such as copy, drawing, or watercolor paper. Use paper that will remain flat when the moist dye is applied but will be thick enough to block heat. The design on the paper will be the reverse of the image on the fabric (lettering will be backward), and successive prints will be lighter. Sublimation ink cartridges are available for inkjet printers, permitting generation of designs on the computer.

Use heat and pressure to transfer the image. A home iron, preferably one without steam vents (see "Resources"), can be used for small projects. If you must use a vented iron, cover the soleplate or press through a Teflon sheet to minimize the marks left by the vents. For larger pieces, use a heat press with Teflon, fiberglass baking sheets, or unprinted newspaper sheets to keep the platen clean and free of ghost images. Experiment to find the temperature that will not melt the fabric or distort the color yet will permit maximum transfer of the dye. Place a piece of paper on top of the sample fabric and iron slowly for 25 to 30 seconds. If the fabric scorches, melts, or becomes brittle, decrease the temperature or choose another fabric. To see how time affects the color, cut a strip painted with disperse dye and apply heat for different lengths of time along the strip (see illustration 7.10).

Transfer Printing Procedure

1. Iron fabric to remove wrinkles as these will interfere with even dye application; however uneven dyeing with pleats may be desired (see illustration 7.6).

2. *Dye* amount based on value
   pale value = 1 teaspoon (2.5 g)
   medium value = 2 teaspoons (5 g)
   dark value = 4 teaspoons (10 g)
   black = 8 teaspoons (20 g)

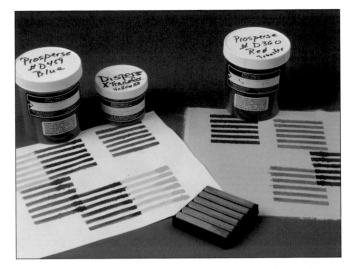

7.7 *Paper stamped with red, yellow, and blue disperse dyes is shown on the left. The resulting heat-transferred polyester fabric is on the right. The design on the paper is reversed when transfer-printed on fabric. Note that the color of disperse dye on the paper is much duller than the resulting transferred color. Photo by Tom Liden.*

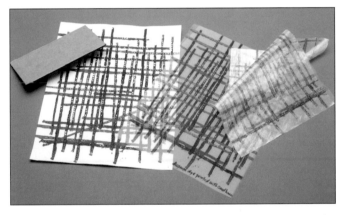

7.8 *Disperse dyes were printed on paper with the edge of a piece of cardboard. The image was transferred to sheer polyester and polyester lamé. Photo by Tom Liden.*

7.9 *Thickened disperse dye was painted in circles with a foam brush on paper and transferred to two weights of polyester. Note the differences between the color effects on the sheer polyester in the middle and the heavier, more opaque polyester on the right. The print on the right was also the second print: a second transfer print is always lighter than the first. Photo by Tom Liden.*

3. Dye colors. Mix the dye with ½ cup (118 ml) *boiling water.* Stir to dissolve. Add a drop or two of *Synthrapol.* Make as many dye colors and mixed colors as needed. For thin watercolor effects on paper, the dye can be used at this stage or thinned with another ½ cup (118 ml) water.

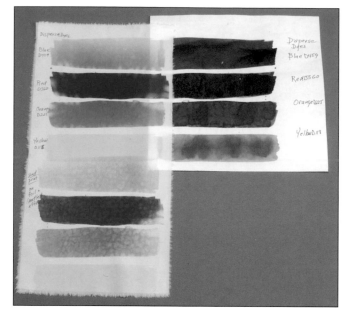

7.10 Disperse dye color test on polyester. On the right are blue, red, orange, and yellow disperse dyes painted on paper. The left shows the colors transfer-printed on polyester. The upper portion shows the colors used with the first transfer printing, and the bottom shows the second, slightly lighter transfer print. Always test colors before undertaking a large project. Photo by Tom Liden.

7.11 Disperse dye transfer using a heat press. A multistep process of transfer printing is shown. First, a paper was painted solid blue. Three leaves were laid between fabric and paper to create the print of white negative leaves surrounded by blue on the right. During heating in the press, blue disperse dye was transferred to the back of the leaves. Next, the leaves were turned over and put on a paper painted with yellow disperse dyes. In the second print, on the heat press platen, the yellow background from the painted paper surrounds the blue disperse dye transferred from the back of the leaves. Photo by Tom Liden.

4. Measure chemicals for thickener paste (thin or thick), depending on the technique you will be using.

Thin paste for painting on paper

1 teaspoon (5 g) *sodium hexametaphosphate* for hard water

2 cups (474 ml) *water*

7½ teaspoons (28.5 g) low-viscosity, high-solids *sodium alginate*

Thick paste for screen printing, stamping, or stenciling on paper

1½ teaspoons (7.5 g) *sodium hexametaphosphate* for hard water

3 cups (710 ml) *water*

7½ tablespoons (85.5 g) low-viscosity, high-solids *sodium alginate*

5. Make the thickener paste. Add sodium hexametaphosphate to warm water in a nonreactive bowl. Slowly sprinkle sodium alginate on the water while stirring with a wire whisk or electric mixer. Let the mixture sit for several hours or overnight to become uniformly thick.

6. Make the dye paste. Mix ½ cup (118 ml) of the thickener paste (thin or thick) with ½ cup (118 ml) of the dye color. These thickened dyes can be stored covered in the refrigerator for about 6 months. Return to room temperature before using.

7. Paint, screen, stamp, or stencil thickened dye on paper. Allow the design to dry, which may take several hours for thick applications. Additional colors may be added to the paper before or after the previous one has dried. The dyes are transparent: additional colors will mix with those underneath to form other colors. Painted paper can be stored in a cool, dry place for several months. Keep painted areas from touching to prevent unwanted color mixing.

8. Image transfer. Wear a respirator and provide good ventilation.

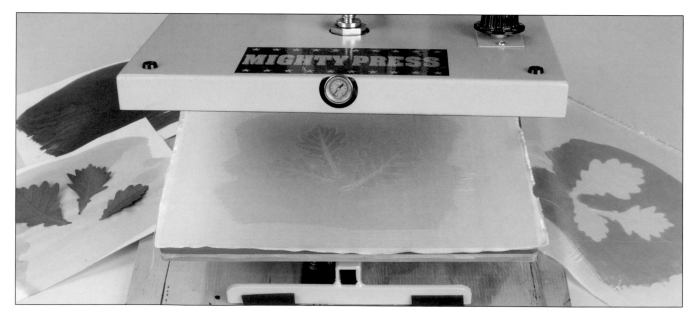

Ironing board method

A. Cover the ironing board with unprinted newspaper or fabric to protect it from dyes bleeding through the fabric.

B. Place the fabric right side up on the ironing board and the design face down on the fabric.

C. Cover with another sheet of paper, a fiberglass baking sheet, or a Teflon sheet to protect the iron and hold the transfer paper in place.

D. Preheat the iron to halfway between "wool" and "cotton" and press each area of the design for 15 to 30 seconds (pale shades) to 5 minutes (dark shades). Do not move an iron without steam vents. If the iron has steam vents, move it slightly to minimize any marks left by the vents.

E. Place the iron on a new location and press. Make sure that the dye transfer paper does not move or the design will be blurred.

F. Check the transfer by lifting a corner of the paper. If the color is not dark enough, apply more heat and pressure. The amount of time and temperature will vary according to the iron, ironing board cover, paper type and thickness, color and depth of disperse dye, and fabric being used.

Heat press method

A. Set the press at 350° to 400° F (177° to 204° C).

B. Protect the platen with a Teflon sheet, a fiberglass baking sheet, or unprinted newspaper sheets.

C. Place the fabric right side up in the press and the design face down on the fabric.

D. Cover with a Teflon sheet, a fiberglass baking sheet, or another sheet of paper.

E. Apply heat and pressure for 30 seconds to 1 minute.
   The dye transfer paper can be used several times, but the color becomes lighter with each use.
   The fabric does not require rinsing or washing. However, washing in warm water will remove any thickener or chemicals that have transferred to the fabric.

9. Line-dry.

Variations with transfer printing

• Use Monagum (carboxymethyl starch) as a thickener instead of sodium alginate, for more textural effects on the paper and with stamps. Measure 1 quart (946 ml) warm water into a nonreactive bowl. Slowly sprinkle ½ cup plus 2 tablespoons (52 g) Monagum on the surface. Stir with a wire whisk or electric mixer. Let the mixture sit for several hours or overnight to dissolve lumps. Add more water for a thinner paste. Add 4 to 8 teaspoons (10 to 20 g) disperse dye per 7 tablespoons (104 ml) thickened paste. Unused Monagum paste can be stored in a clearly labeled, closed container in the refrigerator for months. Return it to room temperature before using.

• Solidly paint an entire sheet of paper with disperse dye.

7.12 Wax transfer crayons were used for rubbings on cement stair grooves, cement cobblestones, and hardware screening. A heavy crayon application is shown on the paper on the right. The resulting heat transfer image on polyester fabric is shown on the left. Note the intensity and vibrancy of the colors on the fabric in comparison to the duller crayon colors on the paper. Photo by Tom Liden.

Cut or tear the paper, then paste the pieces on another sheet of paper to create a pattern for printing.

• Paint thickened disperse dye on a piece of felt to make a stamp pad for use with blocks or stamps.

• Combine disperse dye with wax transfer fabric crayons for different textural effects.

• Place objects such as lace, feathers, a leaf, or torn paper between the fabric and the colored transfer paper to make negative prints. The objects block the disperse dye from reaching the fabric. The result is an image the color of the original fabric surrounded by the transferred color. If the object used to block out the dye absorbs some of the dye, it can be turned over and used to make a positive print on another piece of fabric (see illustration 7.11).

• Apply thickened disperse dye directly to an object such as a fern frond. After the dye dries, place the object dye side down on the fabric with a piece of paper on top for protection. Apply heat and pressure to transfer the image.

• Create a resist design by stitching by hand or machine on paper coated with disperse dye. The dye will not contact the fabric where the stitching occurs.

• Lay a piece of fabric between two pieces of dye transfer paper to print both sides of the fabric in one step (see illustration 7.6).

• Take advantage of polyester's thermoplastic properties. If folded before ironing for transfer printing, it will be permanently pleated and dyed in one step (see illustrations 7.1, 7.6).

Hints for Transfer Printing

■ Disperse dyes are transparent. Printing a blue area over a yellow will produce green.

■ The color of the dye on the paper will look much darker and duller before it is transferred (see illustrations 7.10, 7.11).

Chapter Eight
Discharging

Discharging, the converse of dyeing, is removing, destroying, or stripping color from a dyed fabric, producing light designs on a dark background. Not all fibers can withstand this treatment. Often, the fabric does not return to white but to a lighter or mottled color. Discharging does not remove color all at once but gradually, and the process can be stopped when the desired color is achieved. The darker the original color, the longer it will take to discharge. Results can be unpredictable. A commercially dyed fabric may appear to discharge, but after it is removed from the solution, the original color reappears or a different, unexpected color may result (see illustration 8.4, "Jacket Fabric Sample"). This is especially likely to happen with commercial black cotton fabrics. One sample may discharge to beige, a second sample, even one from the same company, to red, while a third may not discharge at all. Two possible explanations for these results are that manufacturers often overdye colors that did not sell or just use dyes that do not discharge. Test a sample of hand-dyed fabric; question a supplier before buying large quantities of commercial textiles to discharge.

Discharging can occur by reduction or oxidation. Reduction chemicals include thiourea dioxide, Jacquard Discharge Paste, and sodium hydrosulfite. All of these emit strong odors, but they can be used on all fabrics. Another type of reduction discharge is "illuminating," which dyes and discharges in one step, such as with vat dyes. The most common oxidizing chemical is chlorine bleach, which can be used on cellulose but not wool or silk.

Safety Alert
The use of caustic chemicals necessitates working in a well-ventilated place or outdoors and wearing a respirator with cartridges appropriate for the chemicals used. Always wear eye protection, rubber gloves, and an apron.

Opposite: 8.1 Scarf by Edgar Furlong. 79" l × 9¾" w (200.5 cm × 25 cm). Handwoven rayon/cotton black yarn. Woven shibori resist discharged by immersion in Thiox, then dyed with Procion MX. Photo by Joe Coca.
Right: 8.2 Geometry I by Ana Lisa Hedstrom. 95" h × 23" w (241 cm × 58.5 cm). Dyed, discharged, and pieced silk piqué. Photo by Don Tuttle.

8.4 Jacket Fabric Sample *by Holly Brackmann. 18" h × 22" w (46 cm × 56 cm). Handwoven rayon chenille. Two discharges were sampled to see the effects on commercially dyed yarns, Jacquard Discharge Paste on the left and dishwasher gel with bleach on the right. Note how commercially dyed chenille discharged to different colors. The bleach results were chosen for the final jacket fabric. Photo by Joe Coca.*

8.5 Kimono *by Michael Kane and Steve Sells. Stitch-resisted silk charmeuse with ⅛" (3 mm) pleats. Discharged in thiourea dioxide, then dyed with Procion MX and Jacquard acid dyes. The stitched pleats are held in place during discharging and dyeing. One-of-a-kind kimono sewn by hand. Photo by John F. Cooper.*

Discharging can be done by immersion or with a thickened application. Techniques that are especially suited for discharging include shibori, tie-dye, resists, screen printing, stamping, stenciling, and handpainting. Ugly colors can be discharged and overdyed, transforming an undesirable design into something more appealing. The process can be applied to a whole piece of cloth or selected areas. Try tie-dyeing a piece of fabric—discharge it, leaving the ties in place, rinse well, and then overdye (see "Resists" on page 89). The discharge chemicals may penetrate deeper into the bound fabric than the overdyed color, resulting in a halo area of discharge color between the original and overdyed colors.

Thiourea Dioxide Immersion Discharge

Thiourea dioxide smells bad, but it is safer to use than chlorine bleach or sodium hydrosulfite. Developed in the 1940s as a nonexploding alternative to sodium hydrosulfite, it is five to seven times as strong. It can be used to strip colors from most cotton, rayon, linen, and silk, as well as blends that have been dyed with fiber-reactive, acid, or Lanaset dyes. Procion H discharges more easily than MX. Not all colors will go back to white, but many will become light enough to overdye with dark colors. Some colors, including MX turquoise and fuchsia and Cibacron F brilliant blue and gold, will hardly discharge at all. This property can be used to advantage, for example, by dyeing a fabric background with a color blend containing MX turquoise, then discharging a pattern—the discharge area will change to turquoise. Discharging Lanaset colors may change them to different colors, for example, royal blue to yellow-green or violet to yellow. Dry thiourea dioxide has an unlimited shelf life; it is sold under many names, including Thiox and Spectralite.

1. Scour fabric, referring to "Preparing Fabric for Dyeing" on page 120. If the fabric is already clean and dry, soak for at least an hour or longer (overnight) if the fiber is difficult to wet out.
2. Fill a nonreactive pot with 2.5 gallons (9.5 l) *water,* which should be enough for the cloth to move freely. Have a bucket of cold water nearby.
3. Heat water to a simmer, about 185° F (85° C).
4. Add 1 teaspoon (5 g) *soda ash,* 1 teaspoon (3.4 g) *Thiox,* and 1 drop *Synthrapol* (optional). Foaming of the chemicals shows that the sulfur-containing Thiox is decomposing to sulfur dioxide, the actual discharging agent. For a stronger discharge, required by some dye colors, use 2 tablespoons (22 g) Thiox and 2 tablespoons (30 g) soda ash. The pH should be 8 to 8.5.
5. Add 1 pound (454 g) of damp fabric.

Opposite: 8.6 Organized Chaos by Carol Larson. 50" h × 37" w (127 cm × 94 cm). Cotton fabric dyed with Procion MX and discharged with dishwasher gel. Also textile paint, foil, fusing, and free-motion machine stitching. Photo by Lloyd Larson.

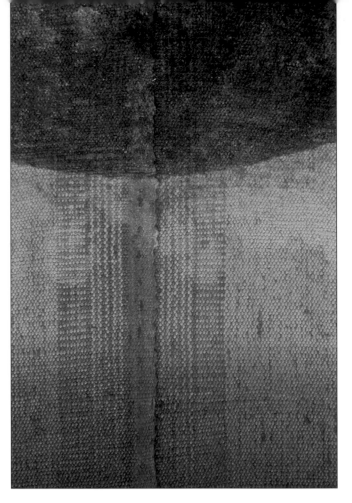

Clockwise, from top left:
8.7 Dream Planet II *by Barbara Shapiro. 38½" h × 39½" w (98 cm × 100.5 cm). Ikat dyed Italian tussah silk warp, discharged with Thiox, dipped in acid dye, and sponged with textile paints. Two handwoven panels stitched together;* 8.8 Dream Planet II *detail. Photos by Sharon Risedorph.*
8.9 Scarf *by Holly Brackmann. 34½" h × 36" w (87.5 cm × 91.5 cm). Black silk folded, clamped, and discharged in Thiox. Soaked in soda ash and painted with Procion MX. Thermofax screen-printed twice with Jacquard Discharge Paste using different amounts of paste. Photo by Joe Coca.*
8.10 Commedia Mask *by Kathy Snyder. 10" h × 12" w (25.5 cm × 30.5 cm). Silk organza clamp resisted, then discharged in Thiox. Textile paint, sewing, and gluing. Photo by Hap Sakwa.*

6. Simmer 20 minutes or less—until sufficient color is removed.

7. Transfer fabric to the bucket of cold water to stop the discharge. Remove more color by returning the fabric to the discharge solution.

8. The solution will weaken in about ½ hour.

9. Neutralize fabric in an acid solution of ¼ cup (59 ml) vinegar in 1 gallon (3.8 l) of water. Soak the fabric for 10 minutes. If any fabric is to be redyed with fiber-reactive dye, this step will prevent premature fixation (the dye will bond immediately to the fabric surface without penetrating the fiber).

10. Follow the instructions for "Rinsing, Washing, and Drying Fabric" on page 122.

11. Discard the discharge bath. These chemicals are not active for very long, and so they can be safely poured into a sewer system. Neutralize the bath with vinegar before pouring into a septic system.

Hints for Immersion Discharge with Thiox

■ To discharge shibori on a pole, heat the bath, add the chemicals, then immerse the pole or pour the hot solution over it.

■ Acid dyes on wool can also be discharged with Thiox, but because wool is harmed by alkali, decrease the quantity of soda ash by 25%. Simmer for only 5 to 10 minutes and immediately rinse in a vinegar solution. Not all acid dyes will discharge.

■ Lanaset dyes require a stronger discharge solution than Procion MX.

Thiox Discharge for Painting or Printing

Thiox can be used thin for painting or thickened for stamping, printing, or stenciling.

1. Paste with a small amount of hot *water* 1 tablespoon (11 g) *Thiox* and 2 tablespoons (30 g) *soda ash.*

2. For painting with a thin solution, add water to the above solution to equal 1 cup (237 ml).

3. For a thick solution, mix 1 to 2 teaspoons (3.8 to 7.6 g) high-viscosity, low-solids *sodium alginate* with ¾ cup (177 ml) water. Wait at least 15 minutes until the alginate thickens to the consistency of a thick milk shake. Add pasted Thiox and soda ash. Do not mix the Thiox and soda ash too far in advance as the combination will begin decomposing in 30 minutes. Add water to equal 1 cup (237 ml).

4. Test the discharge concentration by applying to a sample of fabric. Apply heat with a hair dryer or heat gun, rinse, and evaluate the new color.

5. Stamp, screen, or monoprint the paste on the surface of the cloth, then dry to prevent smearing.

6. Heat is needed to activate the discharge. Small areas can be heated with a hair dryer or heat gun, but ironing with steam is the most easily controlled method. The fabric can also be steamed for 10 to 20 minutes (see "Steaming" on page 126), but this method is hard to control because you can't view the discharged color.

7. Rinse fabric in cool water to stop the discharge action.

8. Neutralize fabric in an acid solution of ¼ cup (59 ml) vinegar in 1 gallon (3.8 l) of water. Soak the fabric for 10 minutes.

9. Follow the instructions for "Rinsing, Washing, and Drying Fabric" on page 122.

Hints for Thiox Painting or Printing Discharge

■ As the chemicals will eventually eat away the Teflon coating on the soleplate, reserve an iron only for this process or protect the soleplate by covering the printed fabric with plain paper or cloth before pressing. Also protect the ironing board with paper or cloth.

■ Try steaming fabric with a steam iron while it is damp. Using the highest "steam" setting, hold the iron just above the printed or painted area without touching it to the fabric.

■ If the recipe above is too strong and the fabric is damaged, especially for protein fabrics, try ½ teaspoon (2.5 g) soda ash and ½ teaspoon (1.7g) Thiox.

■ A solution of Thiox without soda ash will keep for 5 to 7 days with no loss of strength.

■ The Thiox discharge technique can be used several times on cellulose fabrics but only once on silk without damaging the fibers.

■ The discharge paste lasts about a half day and should be discarded when it becomes foamy.

Jacquard Discharge Paste

This is a commercial product with proprietary ingredients that can be applied with a brush or stamp, or screened to penetrate the fabric. It works best on hand-dyed fabrics. Always work in a well-ventilated area.

1. Apply paste to fabric.

2. Allow the paste to dry or iron the paste while damp.

3. Cover the fabric with paper or cloth. Wearing a respirator with acid gas cartridges, iron with steam on "wool," the more steam, the better.

4. Follow the instructions for "Rinsing, Washing, and Drying Fabric" on page 122.

Sodium Hydrosulfite and Color Remover

Commercial color remover contains sodium hydrosulfite. It can be used on cellulose, silk, and wool. Color remover can be purchased in the grocery store and sodium hydrosulfite, from a dye supplier. Both react with air and humidity and have a shelf life of about 6 months. Store away from water as sodium hydrosulfite expands rapidly when wet and can explode. *Always add sodium hydrosulfite to water and not the reverse.*

Clockwise from top left:

8.11 Ethno-Discharge #2 *by Pavlos Mayakis. 48" h × 24" w (122 cm × 61 cm). Handwoven silk. Dyed with Procion MX, overdyed, discharged by stamping with Jacquard Discharge Paste, then stamped with textile paint. Photo by Joe Coca.*

8.12 Wheels *by Cassie Gibson. 56" l × 13" w (142 cm × 33 cm). Silk scarf dyed with Procion MX, then discharged with Jacquard Discharge Paste using Thermofax screens. Metallic textile paint details.*

8.13 Wheels *detail. Photos by Tom Liden.*

8.14 Green Garden *by Marie Plakos. Silk broadcloth garment pieces were cut out, resist stitched, and immersion dyed in WashFast acid dyes. Screen-printed with Jacquard Discharge Paste and textile paint. Hand-quilted details. Photo by Hernan.*

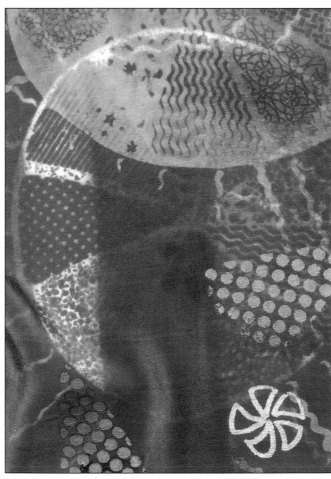

Immersion Discharge with Color Remover or Sodium Hydrosulfite

Wear a respirator with acid gas cartridges and a dust filter. The powder is very fine, and the process smells bad. Provide good ventilation in the studio or work outdoors.

1. Dissolve either 2 tablespoons (30 g) of *color remover* alone or 2 tablespoons (30 g) *sodium hydrosulfite* plus 2 tablespoons (30 g) *soda ash* in a small amount of boiling water. Set aside.

2. Heat 1 to 2 quarts (about 1 to 1.9 l) of *water*. Add the dissolved chemicals.

3. Bring the solution to a simmer and immerse the fabric until the color changes.

4. If the discharge is not acceptable after 20 to 30 minutes, increase the heat or remove the fabric from the pot and add more dissolved color remover or sodium hydrosulfite and soda ash.

5. Rinse the fabric in cold running water. Neutralize by soaking it for 10 minutes in an acid solution of ¼ cup (59 ml) *vinegar* in 1 gallon (3.8 l) of *water*.

6. Follow the instructions for "Rinsing, Washing, and Drying Fabric" on page 122.

Thickened Sodium Hydrosulfite for Painting, Stenciling, Printing, and Stamping

Wear a respirator with acid gas cartridges and a dust filter and work in a well-ventilated area.

1. Dissolve 1 tablespoon (15 g) *soda ash* and 1 tablespoon (15 g) *sodium hydrosulfite* in a small amount of hot *water* and set aside.

2. To 1 cup (237 ml) hot *water* slowly stir in ½ teaspoon (1.9 g) high-viscosity, low-solids *sodium alginate*. Wait 5 minutes to evaluate thickness. If it is too thick, add some water, and if it is too thin, add more sodium alginate.

3. Combine the chemicals and the thickener.

4. Paint, stencil, print, or stamp the thickened solution on the fabric.

5. Cover printed area with plain paper. Iron with a medium-hot iron for 15 to 30 seconds. Remove and discard the paper. The thickened image will be discharged.

6. Rinse the fabric in cold running water. Neutralize by soaking for 10 minutes in an acid solution of ¼ cup (59 ml) vinegar in 1 gallon (3.8 l) of water.

7. Follow the instructions for "Rinsing, Washing, and Drying Fabric" on page 122.

Chlorine Bleach

Chlorine bleach (sodium hypochlorite) aggressively removes color by oxidation. It can be used on most cellulose fabrics, including cotton, rayon, and linen, but will destroy fabrics made of protein, including wool, cashmere, alpaca, and silk. Use the least amount of bleach possible to obtain the desired results as too much bleach will destroy even cellulose fabrics, and traces of bleach left in the fabric will continue to weaken the fibers. The discharged color may be pastel or off-white with a yellowish cast.

To stop the bleach action, rinse the fabric thoroughly, and place it in a solution made from one of the commercially available reducing agents, such as Anti-Chlor (sodium bisulfite, PRO Chemical & Dye) or Bleach-Stop (sodium thiosulfate, Dharma Trading Co.). Do not use vinegar as some recipes recommend. Wear a dust mask when measuring sodium bisulfite or sodium thiosulfate, and keep the container tightly capped as it loses effectiveness as it mixes with air.

Safety Alert
Although household bleach is readily available and will discharge at room temperature, it is toxic and can damage the respiratory system when inhaled. Spraying is thus not recommended. Always wear a respirator, eye protection, and rubber gloves with acid gas cartridges and work in a well-ventilated area or outdoors. Never use bleach to clean dye-stained hands. Instead, use Reduran, a hand cleaner formulated for this purpose.

Liquid Bleach Immersion and Thin Painting Discharge

Bleach can be applied as a thin liquid by immersion, dipping, or painting.

1. Scour fabric, referring to "Preparing Fabric for Dyeing" on page 120. Prewashing is important as fabric finishes can combine with bleach to produce noxious fumes.

2. Pin or tape ironed, smooth fabric to a padded surface (see "Print Surfaces and Print Tables" on page 70).

3. Fill a nonreactive pot using a ratio of 1 part *bleach* to 5 parts hot *water*. A solution stronger than equal parts bleach and water can damage fabric. Heat speeds up the bleaching action. To retard bleaching, use room-temperature water.

4. Choose a method for application, including
   A. immersing the fabric in the pot
   B. painting designs on the fabric with a synthetic brush
   C. brushing the edges of fabric wrapped on a pole

5. Discharging with a solution of 1 part bleach to 5 parts water may take 15 minutes to an hour to discharge, while a strong (1:1) solution should take about 3 minutes and not longer than 5 minutes.

6. Rinse fabric immediately in running water. Do not let the fabric soak in water since the chlorine will migrate into the water and continue the bleaching action.

7. Stop the discharge by placing fabric in a solution of 1 tablespoon (20 g) *sodium bisulfite* (Anti-Chlor) per gallon (3.8 l) room-temperature water. Soak fabric for 10 minutes. Do not inhale vapors from the neutralizing solution. Discard sodium bisulfite solution after 1 day.

8. Follow the instructions for "Rinsing, Washing, and Drying Fabric" on page 122.

9. After rinsing, the fabric may be dyed without drying.

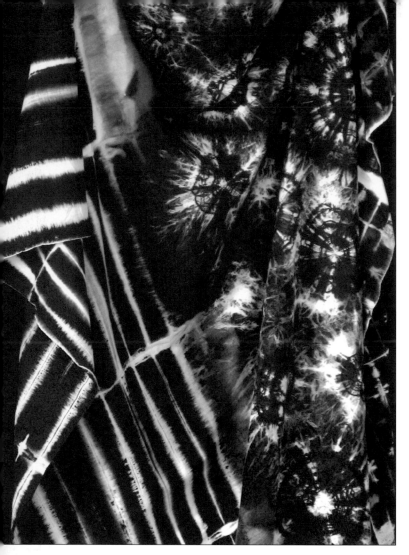

Thickened Bleach Discharge

Adding a thickener to bleach will provide more control for printing, stenciling, stamping, and painting. There are two preferred thickeners for bleach. Monagum (a carboxymethyl starch) will remain thick for a few hours, while a bleach thickener sold by Rupert, Gibbon & Spider will remain thick for 24 to 36 hours. Sodium alginate can be used, but it is composed of proteins and thins rapidly. The thickness can be adjusted as long as the mixture does not contain more than equal parts bleach and thickener. Monagum powder will keep indefinitely in a cool, dry place. Thickened Monagum and bleach thickener will keep for several months in the refrigerator, but once mixed with bleach, they will begin to thin and disintegrate.

Monagum or Bleach Thickener

1. Scour fabric, referring to "Preparing Fabric for Dyeing" on page 120. Prewashing is important since fabric finishes can combine with bleach to produce noxious fumes.
2. Pin or tape ironed, smooth fabric to a padded surface (see "Print Surfaces and Printing Tables" on page 70).
3. Make the thickener.

Monagum

A. Mix *Monagum paste*. Put 1 cup (237 ml) warm *water* in a nonreactive bowl. Slowly sprinkle 2 to 3 tablespoons (10.4 to 15.6 g) Monagum over the water while stirring with a whisk or electric mixer. Let stand at room temperature for several hours or overnight (preferred) until thick, smooth, and translucent. Place in a lidded, labeled, and dated container. Store in the refrigerator. Return to room temperature before using. Adjust thickness according to technique to be used.

B. Mix discharge paste. Put ½ cup (118 ml) room-temperature Monagum paste into a nonreactive bowl. Stir in 1 tablespoon (15 ml) *chlorine bleach*. Adjust thickness by adding more bleach, up to ½ cup (118 ml) total. The more bleach added, the thinner the solution and the faster the discharge. A weaker solution takes longer to discharge but is kinder to the fabric.

Bleach Thickener

A. Mix thickener. Add bleach thickener to room-temperature water, mixing in a blender or with a whisk in a nonreactive bowl. The mixture will be thick. Place in a lidded, labeled, and dated container. Store in the refrigerator. Return to room temperature before using.

B. Mix discharge paste. Add bleach according to the technique to be used and the measurements below. Vary the amount of water to obtain the consistency required. More bleach can also be added but not more than 1 part bleach to 1 part thickener.

8.15 Bleach Discharge Fabric *by Anita Sison. 60" h × 73" w (152.5 cm × 185.5 cm). Black cotton fabric clamped, tied, and folded, then discharged with bleach. This Lunn fabric is made to discharge to white, which is not possible with all black cotton fabric. Photo by Amy Melious.*

8.16 *Thickened bleach and dishwasher gel discharge on cotton dyed with Procion MX. Thermofax-screened and stamped fabric. Fabric on the left was discharged with dishwasher gel. The dishwasher gel worked better with the stamp, but was too runny for the fine detail of the Mehndi screen, resulting in a blurred image. The fabric on the right was discharged with bleach thickened with Bleach Thickener from Rupert, Gibbon & Spider. The thickened bleach blobbed up on the stamp but produced a clear image with the screen. Both fabrics were placed in the sun to speed up discharging. Photo by Tom Liden.*

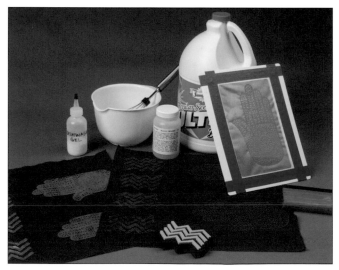

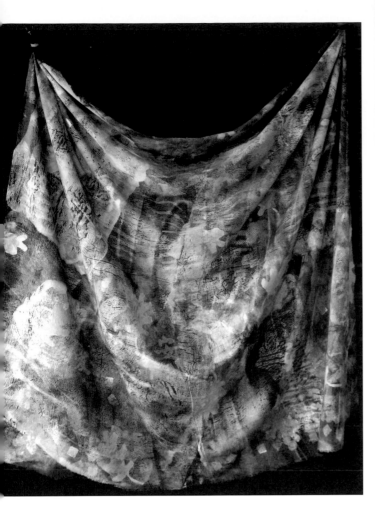

i. For painting, mix ½ cup (118 ml) water, 1 tablespoon (15 ml) thickener, and 1 to 2 tablespoons (15 to 30 ml) bleach.

ii. For printing, mix ½ cup (118 ml) water, 1 tablespoon plus 2 teaspoons (25 ml) bleach thickener, and 2 tablespoons (30 ml) bleach.

4. Test the mixture on a scrap of fabric to see how fast the discharge occurs.

5. Apply the thickened bleach to the fabric.

6. Let the fabric sit until the color changes to the desired shade, about 5 to 10 minutes, but not longer than a few hours.

7. Rinse fabric immediately in room-temperature running water. Do not let the fabric soak in water since the chlorine will migrate into the water and continue the bleaching action.

8. Neutralize the fabric in a solution of 1 tablespoon (20 g) *sodium bisulfite* (Anti-Chlor) per gallon (3.8 l) room-temperature water. Soak fabric for 10 minutes. Do not inhale fumes from the neutralizing solution. Discard sodium bisulfite solution after 1 day.

9. Follow the instructions for "Rinsing, Washing, and Drying Fabric" on page 122.

10. The fabric may be redyed without drying.

8.17 Forest Floor *by Anita Sison. 68" h × 61" w (172.5 cm × 155 cm). Black cotton fabric discharged with bleach, overdyed with Procion MX, stenciled, handpainted, and foiled;* 8.18 Forest Floor *detail. Photos by Amy Melious.*

Hints for Bleach Discharge

▪ Use foam or synthetic brushes because natural bristles, which are made of protein, will be destroyed by bleach.

▪ Thickened bleach can be applied by a squeeze bottle, stamp (use thicker paste), stencil (contact paper or freezer paper), or screen print. The bleach will dissolve photo-emulsion but not Thermofax screens.

▪ Apply thickened bleach over cassava paste, dextrin, or other water-soluble resists. Because the contact time between the resist and thickened bleach is short, these resists will not break down.

▪ Work quickly when applying thin or thickened bleach, and apply to no more than 2 yards (1.8 m) fabric at a time, or one end will be ready to rinse before the other is discharged.

▪ Discharging can be done over stamped dye patterns, or dye can be painted over discharged designs.

▪ Chlorine bleach is a component of dishwasher gel, bleach pens, and some household cleansers. Apply these products for discharge effects, allowing up to several hours to discharge. Placing the fabric in the sun can speed up discharging.

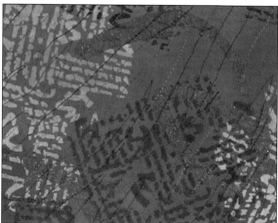

8.19 Whole Nine Yards by Carol Larson. 62" h × 48" w (157.5 cm × 122 cm). A variety of cottons were dyed in Procion MX and discharged with dishwasher gel. Printed with textile paints. Free-motion machine quilting.
8.20 Whole Nine Yards detail. Photos by Lloyd Larson.

Chapter Nine
Screen Printing

Screen printing, or serigraphy, was developed from the craft of stenciling. A screen holds the design while a printing medium is pulled across openings in the screen, forcing color onto fabric. Because traditional stencils cannot accommodate designs with floating, or island areas, Japanese artists cut stencils from two sheets of mulberry paper and used strands of human hair or gossamer silk sandwiched between the two layers to support the isolated areas. This practice evolved into screen printing. The technique at first had limited use. Until the 1930s, most European and American fabrics were printed with engraved rollers or wood blocks. Lack of economic incentive kept manufacturers from coming up with a less labor-intensive process, and they were unwilling to produce small quantities of fabric in a particular design because of the cost and time involved in carving the rollers or blocks. The advent of knife-cut film in 1929 made commercial screen printing cheaper and more versatile. By the 1950s, screen printing had become the major method for printing all types of fabric. Screen printing offers many advantages, including lower cost and the possibility of printing a wide range of sizes with intricate design details.

Safety Alert
The use of caustic chemicals necessitates working in a well-ventilated place or outdoors and wearing a respirator with cartridges appropriate for the chemicals used. Always wear eye protection, rubber gloves, and an apron.

Left: 9.1 Golden Coins Kimono Jacket *by Suzanne Perlman. Silk organza with screen print, discharge, Sennelier dyes, and foiling. Imagery based on personal travels. Photo by Neil Silverman.*
Above: 9.2 Cotton fabric screen-printed by Tiwi aboriginals, Northern Territory, Australia. Textile paint colors are blended in the screen to add variation and depth. Photo by Joe Coca.

9.5 Dancing Vegetables Quilt *by Dede Ledford. 72" h × 72" w (183 cm × 183 cm). Vegetables printed with thickened Procion MX using the polychromatic screen technique (see Joy Stocksdale's* Polychromatic Screen Printing *in the "Bibliography"). Background fabric is random-dyed in a washing machine with Procion MX. Materials include textile paints, watercolor and fabric pens, and machine embroidery. Photo by Roger W. Foote.*

9.3 The Magic Flute Scarf *by Lolli Jacobsen. 36" h × 36" w (91.5 cm × 91.5 cm). Designed for the San Francisco Opera by Ariel. Silk habotai printed with four colors of thickened Procion MX. Note how overlapping the transparent dyes create other colors. Photo by Joe Coca.*
9.4 Pines Scarf *by Lolli Jacobsen. 34" h × 36" w (86.5 cm × 91.5 cm). Silk charmeuse dyed in Procion MX, soda soaked and squirted with MX, screen-printed with thickened MX, then discharged with Jacquard Discharge Paste, screen-printed with metallic textile paints, and foiled. Photo by Joe Coca.*

Tools and Equipment

Equipment includes a frame covered with stretched fabric mesh and a squeegee. You can purchase ready-made screens or construct your own; beginners should start with a well-crafted prestretched screen. Thermofax machines, which use a quick-and-easy process to prepare screens, are discussed later in this chapter.

Screen Fabric

Originally, silk was the most common screen printing mesh, but it has lost favor because it does not withstand harsh chemicals and long use. Today's artists prefer polyester mesh, either monofilament or multifilament. Monofilament is smoothly woven from single strands. It is more costly than multifilament and used mainly for oil-based printing media and very fine details. Multifilament fabric, made from multiple plied yarns, has more "tooth" (is better able to hold water-based products) and is the choice of textile artists. Numbers denote the size of the mesh—the larger the number, the finer the mesh—while x's denote its strength, with most screen fabric being xx, or double strength. Common multifilament mesh sizes are 8xx and 10xx, used for pigments, and 10xx and 12xx, used with thickened dyes. My favorite is 10xx as it can be used with both of these media.

Stretch the screen mesh across the frame with the warp and weft parallel to the sides and secure it with either a hand-operated staple gun or (easier) the groove-and-cord method (see illustration 9.6). Lay the wood on a flat sur-

9.6 Making a screen. Polyester fabric is stretched over a grooved wood frame and a cord is pressed into the groove using a screen and spline installation tool. Another way to attach the screen is to place half a hinge with rounded corners over the groove and bang it with a hammer. After the screen fabric has been secured, it is degreased and taped. Photo by Tom Liden.

9.7 A taped screen showing the trough at either end and the 1" allowance on sides. The image used in screen printing must always be smaller than the actual screen size. The nails in either end of the squeegee handle keep it from falling into the printing medium between prints. The portable padded print board below the screen is made of plywood covered with felt and cotton muslin. Photo by Tom Liden.

face with the grooved side up. Cut the screen fabric 1 to 2 inches (2.5 to 5 cm) larger than the frame on all sides. Wet the fabric to ensure a tight fit. Using pushpins, pin the fabric to the frame, covering the groove and making sure that the warp and weft are parallel to the sides. Cut a length of cord slightly longer than the length of the groove; the cord should fit snugly in the groove. Begin in the middle of one side of the frame. Using one half of a door hinge that has been ground to round the corners or a screen and spline installation tool (available in hardware stores), begin forcing the cord into the groove. Do not drive the cord to the bottom of the groove yet. Continue all the way around the frame, forcing the cord into the frame. When the cord is in place, remove the pushpins. Complete the final tightening by driving the cord to the bottom of the groove with a hammer and the hinge or spline tool. The cord does not have to be hammered into the groove at the corners. Cut the cord so that the ends meet in the middle of one side of the frame. The screen mesh must be as tight as a drumhead and free of soft spots or ridges. Trim off excess mesh and loose threads, which will interfere with printing.

Clean new screens before use to remove manufacturing oil and sizing. Use a commercial screen degreaser, kitchen cleanser, or a solution of 1 tablespoon (13.1 g) trisodium phosphate (TSP) dissolved in 1 quart (946 ml) of water. This solution can be stored in a lidded, labeled container indefinitely. First, rinse the screen with water, then spread on the solution on both sides with a foam brush. Rinse the screen with water and air-dry.

Wooden Frames

Screen-printing frames are traditionally made from knot-free, kiln-dried wood that is soft enough to easily accept staples. The dimensions of the boards should be in proportion to those of the frame and should have dove-tailed or mitered corners, the latter secured with corrugated fasteners. Very large screens should be reinforced with metal corner angles. The frame must remain flat (unwarped) for good contact between the screen and fabric during printing.

Frames can be reused after removing the design from the mesh and cleaning the screen. Both cleaning and fabric printing use water; to protect the wood from liquids, dye penetration, and warping, apply a waterproof coating, such as polyurethane. If using a prestretched screen, cover the polyester mesh with paper and tape while coating the frame. Coat studio-constructed wooden frames before applying the mesh.

Seal the area where the frame and mesh meet to keep the printing medium from leaking out. Sealing also further protects the wood from moisture. Tape the front or flat side of the screen, covering up part of the frame and the mesh (see illustration 9.7). Choose from silver duct tape, clear packing tape, or special printing tape. Duct tape leaves a sticky residue when removed to reuse a screen.

To determine the proper frame size for a given project, remember that the design must always be smaller than the wood frame. As a general rule, allow 3 to 4 inches (7.6 to 10.2 cm) at the top and bottom of a design for the trough (the area holding the printing medium between passes of the squeegee) and 1 inch (2.5 cm) on each side as the squeegee does not occupy the entire width of the screen (see illustration 9.7).

Squeegees

A squeegee forces paint, dye, or chemicals through the screen and onto the fabric; and should fit inside the frame with ½ to 1 inch (1.3 to 2.5 cm) leeway on either side. It has a blade made of synthetic rubber mounted in a wooden, metal, or plastic handle. The handle should be comfortable for use with one hand except for the very largest, which requires two hands. Coat wooden handles with polyurethane so they do not absorb dyes or chemicals. Squeegee blades used for fabric printing have slightly rounded edges as these work best on the pliable fabric. Squeegees used on paper should have a square edge. Tap a finishing nail or drill a hole and insert a dowel into either end of a wooden-handled squeegee so that the handle can rest on the sides of the frame when not printing and out of the printing medium in the trough (see illustration 9.7). To avoid damaging the blade and risking uneven prints, always store squeegees by hanging from a screw-eye in one end of the handle or setting them handle down, blade up. For the same reason, never allow objects to press against the blade. If the blade does get a nick, run it across fine sandpaper on a flat hard surface to smooth and repair.

Printing Surfaces and Printing Tables

Printing surfaces for fabric need to be padded and resilient because cloth gives and does not remain flat during print application. A printing surface should consist of three layers: foundation, padding, and cover cloth. Many professional padded printing tables are 100 to 200 feet (30.5 to 61 m) long, but most artists have neither the money nor studio space for this type of setup. A smaller, but ideal printing table for yardage measures 3 yards (2.7 m) long and 6 inches (15.2 cm) wider than the fabric to be printed.

Another option is a sheet of plywood 4 by 8 feet (121.9 by 243.8 cm) reinforced on the back with two-by-fours and padded. Place the sheet on sawhorses, file cabinets, or folding legs to make a temporary printing table; lean it against the wall when not in use. For a permanent table, a base with metal or wood legs on locking wheels makes repositioning easy. Dividers in the base provide vertical screen storage. The printing surface should be 3 to 6 inches (7.6 to 15.2 cm) larger than the base all around to permit clamping fabrics to the table as well as providing foot room while standing at the table. The height of the printing surface should be 30 to 40 inches (76.2 to 101.6 cm) or whatever height will allow you to bend at the hips and not at the small of the back. The simplest padded surface for a studio is a small board (see illustration 9.7) that can be repositioned during printing.

To pad a printing surface, cut a piece of felt ½ inch (1.3 cm) thick and the size of the wooden board, or use smooth carpet felt or several layers of craft felt. Place the felt on the board, wrap smooth cotton muslin or light canvas over the padding, and staple it to the underside of the board. The fabric should be pulled tight and smooth across the surface. To waterproof the printing surface, cover it

with a sheet of heavy plastic. Some artists prefer to print on plastic or a nonabsorbent surface whereas others cover the printing surface with an old sheet to absorb migrating dye; wash the sheet after each use. Placing a self-healing cutting mat on top of the printing table when you are not using it will convert it into a cutting surface while protecting the padded surface from dents that would interfere with good contact in printing. Some artists mark a grid with a permanent marker directly on the printing surface to assist in laying out fabric on the straight grain.

Professional printing tables have a metal guide rail along the edge to ensure correct registration and enable printing of one color next to another without spacing or overlapping. The screen printing that I do focuses less on exact repetition of a design and more on letting a design overlap indiscriminately with other design elements. For information on screen printing with photo emulsion, knife-cut film, PhotoEZ (light-sensitive emulsion precoated on a nylon screen) and repeating design patterns on professional printing tables, consult the "Bibliography" and "Resources."

Freezer, Contact Paper, and Plastic Screen Techniques

Freezer paper, which is plastic coated, provides the easiest, most economical, and fastest way to make a design for a screen print. It is an excellent material for beginners. Advanced printers often use it for experimental designing. Usable for a day, after which it begins to absorb liquids, freezer paper is not rugged enough for quantity printing. Freezer paper is available at the grocery store.

Contact paper is more durable than freezer paper and will allow many more prints. Although its adhesive fails after numerous washings, water will still adhere it to the

9.8 Contact paper stencil. Clear contact paper marked with a design is being cut with an X-Acto knife on a mat. The finished design is shown adhered to a screen on the right. Cotton fabric on the left was resist-dyed in Procion MX and printed with the contact paper screen and textile paint. Photo by Tom Liden.

screen. To eliminate washing the screen between prints and to get a longer run out of a single design, try starting with a light color and printing with progressively darker colors. An elegant variation of this approach is to mix colors during printing by continually adding new colors to the trough (see illustration 15.3, page 108). Buy clear contact paper at grocery, hardware, or craft stores.

Plastic designs are similar to those made with freezer or contact paper but can be cleaned and reused. Use plastic sheeting, plastic sold by the yard, or plastic file folders. Thinner plastic works well on a screen while thicker plastic is more suited as a conventional stencil printed with a brush.

1. Cut freezer, contact paper, or plastic to the outside dimensions of the screen frame.
2. Draw the design, remembering to leave a 1-inch (2.5 cm) border on each side and 3 inches (7.6 cm) at the top and bottom of the screen. *Freezer paper* has dull and shiny sides; draw on the dull side. For *contact paper,* draw on the backing that covers the sticky side. Draw on either side of *plastic.*
3. Lay the design on a piece of cardboard or cutting mat and cut it out with an *X-Acto or matte knife.* Remove the backing from the contact paper.
4. Tape the design to the outside or flat side of the screen with the dull side of the freezer paper or the sticky side of the contact paper against the screen. You don't want anything on the inside of the screen that will interfere with the motion of the squeegee.
5. Position the screen on a piece of newspaper or scrap fabric.
6. Pour the *thickened dye, paint,* or *chemical* into the trough at the far end of the screen.
7. Make a trial print, following "Screen Printing Procedures" on page 74. The first print will moisten the stencil, adhering it to the screen.
8. Make the actual print(s).
9. When printing is complete, remove the stencil and wash the screen and squeegee before the printing medium dries on them.

Hints for Freezer, Contact Paper, and Plastic Screens

■ The most successful designs have simple, large design areas.

■ Screen designs are negative—it is the cut-out areas that will print.

■ Other possibilities for freezer paper stencils include burning the edges, punching holes, and tearing shapes rather than cutting them out.

■ Contact paper and plastic stencils can be reused. After drying, roll them without creases onto a cardboard tube or store them flat in a manila folder.

Thermofax Screen Printing

Thermofax or thermal imagers were developed in the 1940s to make stencils for mimeograph printing. With the advent of copy machines in 1950, many Thermofaxes were sent to the landfill. The others—survivors and newly manufactured machines—provide a simple and effective way to make screens without many steps or chemicals. The largest screen measures 8.5 by 14 inches (21.6 by 35.6 cm), the size of legal-size paper.

A Thermofax machine has a slot opening to an internal conveyor belt that passes by a very hot bulb. The Thermofax screen, a plastic-coated polyester mesh, is placed on top of an image made in a copy machine or laser printer using carbon toner (not inkjet ink). As the mesh and image pass together through the machine, the bulb heats the carbon, melting the plastic in the image area. The process takes only a few seconds. After emerging from the machine, the screen is separated from the copy. Wherever there was black toner on paper, the plastic has fused to the carbon and open mesh is exposed. The screen is ready to use after taping it to a plastic frame.

Thermofax machines can be purchased new or reconditioned (see "Resources" on page 136). The screens can be purchased as separate sheets or as a roll. Rolls cost more initially but yield many screens at a lower cost per screen than the sheets.

1. *Photocopy* or *laser-print* artwork on a sheet of paper.
2. Cut a piece of *Thermofax screen* to cover the artwork plus a border area. Four sizes of plastic frames are commercially available. The image should be at least 1 inch (2.5 cm) smaller than the frame on all sides. If the image is too large, you can reduce it on the copy machine or computer.
3. Lay the photocopy with image side up. Place a screen on top with the curling or shiny side against the design. Slide these into an *acetate carrier,* which is supplied with every roll of screen or built in with single sheets. The carrier keeps the image and screening correctly aligned.
4. Insert the carrier into the upper slot on the Thermofax machine. The conveyor belt will pull it in, and the finished screen will emerge from a lower slot at the front of the machine.
5. Remove the screen from the carrier. Pull back a corner of the screen to see if the mesh is open in the image area. If it is not, put it back in the carrier with the image in place and run through the machine again. Separate the design and the screen by gently pulling them apart.
6. Place the curling or smooth side of the screen against a *plastic frame.* Stretch slightly and tape as tightly as possible, without any ridges or slack areas. Using blue *painter's tape* allows one screen to be removed and another easily positioned in the frame and does not

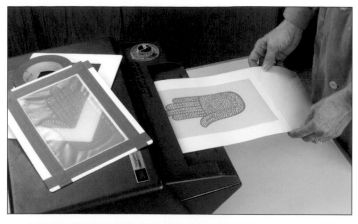

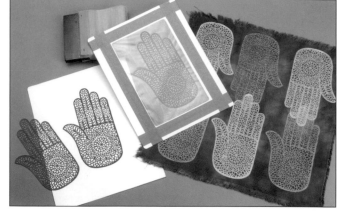

Clockwise from top left:

9.9 Making a Thermofax screen. A machine-copied mehndi design is being fed into a Thermofax machine. After copying, the Thermofax screen is separated from the copy and mounted in a plastic frame with tape, shown on the left. Photo by Tom Liden.

9.10 Making of the mehndi screen. On the left is the green mehndi stencil, used to print henna on hands in India. This was made into a black-and-white image on a copy machine and converted into a Thermofax screen. Fabric dyed with Procion MX and printed with the screen in two colors of textile paint is shown on the right. Photo by Tom Liden.

9.11 Machu Picchu Terraces #4 by Holly Brackmann. 12⅞" h × 14⅞" w (33 cm × 38 cm) fabric, 23½" h × 23¼" w × ¼"d (59.5 cm × 60.5 cm × 6 mm) mounted. Two screens were used to print the dévoré solution combined with disperse dye for the foreground and background layers. The two layers were then dyed with different colors of Procion MX. Photo by Hap Sakwa.

9.12 Machu Picchu Terraces by Holly Brackmann. A sequence for making print screens. A color photograph taken at Machu Picchu was converted to a black-and-white image, the contrast heightened, the image converted to a negative, and separated into foreground and background screens in Photoshop.

9.13 Old Passports by Holly Brackmann. Thermofax screens made from photos, visas, and stamps in passports. Shown are an old passport photo with an enlarged photocopy used to make the Thermofax screen, copies of passport pages used to make screens, strike-offs to test the screens, and a textile paint color test swatch. Screens and images used for 9.15, Passport to Travel. Photo by Tom Liden.

9.14 Great-Grandmother Mattie and Great-Aunt Ivah. Original photos can also be used to make Thermofax screens. High-contrast photos are best. An old photo of Holly's relatives was photocopied, the copy made into a screen, and the screen printed with textile paint on cotton knit fabric. Photo by Tom Liden.

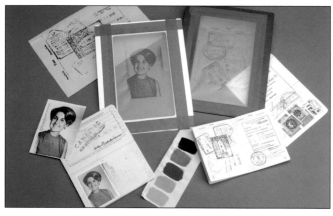

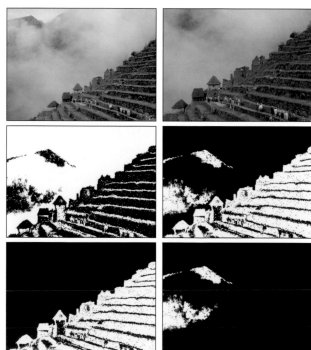

Hints for Thermofax Printing

■ Adjusting the dial on the Thermofax makes the internal conveyor belt go faster or slower, increasing or decreasing contact time between the toner and screen mesh.

■ To test the setting, begin at the midpoint on the dial. Run a piece of artwork through the machine. Lift a corner to see if the mesh is open. If it is cloudy and not open, change to a slower, darker setting. If the setting is too dark, the screen could burn and tear when separated from the photocopy, or melt the conveyor.

■ As an alternative squeegee for a small Thermofax screen, try a credit card or plastic grout spreader.

■ Thermofax screening comes in two mesh sizes, 70 and 100. The 70 is suitable for all but very detailed designs. Metallic paint will clog the 100.

■ Because every black area of an image will result in an opening in the mesh, cover unwanted black dots with correction fluid or tape before putting the image through the machine.

■ Drawings made with carbon-based India inks can be used in the Thermofax, but the quality will not be as good as that of photocopies or laser prints.

■ A photocopy or laser print can be used only once in the Thermofax.

■ Thermofax screens can be removed from a frame, stored flat in a manila file folder, and reapplied to a frame later.

■ One to three passes of the squeegee should be sufficient to produce a good print. Too many passes will result in lost detail or a blurred image.

■ If the screen becomes clogged during printing, especially with textile paint, wash with lukewarm water and air-dry before resuming.

■ To make an impromptu frame, fold and adhere duct tape around the edges of the screen.

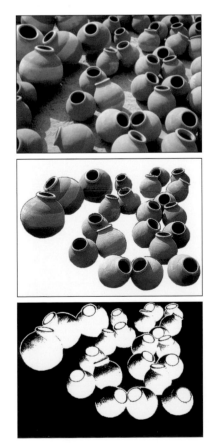

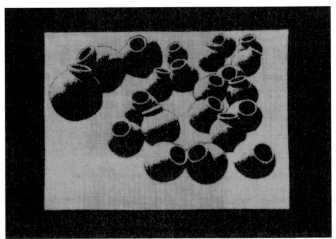

Above: 9.15 Passport to Travel by Holly Brackmann. 70 ½" h × 55½" w × ¾ d (179 cm × 141 cm × 2 cm) when opened flat. Folding screen imagery made from enlarged images in old passports that were converted to Thermofax screens. Printed with textile paint on cotton. Photo by Tom Liden.
Left: 9.16 Bagru Pots by Holly Brackmann. Photo taken in Bagru, India, manipulated as a black-and-white image in Photoshop, and the negative image used to make a screen.
Below: 9.17 Bagru Pots #2 by Holly Brackmann. 4½" h × 6" w (11.5 cm × 15 cm) image, 11" h × 14" w × 1" d (28 cm × 35.5 cm × 2.5 cm) mounted. Handwoven plain-weave fabric from polyester/cotton sewing thread with dévoré. Dyed with Procion MX. Photo by Joe Coca.

leave a sticky residue like the double-sided tape that some artists use.

7. Print the design on a padded surface with an appropriate medium and a squeegee that fits the frame. Refer to "Screen-Printing Procedures" below. Do not apply too much pressure on the squeegee because the screen is not as secure as mesh on a wooden frame.

8. After printing is completed, wash the screen with lukewarm water and a sponge. Do not scrub with a brush or the design may be damaged.

Screen-Printing Procedures

Screen printing requires dexterity to force consistent amounts of dye, paint, or chemicals onto the fabric surface. Variables include the angle of the squeegee, density of table padding, weave structure of the cloth being printed, ability of the fabric to accept chemicals, size of the screen mesh, number of passes made with the squeegee, and thickness of the printing medium. Always

9.18 Printing on fabric with textile paint and a Thermofax screen. Note the 45-degree angle of the squeegee. Photo by Tom Liden.
9.19 Two screen-printed fabrics folded and resist-dyed in Procion MX and then screened with textile paint through the same screen. One fabric uses a single color of paint. The other fabric uses two colors, showing the effects of a randomly placed overlapping design. Photo by Joe Coca.

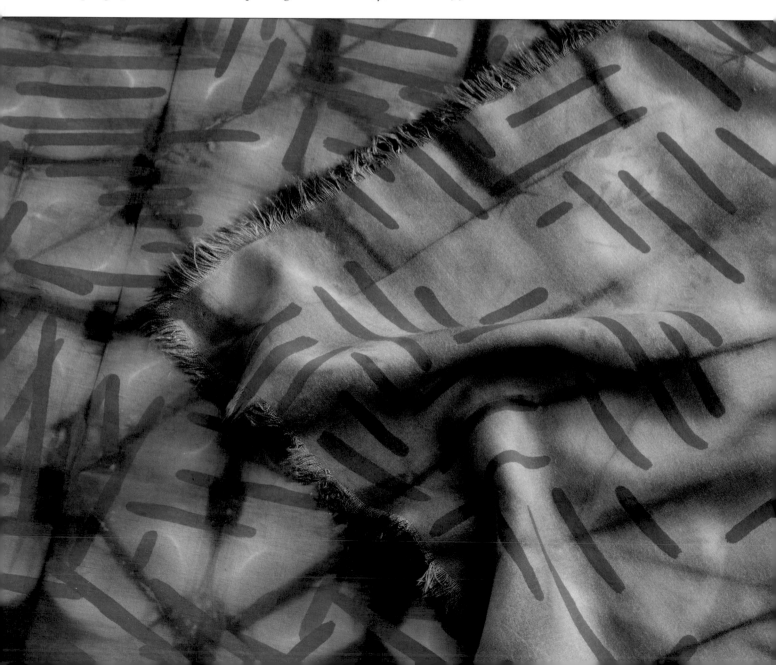

test a design and screen on a scrap of the fabric you will be using before printing large areas or expensive fabric. Since the screen frame is larger than the design, you must carefully plan the order of printing. Contaminating the underside of the screen with wet printing medium from an image will result in a "ghost image" with the next print.

1. Tape or pin clean, smoothly ironed fabric to the *padded printing surface.* If a padded printing table is not available, use a smooth folded towel, fabric length, or sheet.

2. Before you start printing, the *screen* must be wet out to produce a trial print ("strike-off"). This coats ("charges") the screen with printing medium and shows if the screen is printing properly. Trial prints indicate the number of passes and pressure required for a particular technique or design and fabric. Heavier fabrics may need four or more passes while thin fabrics require fewer. After a successful trial print, proceed to the actual fabric.

3. Position the screen on *newspaper* or a *fabric scrap* larger than the screen.

4. Rest the *squeegee* 2 to 3 inches (5.1 to 7.6 cm) from the end of the screen.

5. Pour the *thickened dye, paint,* or *chemical* into the trough at the far end of the screen between the squeegee and frame.

6. Hold the screen in place with one hand and put the other hand on the squeegee. Printing with a large screen may require two people, with one person holding the screen and the other moving the squeegee.

7. Place the squeegee behind the printing medium and pull down toward you, across the screen, at a 45-degree angle with a firm, consistent stroke. Scoop up the printing medium on the squeegee, lift and put the squeegee back at the top of the screen, then repeat. Some artists prefer to stroke down, then reverse the direction of the squeegee and stroke upward without picking up the squeegee. The screen may alternatively be positioned to stroke sideways, maintaining a 45-degree angle with the squeegee (see illustration 9.19). Jerky motions can result in an uneven print.

8. After the print has been made, rest the squeegee in the trough, raise one edge of the frame and peel from the fabric. Never lift the screen straight up since this will lift the printed fabric off the table and cause wrinkles.

9. In between prints, lay the screen on a clean piece of newspaper or rest it on a small container to keep it elevated, leaving the squeegee and printing medium resting in the trough.

10. Wipe gloved hands often to reduce the risk of transferring smudges to fabric.

11. Refill the trough with medium as needed between prints.

9.20 Trails *by Cassie Gibson. 58" l × 14" w (147.5 cm × 35.5 cm). Silk charmeuse dyed with thickened Procion MX. Thermofax-printed with metallic textile paint. The imagery is based on topographic maps of Cassie's neighborhood and the route she takes on her daily walks. 9.21 Trails detail. Photos by Tom Liden.*

12. Printing should be done as quickly as possible, especially if using paints. Acrylic paints dry very quickly, and once dried in the screen, cause permanent clogging, requiring replacement of the mesh. If printing must be interrupted briefly, leave the screen in the last position on the fabric to keep the mesh damp. Thickened Procion MX dyes need to be used within 4 hours.

Hints for Screen Printing

■ Because dyes and most textile paints are transparent, printing one on top of the other will result in a color mixture (for example, red + blue = purple).

■ Two or more colors of thickened dye or paint can be poured on the screen at once for blended color effects (see illustration 15.3).

■ Use a hair dryer to dry a still-damp design area if the screen frame will overlap, and possibly smudge, any part of it when the next print is made. You could cover the wet print with a paper towel or newsprint to keep medium from transferring to the underside of the screen, but this might remove some of the image.

■ Print a design randomly across a fabric, then print one or more layers of the same or different designs on the fabric for visual depth.

■ Offsetting or rotating the same screen can produce different image effects.

■ The printing medium must be viscous enough to hold together while being forced through the screen. It should not be runny.

■ Uneven printing can be the result of too few passes of the squeegee or not enough printing medium.

Screen Cleanup

1. Scrape unused printing medium from the screen with a rubber spatula or piece of cardboard and return it to the container.
2. Remove the freezer paper, contact paper, or plastic stencil from the flat side of the screen (see "Freezer, Contact Paper, and Plastic Screen Techniques" on page 70).
3. Wash the screen and squeegee thoroughly in a deep sink or tub with a hose fitted with a spray attachment.
4. Paints or dyes may stain the screen but won't affect future prints if they don't clog the mesh. To check for clogging, hold the screen up to the light. Scrub any blocked areas with a brush.
5. Dry and store screens vertically and squeegees with the blade up. Hasten drying with a fan.
6. Dry the screen completely before printing another color or chemical.

9.22 Sunflower Scarf *by Leila Kazimi. 60" long × 15" w (152.5 cm × 38 cm). Silk dyed with random and soda soak techniques in Procion MX. Thermofax-printed with Jacquard Discharge Paste and with transparent and metallic textile paints.*
9.23 Sunflower Scarf *detail. Photos by Neal Mettler.*

Opposite: 9.24 Guggenheim #1 *by Holly Brackmann. 8½" h × 9" w (21.5 cm × 23 cm) fabric, 13" h × 13" w × ¼" d (33 cm × 33 cm × 35.5 cm) mounted. Dévoré on commercial polyester/cotton fabric. The same screen was used three times on two pieces of fabric, once on the front piece (dévoré) and twice on the back piece (dévoré and textile paint). Procion MX and disperse dyes and textile paint. Embroidered with cotton thread and mounted on fiberglass screening. Photo by Hap Sakwa.*
9.25 Guggenheim *by Holly Brackmann. Photo taken in the Guggenheim Museum in New York City. Converted to a black-and-white image and manipulated in Photoshop. Contrast heightened and inverted to make a screen. It is advantageous to invert images before using the dévoré process.*

Chapter Ten
Monoprinting

Monoprinting ("mono," from the Greek, means "one") is the process of making a single print. Dyes, paint, or chemicals are applied to a nonporous printing plate of acrylic or glass, a design is drawn on the plate with fingers evoking memories of childhood finger painting or tools, and the plate applied to the fabric. Monoprinting can be done with thickened Procion MX, Cibacron F, disperse dye, textile paint, or discharge paste.

Thickened Procion MX, Cibacron F, or Textile Paint Monoprinting

1. Work on a padded printing surface (see "Printing Surfaces and Printing Tables" on page 70).
2. Stretch clean, ironed fabric tightly on the printing surface and secure.
3. Choose one to three colors of *thickened Procion MX* or Cibacron F (see "Thickened Procion MX or Cibacron F on Cellulose and Silk" on page 23). Prepare ½ cup (118 ml) of each color. Thick *textile paint* can also be used.
4. Apply a thin layer of dye or paint to the *printing plate*, with a *brayer, foam roller, or bristle or foam brush*.
5. Draw a design with a gloved finger or tool.
6. Place the printing plate, design side down, on the stretched fabric. Press evenly on the back for good contact between image and fabric.
7. Carefully lift one side of the printing plate and peel off the fabric.

Hints for Monoprinting with Thickened Procion MX, Cibacron F, or Textile Paint

■ Sand a smooth plastic printing plate to improve adhesion of paint or dye.

■ Tools for making designs on the printing plate include faux-finish or grout tools, hair pick, comb, kitchen utensils, and a gloved finger.

■ To prevent muddy colors, do not use too many colors on the printing plate at once.

■ Work from light to dark when applying colors to the printing plate.

■ To add texture to the print, apply color to the printing plate with a sponge or wadded paper towel.

■ Placing leaves, paper shapes, or doilies on fabric before placing the print plate will produce a negative design surrounded by color.

■ Try printing on dry, damp, or wet fabric for different effects.

10.1 Monoprinting tools. Shown on an acrylic sheet are a wadded paper towel, faux-finish tools, natural sponge, hair pick, comb, wadded plastic wrap, and a foam brush. Photo by Tom Liden.

10.2 After textile paint has been applied to an acrylic sheet with a brayer, the wet paint is combed with a faux-finish tool and printed on fabric. Photo by Tom Liden.

Opposite: 10.3 Floating Head by Daphne Gillen. 12" h × 12" w (30.5 cm × 30.5 cm). Procion MX used as a random dye, then fabric monoprinted with textile paint. Stitch embellishments. Photo by Joe Coca.

10.4 Combed Disperse Dye Monoprints *by Holly Brackmann.*
*Thickened disperse dye was applied to paper and combed. The print
was transferred to polyester lamé using four leaves as a resist, resulting
in blank leaf shapes on a combed background. A second print, made
using the transferred side of the leaves and paper coated with a solid
red disperse dye, yielded a solid red background with patterned leaves,
shown on the left. The thickness of the leaf stems held the transfer
paper away from the polyester, forming a halo effect. Finally, the
leaves, which now were red on the other side, were used to transfer
red to the original lamé print, shown at right. Photo by Tom Liden.*

8. Wipe off or wash the plate with water before applying
more medium. Print on top of the first design or on
another area of the fabric.

9. Dye or paint must be fixed to the fabric (see "Fixing
Thickened Procion MX and Cibacron F Dyes" on page
24 and "Heat Setting or Fixation" on page 112).

10. Wash residue from the fabric (see "Rinsing and Washing
Out Unfixed Dye" on page 15 and "Rinsing, Washing,
and Drying Fabric" on page 122).

Hints for Disperse Dye Transfer Monoprinting

■ Lay a piece of fabric between two pieces of dye transfer paper to
print both sides of the fabric in one step.

■ Overprinting can rescue a weak piece or tone down colors that are
too bright.

■ Try using aluminum foil, plastic wrap, or a plastic bag as the printing plate for a textural design.

Disperse Dye Transfer Monoprinting

1. Follow Steps 1 and 2 above.

2. Make *thickened disperse dye* (see "Transfer Printing
Procedure" on page 53).

3. Follow Steps 4 and 5 above.

4. Place a sheet of plain, smooth *paper* on top of the *printing plate.* Gently press or lightly roll a *brayer* on the
back of the paper. Too much pressure will obliterate fine
design details.

5. Peel the paper from the printing plate and set aside to
dry.

6. Transfer the image to *polyester, nylon, or acetate fabric*
with an *iron or heat press* (see "Transfer Printing" on
page 51).

7. The fabric does not require rinsing or washing; however,
washing in warm water will remove any thickener or
chemicals transferred to the fabric.

Chapter Eleven
Stamping

Stamping is a fast way to apply designs on fabric. Coat a stamp with thickened dye, paint, discharge paste, or resist, and press it on the fabric. Designs can be repeated with regularity or placed randomly. Stamping requires minimal supplies: a foam brush or brayer for applying medium to the stamp, a printing surface, and fabric. Stamps can be purchased ready-made or created from a variety of materials, including found objects.

Commercial Stamps

Stamps for fabric need to have large, bold designs because the weave structure can fracture fine details. The rougher the weave, the less detail will show. Only finely woven fabric such as silk habotai will work with commercial rubber stamps made for stamping on paper. Stamps intended specifically for fabric are usually made from foam for flexibility. They are available from craft, art, and hardware stores in a wide variety of styles, shapes, and sizes. After trying commercial foam stamps and learning how to stamp on fabric, try making your own stamps.

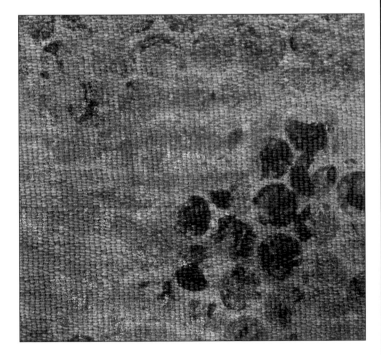

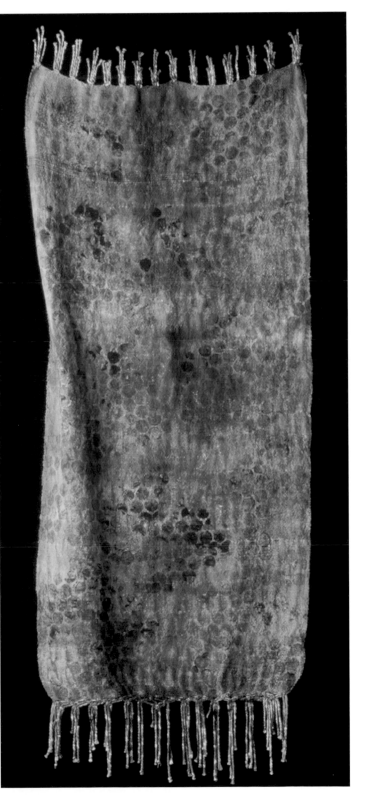

11.1 Shibori Bingo by Pavlos Mayakis. 60" h × 28" w (152.5 cm × 71 cm). Handwoven shibori with ramie warp and cotton weft, immersion-dyed with Procion MX, then stamped with bubble wrap. 11.2 Shibori Bingo detail (above) by Pavlos Mayakis. Photos by Black Cat Studios.

11.3 *Foam weather stripping glued to an acrylic backing is being charged with textile paint for printing. Patting the stamp with a foam brush filled with printing medium applies a sufficient quantity of paint to the stamp without clogging the indented areas. The resulting stamped design is shown on the cotton fabric. Photo by Tom Liden.*

11.4 *Heating a precut shape with a craft heat gun, then pressing it onto a textured surface, makes a heat-moldable foam stamp. Here, heat-moldable foam was pressed on a faux-finish tool to make a stamp with parallel concentric lines. Photo by Tom Liden.*

Foam Weather-Stripping Stamps

1. Plan your design and mark it on a 3-by-3-inch (7.6 by 7.6 cm) or larger piece of *clear plastic acrylic* such as Lucite or Plexiglas with a *permanent marker.* When making a print, you will be able to see through the plastic exactly where you're placing the stamp on the fabric.
2. Cut lengths of *foam weather stripping* for each design element with scissors.
3. Remove the adhesive backing and apply the stripping to the plastic.

Heat-Moldable Foam Stamps

PenScore, a heat-moldable foam, can be softened with heat and pressed on textured objects to create designs. It can be purchased in sheets or precut shapes from art and craft suppliers.

1. Hold *heat-moldable foam* 4 to 6 inches (10.2 cm to 15.2 cm) from a 300° F (149° C) *heat source* (heat gun, electric hot plate, or iron) for 20 to 30 seconds, depending on the size of the block. Take care not to burn yourself or scorch the foam.
2. Within 5 seconds, press the foam on any *textured object* such as a piece of lace, jewelry, pasta, button, shell, or plant material. Hold in place for 10 to 25 seconds. As the foam cools, it will form a mold of the part of the object that it is touching.
3. Lift the mold off the object. It is now ready to be used as a stamp.
4. To reuse the foam, reheat it for 30 to 60 seconds to erase the design, then repeat Steps 2 and 3.

Ideas for Improvised Stamps

- Draw a shape on a compressed cellulose sponge and cut it out while the sponge is still compressed. Put the sponge in water to expand to its full size before stamping.
- Glue thick string to a wooden or plastic base. Coat the string and backing with polyurethane to waterproof.
- Cut or carve Styrofoam packing material or food trays into shapes.
- Carve art gum, white art erasers, or soft printing blocks.
- Cut sheet foam from craft stores into shapes and adhere to clear plastic or wooden blocks.
- Use vegetables such as cut carrots, halved artichokes, cut green peppers, or celery. Veggie stamps can be stored overnight in plastic wrap. If they start to dry out, cut off the dried surface and reuse. Let carved potatoes sit for a few hours to dry slightly before printing.
- Use flat leaves. Apply medium to the leaf and press on fabric. Leaves that have prominent veins on the back make interesting prints.
- Try whole raw fish, as in Japanese fish printing (*gyotaku*). Wash and dry a fish, apply printing medium to the surface, then roll it on fabric. Rubber fish are available from art suppliers (see illustration 11.5).
- Use kitchen utensils such as potato mashers, meat tenderizers, and wooden spaghetti lifters. Do not use them again for food.
- Cut or carve inexpensive foam thongs or computer mouse pads into shapes with scissors and adhere to a plastic or wooden backing.
- Try plastic bubble wrap (see illustrations 11.1 and 11.2); empty thread spools; wine corks; children's carved

11.5 *A variety of stamps, including rubber fish, African gourd, India woodblock, commercial fabric, bubble wrap, natural sponge, insulation foam mounted on acrylic block, and heat-moldable foam. Photo by Tom Liden.*

11.6 *Stamps and the impressions made by them, including from left to right, commercial foam, heat-moldable foam, bubble insulation from a hot tub cover, and carved erasers glued to an acrylic backing. Photo by Tom Liden.*

wooden blocks; rubber-gloved hands; footprints (do not use bleach discharge on skin); sink or tub stoppers; or synthetic sponges sold for children's craft projects, cosmetics, or upholstery.

Stamp-Printing Procedure

1. Prepare a *padded printing surface* (see "Printing Surfaces and Printing Tables" on page 70).
2. Stretch clean, ironed fabric tightly on the printing surface and secure.
3. Pour a small amount of *medium* into a container.
4. Apply medium to the stamp by patting with a *foam brush, rolling with a brayer or sponge roller,* or pressing the stamp into it.
5. Press the stamp firmly and evenly on the fabric. Rocking or moving the stamp will cause a blurred image. If the image is pale, you need to apply more medium. If details are lost, you used too much medium, which filled recessed areas of the stamp and blurred the image.
6. Wash stamps with soap and water and scrub with a *toothbrush* immediately after stamping as dried textile paint is not water soluble and can be impossible to remove. A stamp can be ruined if paint is allowed to dry in the recessed areas.
7. Fix the dye or paint. If using thickened fiber-reactive dye, see "Fixing Thickened Procion MX and Cibacron F Dyes" on page 24. If using textile paint, see "Heat Setting or Fixation" on page 112. Process discharge chemicals according to "Thiox Discharge for Painting or Printing" on page 61, "Jacquard Discharge Paste" on page 61, "Thickened Sodium Hydrosulfite for Painting, Stenciling, Printing, and Stamping" on page 63, "Thickened Bleach Discharge" on page 64, and resists according to "Stamping with Presist or Inko Dye Resist and Thin Textile Paint" on page 89.

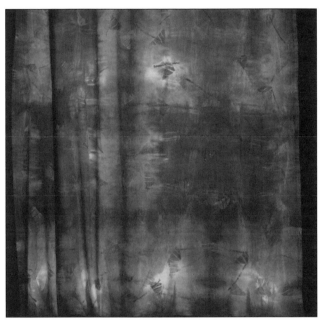

11.7 Golden Medlee *by Pavlos Mayakis. 36" h × 36" w (91.5 cm × 91.5 cm). Commercial cotton knit massage wrap dyed with Procion MX, overdyed with folded resist, then stamped with textile paints. Stamps used include licorice sticks, which were inspired by the cables on the Golden Gate Bridge. Photo by Black Cat Studios.*

Hints for Stamping

■ For letters and numbers to read correctly in the finished piece, they must be reversed on the stamp.

■ Apply two or more colors at once to a stamp for a blended effect.

■ Print once with a stamp, and then rotate it and print again on the same fabric.

■ Vary the sizes of stamps on a single fabric for increased visual interest.

■ Create blended colors by overlapping images made with different transparent dyes or paints.

■ To plan the placement of stamps, mark locations on fabric with disappearing ink.

■ Print dye or textile paint without washing the stamp between color changes, starting with light and progressing to dark colors. Subsequent stamp impressions will be a mixture of colors.

■ Store stamps so that the surface is not compressed or indented.

Chapter Twelve
Stenciling

Stenciling involves applying dye, paint, or chemicals to a surface through openings in a sheet mask. It is an ancient form of printing, developed to a high level in Japan and believed to be the precursor of screen printing. Stenciling is fast and portable and requires only a stencil, printing medium, and applicator. Commercial plastic stencils have laser-cut voids. Try using a purchased stencil to familiarize yourself with the application technique before making your own.

A stencil can produce either a positive or a negative image. Stencils need bridges to connect areas of a design. Think of an "O" design. It is impossible to cut the "O" and retain the center area, which would just fall out of the mask material; however, the "O" design could be cut with four bridges to connect the center of the circle and the outer area. Stencil designs should be fairly simple because the weave structure of all but the most finely woven fabric distorts and obscures fine details.

Stencil Applicators

Applicators for stenciling include brushes, sponges, and sprayers. Stencil brushes have a wide, flat surface, providing good contact between the open areas of the stencil and the fabric. Square or round foam brushes or cellulose, cosmetic, or natural sea sponges are good for applying thick dyes, discharge pastes, textile paints, resists, dévoré, or other chemicals. Keep in mind that bleach discharge will destroy natural bristle brushes and cellulose sponges. Thin dyes, discharge, or textile paints can be sprayed through the openings in a stencil. Wear a respirator when spraying.

Cutting the Stencil

1. Lay the *stencil material* flat on a *cutting mat* or heavy piece of *cardboard* to protect the table surface.
2. Position the *design* under the stencil and mark its outline on the plastic. If needed, include bridges between the negative and positive areas to hold the stencil parts in place during printing.
3. Cut along lines with an *X-Acto knife,* which is easier to use and has a finer blade than a matte knife. Cut away from right-angle design corners to prevent overcutting. *Tape* on both sides of the stencil to repair mistakes. The cutout design will be the positive, printed shape.

12.2 *Commercial plastic stencils are shown with stencil applicators, including natural bristle and foam stencil brushes, foam paint roller, cellulose sponges, and natural sea sponge. Photo by Tom Liden.*

Interfacing-and-Net Stencil

Artist Jane Dunnewold introduced this technique, which uses fusible interfacing and nylon netting in a modern adaptation of the Japanese stencil.

1. Cut two pieces of *fusible heavyweight or window-shade interfacing.*
2. With the fusible sides of the pieces held together, draw, then cut out the design with *scissors* or an *X-Acto knife.* A design with bold lines and strong negative and positive areas is best.
3. Cut a piece of *nylon net or tulle* that is slightly larger than the interfacing.
4. Place the netting between the two pieces of interfacing, matching the areas of cutout design, and *steam iron* together, following the instructions of the interfacing manufacturer.
5. Waterproof both sides of the stencil with *acrylic craft paint* by rolling with a *foam roller.* The mesh of the net or tulle will not clog.
6. Line-dry.
7. If the stencil begins to come apart with use, wash out the stenciling medium, allow the stencil to dry, then iron the interfacing layers together to re-fuse and reuse.

Opposite: 12.1 Heavenly Bamboo by Jane Spanbauer. 72" l × 14" w (183 cm × 35,5 cm). Silk crepe de chine scarf folded and clamped twice, then dyed with Cibacron F. Finally, printed twice with two handmade net-and-interfacing stencils using textile paint. Photo by Joe Coca.

12.3 *Interfacing-and-net stencils with resulting images. The components for making a stencil include pieces of fusible interfacing, netting, an X-Acto knife, and an iron. On the right, a completed stencil has been waterproofed by coating both sides with turquoise acrylic paint. Next to it is a rectangular print made with the stencil using opaque blue textile paint. If the stencil separates during printing, it can be ironed to re-fuse the two pieces of interfacing. On the left, a ginkgo design stencil and the resulting print. Photo by Tom Liden.*

12.4 *Half Bulls-Eye by Holly Brackmann. 73" l × 8" w (185.5 cm × 20.5 cm). Handwoven polyester/cotton using an interfacing-and-net stencil to apply disperse dye mixed in the dévoré solution, to dye and burnout in one step. Disperse dye was handpainted on paper for transfer-printing the same half-bulls-eye image on the fabric. Background dyed with Procion MX. Photo by Tom Liden.*

12.5 *Negative and Positive Sample by Holly Brackmann. Black rayon challis was stenciled with two interfacing-and-net stencils. First a regular stencil was made, and the resulting cutout design was used to make a second stencil. Both designs were printed with Jacquard Discharge Paste. The fabric was then wrapped on a pole for arashi shibori, soaked in soda ash, and dyed with Procion MX. Photo by Tom Liden.*

Clear Plastic or File Folder Stencils

Clear acetate or Mylar sheets, available from art suppliers; overhead projector sheets; and file folders from office suppliers make strong stencils. Blank stencil sheet plastic is also available in craft stores.

1. Draw or trace the design.
2. Cut along the lines with an X-Acto knife. Acetate, Mylar, or plastic stencils can be cut with a stencil-burning tool.
3. Seal and waterproof a stencil made from a manila file folder by spraying with polyurethane outdoors or in a well-ventilated space. Place the stencil on plastic sheeting and spray one side. When that side is dry, turn the stencil over and spray the other side. Give each side a second coat.

Stencil Printing

1. Tape or pin smooth fabric to a *padded print surface* (see "Printing Surfaces and Printing Tables" on page 70).
2. If spraying on the printing medium, tape or pin the fabric to a board and lean it against a wall. Spray in a well-ventilated space or outdoors, wearing a respirator and eye protection. Spraying is especially appropriate for large pieces of fabric, such as costumes, wall hangings, or rugs.
3. Mark the *fabric* with disappearing ink or place the stencil randomly on it.
4. You may spray the back of the stencil with a spray stencil adhesive to help the stencil stay in position on the fabric, but be aware that small amounts of adhesive may be transferred to the fabric.
5. Position the stencil on the fabric, use masking or painter's tape to secure in place on the fabric.
6. Pour the *stenciling medium* into a *small container* or onto a *palette*.
7. Dip the *applicator* into the stenciling medium. Only a very small amount of medium is required for stenciling. If there is too much medium, tap the charged applicator on a paper towel, jar lid, or scrap of fabric.
8. Holding the stencil in place with one hand, use a pouncing (up-and-down) motion on the stencil, either begin in the middle of the stencil and work outward or start at the edge and work inward. Avoid using a stroking motion, which can force medium under the edges of the stencil.
9. Peel off the stencil from the fabric by lifting one corner, taking care not to blur the image.
10. Check the underside of the stencil for excess stenciling medium. If it has become contaminated, wipe with a sponge or paper towel, or thoroughly wash and dry the stencil.
11. Reposition the stencil and repeat the application. Make sure that it is not placed on top of a wet area.
12. If using thickened fiber-reactive dye, see "Fixing Thick-

12.6 A commercial plastic stencil being used to print on cotton fabric with a foam stencil brush and acrylic paint. The brush is first tapped on the plastic lid to remove excess paint, then tapped on the stencil to force paint through the stencil onto the fabric. Photo by Tom Liden.

ened Procion MX and Cibacron F Dyes" on page 24. If using textile paint, see "Heat Setting or Fixation" on page 112. Process discharge chemicals according to directions "Thiox Discharge for Painting or Printing" on page 61, "Jacquard Discharge Paste" on page 61, "Thickened Sodium Hydrosulfite for Painting, Stenciling, Printing, and Stamping" on page 63, and "Thickened Bleach Discharge" on page 64. Dévoré chemicals must be heated: see "Dévoré Screen Printing or Stenciling" on page 103.

Stencil Cleaning and Storage

Stencils will last a long time if properly maintained. Immediately after printing, lay the stencil flat in the sink and gently remove the stenciling medium with water and a sponge or soft brush. Allow the stencil to dry after each use. Dried paint will not affect it. Store stencils vertically in file folders or folded paper. Stacking stencils horizontally can cause warping, which in turn can cause blurred prints.

Hints for Stenciling

■ When repeating the same stencil on a fabric, change its orientation and/or vary colors to make the fabric more interesting.
■ Try enlarging, reducing, or reversing a stencil design on a copy machine.
■ Print only parts of a stencil to create a new design.
■ Mix colors by applying more than one color to the stencil during application for a blended effect.

12.7 Military Twill by Pavlos Mayakis, 60" h × 28" w (152.5 cm × 71 cm). Cotton warp painted with fiber-reactive dyes and hand-woven. Overdyed, then discharged with Jacquard Discharge Paste using commercial letters and stencils randomly placed on the weaving. Photo by Black Cat Studios.

Chapter Thirteen
Resists

Resists are treatments that prevent dye or paint from reaching and penetrating fabric, thus protecting the current color. If beginning with white fabric, the resisted area will be white. If beginning with a colored fabric, the dye color should be harmonious with the background color because both are transparent and will affect one another. Resists can also be used with discharge and scouring silk. There are two main types of resists, mechanical and physical.

Mechanical Resists

Mechanical resists employ wax, starch, or glue to form a barrier preventing penetration of the dye into the fabric. The result is a shape surrounded by a colored area. Mechanical resists include water-soluble resists and cold wax. They are best suited for direct painting techniques.

Water-Soluble Resists

Water-soluble resists present few health hazards and are easy to remove from fabric but are not appropriate for use with immersion techniques. They can also be used with thickened discharge on dark fabrics. Commercial brands include Cerulean Blue Presist, Inko Resist, Silkpaint! Water-soluble Resist, Jacquard Water-based Resist,

Sennelier Aqua Gutta, Pebeo Water-based Gutta, DuPont Colored Gutta, Sabra Silk Resist, and Elmer's Glue Gel.

Begin with lightweight cotton, rayon, wool, or silk for best penetration. Heavier fabrics, such as silk noil, cotton velvet, or textured linen may need extra applications of resist. Stamp, stencil, print, or paint the resist on fabric, allow it to dry, then apply thickened dyes or thin textile paints. After the dye or paint has dried and cured, preferably for 24 hours, rinse the resist from the fabric.

Stamping with Presist or Inko Resist and Thin Textile Paint

1. Work on a *padded printing surface* (see "Printing Surfaces and Printing Tables" on page 70).
2. Follow directions for "Stamp Printing Procedure" on page 83.
3. Allow the *Presist* or *Inko Resist* to air-dry for 24 hours.
4. Brush *thin textile paint* across the stamped areas and dry.
5. Heat-set *textile paint* (see "Heat Setting or Fixation" on page 112).
6. Soak the fabric in plain *water* to soften and remove resist. Wash residue from fabric.

13.2 Presist water-soluble resist was stamped on cotton fabric at left. Thin, transparent textile paint was sprayed over the resist on the fabric in the center. In the fabric shown on the right, the paint was fixed with an iron and the Presist washed out. The original white of the fabric was resisted and is now surrounded by color. Photo by Tom Liden.

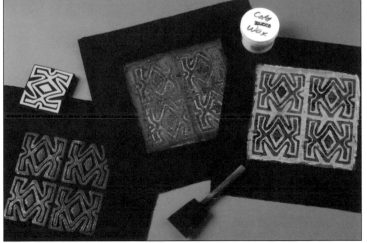

13.3 Cold wax resist was stamped on black cotton on the left. The fabric in the center was painted with thickened bleach and still contains wax. The resulting fabric, shown on the right, was boiled in water with soap to remove the wax. The dark area was resisted by the cold wax and is now surrounded by the lighter discharge. Photo by Tom Liden.

Opposite: 13.1 Turban cloth from Rajasthan, India. The binding has been partially removed. Because the cotton fabric is so thin and loosely woven, the dye penetrated through multiple layers. Photo by Joe Coca.

Cold Wax Resist

Cold wax, an alternative to hot wax, produces a batik-like crackle pattern. It works best with thickened dyes or discharge chemicals and thin textile paints. Use lightweight fabric because cold wax will not penetrate heavy fabric.

1. Stretch clean, smooth fabric tightly on a *padded printing surface* covered with *plastic* and secure (see "Printing Surfaces and Printing Tables" on page 70). The fabric can also be stretched on a *frame,* which allows better wax penetration and keeps the waxed fabric from sticking to the plastic covering the printing surface.

2. Apply the *cold wax* by brushing, stamping, or squeezing from a bottle. Cold wax will permanently coat a *brush, stamp, or bottle.*

3. If the wax hasn't penetrated the back of the fabric, apply more wax to that surface.

4. Allow the cold wax to dry.

5. Apply thickened dye, thin textile paint, or bleach discharge.

6. If using thickened fiber-reactive dye, see "Fixing Thickened Procion MX and Cibacron F Dyes" on page 24. Allow textile paints to air-cure (allowing the polymer bond to form) for a week as they cannot be heat-set before removing the wax. If discharging with bleach, see "Chlorine Bleach" on page 63 to stop the bleach action.

7. To remove the wax from the fabric, place it in a *large pot* (not used for cooking) of water. Heat to boiling and add a small handful of *soap flakes* (not detergent) or shavings from a bar of Ivory soap. The soap keeps the wax suspended in the solution. Boil for 5 to 15 minutes. Allow the submerged fabric to cool in the pot and the wax to congeal on the surface. Skim the hardened wax from the surface and discard.

8. Rinse the fabric. If any wax residue remains in the fabric, boil again in a fresh pot of water with soap and rinse.

13.4 *Wrapped and bound designs in fabric from Japan and India. Wrapped areas resist dye penetration. Dye applied locally to the Indian fabrics before wrapping resulted in dots of color after the wrapping was removed. Photo by Joe Coca.*

Physical Resists

Physical resists use binding, clamping, wrapping, stitching, knotting, or folding to prevent penetration of dye, paint, or chemicals into the fabric. This technique is also referred to as tie-dye, shibori (Japan), *plangi* (Indonesia), and *bandhani* (India). Physical resists have been used in many parts of the world, including pre-Columbian Peru, but most extensively in Asia and Africa. In the 1960s, the technique became associated with tie-dyed T-shirts. Physical resists squeeze flat fabric into a three-dimensional form, which is then immersed in, dipped into, or painted with dye or discharge solution. The resulting negative or positive shapes have blurred edges between the resist areas and the dyed or discharged portions. Wet the fabric thoroughly before dyeing to swell the fiber, which keeps out dye and enhances the resist; dry fabric wicks dye into resisted areas. For inspiration on using physical resists, see books by Karren Brito and Yoshiko Wada in the "Bibliography."

13.5 *A bound resist using marbles tied with rubber bands is shown on the left. The resulting fabric on the right was soaked in soda ash and dyed with Procion MX. Photo by Tom Liden.*

Fiber-reactive, acid, vat, and disperse dyes are all appropriate for this technique. Fiber-reactive dyes can be thin (soda soak and random recipes) or thickened (painted on the edges). Using an immersion dyebath with fiber-reactive dyes requires that the resist be very tight, or the dye will migrate into the folds and obscure the design (see illustration 13.17). Acid dyes are especially suitable for physical resists with immersion techniques. Vat dyes attach to the fabrics very rapidly and work well with immersion dyeing of cellulose and silk fabrics. A special technique of scouring sericin silk with alkali or vat dyes is discussed below. Disperse dyes used for transfer printing are also compatible with physical resists.

Bound Resists

For this technique, fabric is knotted on itself or pulled up and tied with string, thread (polyester, or button and carpet), crochet cotton, rubber bands, raffia, or nonsticky Japanese plastic tape. The binding material should suit the weight of the fabric—thread for fine cotton, string for loose-weave linen. Objects such as pebbles, seeds, glass marbles, shells, corks, buttons, or beads can be inserted into the fabric folds, affecting the size and shape of the bound pattern. Choose objects that will not rust and stain or swell and split the fabric.

1. Iron the *washed fabric* for a smooth working surface.
2. Mark the placement of wrappings with *disappearing ink.*
3. Gather the fabric on itself or around an *inserted shape.* Wrap the fabric with thread, rubber bands, or other material. The ties must be very tight. To protect your fingers, pull the ties against scissors or a pencil, or wear bandages.
4. Soak fabric in plain *water* for ½ hour or overnight.
5. *Dye* with fiber-reactive, acid, or vat dyes, then batch cure, or steam as the method requires.
6. Unwrap, rinse, and wash the fabric.

Bound Resist Hints

■ Place wrappings close together to completely exclude the dye; widely spaced wrappings allow dye to seep between the wraps, creating a banded effect.

■ Carry the wrapping material from one resist area to the next, if wrapping small areas that are close together.

■ Fabric can be dyed and washed, then rebound in other areas and dyed with another color to produce new color combinations.

■ Braiding, twisting, knotting, or randomly scrunching fabric gives interesting effects.

■ Drying the fabric thoroughly before untying helps keep dye from bleeding into resist areas.

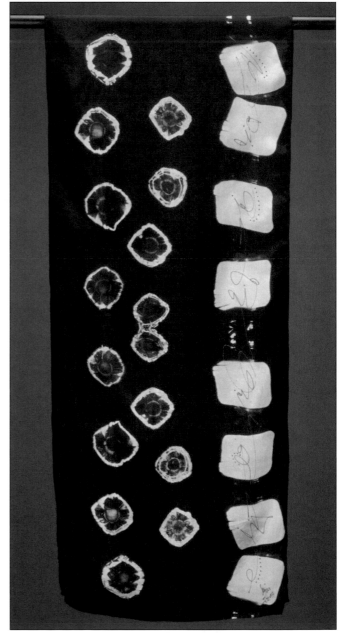

13.6 Black Shibori *by Kathy Snyder. 72" l × 14" w (183 cm × 35.5 cm). Bound and clamp resisted with Procion MX dyes and textile paint on silk fabric. Photo by Hap Sakwa.*

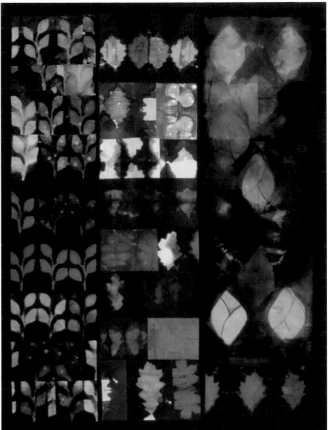

Clockwise from top left:
13.7 Holly Brackmann used wooden leaf shapes designed by Carol LeBaron to resist a worsted-wool scarf. 63" *l* × 8½" *w* (160 cm × 21.5 cm). The shapes were clamped to the fabric, which was then immersed twice in WashFast acid dye. Note how the dye permeated the fabric through an opening cut in one of the shapes. Photo by Tom Liden.

13.8 Stony Creek September Triptych *by Carol LeBaron. Three panels, each 108" h × 28" w 274.5 cm × 71 cm). Wooden shapes clamped to folded wool as a resist for WashFast acid dyes. Smaller pieces hand-stitched together. Photo by Cathy Carver.*

13.9 Four clamp-resisted scarves by Holly Brackmann. 59" *l* × 11½" *w* (150 cm × 29 cm) each. Silk habotai was clamped and dip dyed in acid dye. Photo by Joe Coca.

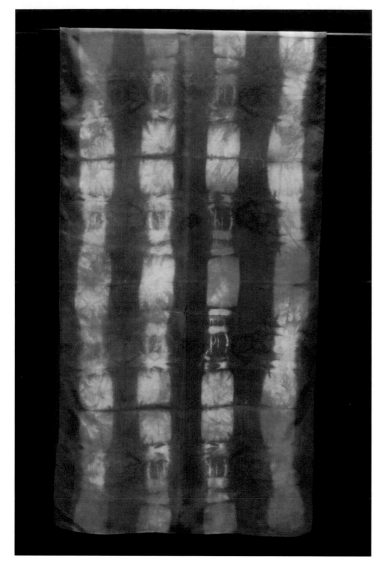

13.10 Red Shibori Twice *by Kathy Snyder. 85" l × 22" w (216 cm ×
56 cm). Clamp resist using metal Altoid boxes and rubber bands.
Procion MX on silk fabric. Photo by Hap Sakwa.*

Hints for Clamping

◼ Simple shapes are best for resist blocks.

◼ Dye applied to dry fabric wicks into the fabric, producing less resist than wet fabric.

◼ Clothespins applied to thin fabric produces dots of resist.

◼ Clamping blocks made from hard woods will last longer than those made of plywood, which tends to delaminate on exposure to water.

◼ To keep wooden blocks from transferring dye from a previous dyebath to the fabric, place a layer of plastic between the block and fabric.

◼ Clamps made of wood, polypropylene, or acrylic at least ¼ inch (6 mm) thick work best in hot dyebaths because they do not distort in heat.

◼ Clamped fabric edges can be dipped in different colors of dye. Clear acrylic blocks allow dye absorption to be viewed.

◼ Fabric can be discharged, overdyed, dyed and discharged, or treated in any combination with clamping resists, creating layers of imagery.

Clamping

For the technique called *itajime* in Japan, fabric is folded in two or more directions before clamping between paired blocks of shaped wood, acrylic, or plastic. The compressed fabric retains the original color while the projecting fabric takes up dye or discharge. The size of the blocks and placement on the pleated fabric will affect the resist pattern.

1. Iron the clean *fabric* for a smooth working surface.
2. Accordion-fold the fabric lengthwise, pressing the pleats with an iron for more precise lines. Larger pleats will produce a bolder design.
3. Fold and iron the fabric again into squares, rectangles, or triangles.
4. Place the stack of fabric between matching *blocks,* which can be larger or smaller in size than the area of the folded fabric.
5. Clamp the blocks together with one or more spring-loaded *plastic clamps.* Metal C-clamps can be used but will rust and need oiling.
6. Soak in water for ½ hour to overnight.
7. Dye with *fiber-reactive, acid, or vat dyes, or discharge.* If the fabric folds are thick, work the dye into the protruding edges during dyeing.
8. Unwrap, rinse, and wash the fabric.

Pole Wrapping

In pole wrapping (*arashi shibori* in Japan), fabric is wrapped around a pole or pipe, wound with yarn, dental floss, string, or rubber bands, then pushed down to compress and resist. The fabric can be wrapped straight or diagonally, flat, folded, or as a tube that has been stitched the circumference of the pole. For poles, you may use PVC irrigation pipe, plumbing pipe, polypropylene pipe, or large wine bottles. The circumference of the pole should be in proportion to the width of the fabric—larger widths need wider poles.

1. Place clean, ironed *fabric* straight or at an angle around the *pole.* Hold in place temporarily with *painter's tape.*
2. Wrap a piece of strong *string* twice around one end of the pole, tie a knot, and secure the free end of the string to the inside of the tube with painter's tape.
3. Wrap the string around the fabric and pole for several inches (centimeters), leaving spaces between wraps. Remove the tape holding the fabric.
4. While maintaining tension on the wrapping string, push the fabric toward the end of the pole from which you started. Repeat wrapping and compressing until the fabric ends.
5. Secure the outer end of the string with a knot, or wrap back across the compressed fabric and knot the ends together.
6. Give the fabric one last compression without pushing it off the pole.

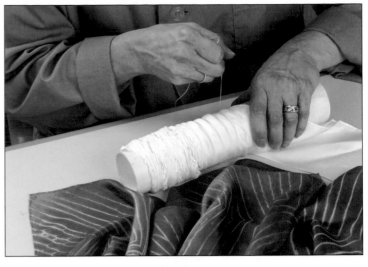

Clockwise from top left:

13.11 Ripple in a Pond Field Jacket *by Michael Kane and Steve Sells. Silk charmeuse and crepe de chine. Discharged and dyed using Procion MX and Jacquard acid dyes. Clamping and pole-wrapping techniques. Coat pieced and constructed using a matchstick format developed by the artists. Photo by John F. Cooper.*

13.12 *A white silk scarf was folded in half and wrapped on a pipe with dental floss, then soaked in soda ash and painted with Procion MX dyes. The resulting scarf is shown in the foreground. Folding the scarf before wrapping produced the white chevrons in the dyed fabric. Photo by Tom Liden.*

13.13 Blue Ripples Field Jacket *by Michael Kane and Steve Sells. Silk fabric wrapped on a pole with ⅛" (3 mm) pleats, then colored with Procion MX and Jacquard acid dyes and textile paints. Michael and Steve laid out the garment pieces to suggest water ripples and cool sensations. Photo by John F. Cooper.*

7. Soak fabric in plain *water* for ½ hour to overnight.

8. Dye with fiber-reactive, acid, or vat *dyes, or discharge,* following the appropriate procedures.

9. Unwrap, rinse, and wash the fabric.

Pole Wrapping Hints

■ Mixed dye colors may halo or separate into component colors as they penetrate into the fabric at different rates. Purple, for example, may separate into gradations of red and blue.

■ Thin dyes can be applied with a brush, squirt bottle, or turkey baster; poles may also be dipped.

■ Coating the pole with silicone spray (wipe off the excess before wrapping) aids in compressing the fabric.

■ For more complex effects, the fabric can be rewrapped in another direction and redyed.

■ PVC pipes will distort in hot liquids; polypropylene pipes will not.

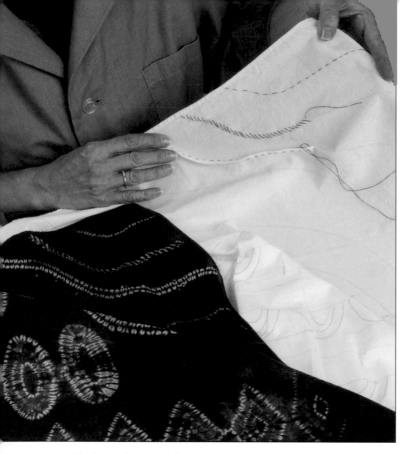

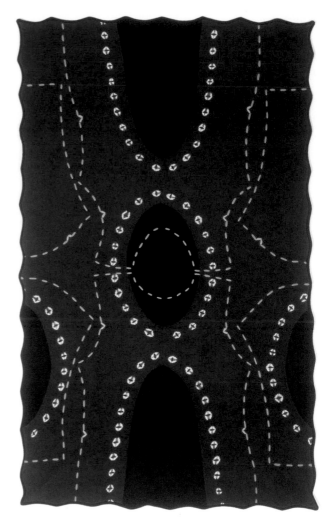

Clockwise from top left:
13.14 Stitching lines were marked on cotton fabric with a water-soluble pen. Running and whipstitch as well as fabric fold with a running stitch were used. The stitching was then gathered and the fabric dyed in indigo. The finished fabric shows the effects of stitching resists on flat and folded fabric. Photo by Tom Liden.
13.15 Markers by Jean Cacicedo. 60" h × 48" w × ¼" d (152.5 cm × 122 cm × 6 mm). Resist-dyed shibori with acid dyes on fulled wool. Pieced, dyed, and quilted to a linen backing. Photo by Kate Cameron.
13.16 Sample fabric. 54" l × 8½" w (137 cm × 20.5 cm). Stitched-resisted wool flannel dyed with Washfast acid dye. Photo by Joe Coca.
13.17 Stitch resists must be drawn very tight. The cotton handkerchief on the right was gathered tightly, producing a clear image; the one on the left was gathered loosely, resulting in a resist that is barely visible. Photo by Joe Coca.

Stitching

Hand or machine stitches gathered very tightly to resist dye can form stripes or geometric or representational shapes. Stitches can be made in flat or folded fabric. The thread should be strong enough to be pulled tight but fine enough so that no large holes will be visible when it is removed. Doubled carpet thread, buttonhole thread, or waxed sewing thread sewn with a thin, sharp needle works best.

1. Draw a design on clean, ironed *fabric* with *disappearing ink or tailor's chalk*.

2. Sew design area, leaving a tail of *thread* 2 to 3 inches (5 to 7.6 cm) long at the beginning and end. Complete all stitching before gathering the fabric: sewing on partly gathered fabric is difficult.

3. Tightly gather all stitched areas. Stitches should not be visible between the folds. Tie the ends of gathering threads together, backstitch, or knot at the end of each gathered area. Trim off the long ends.

4. Soak fabric in plain *water* for ½ hour to overnight.

5. Dye with fiber-reactive, acid, disperse, or vat *dyes or discharge*. Batch cure or steam the dyes. While the fabric is still gathered, rinse to remove dye residue and dry.

6. Remove the stitches from dry fabric with sharp-pointed scissors or a seam ripper, then rinse and wash the fabric.

Stitching Hints

■ Doubling or tripling sheer cottons and silk will yield symmetrical designs.

■ The most common hand stitches are running (in-and-out) and whip (diagonal rows). The whipstitch looks best on single layers of fabric, creating a small pleat in the fabric when gathered (see illustration 13.14).

■ Machine stitching is good for long, straight lines. Use buttonhole thread on the bobbin and regular cotton/polyester sewing thread on the top. Sew with a long, loose stitch. Pull up and gather the stronger bobbin thread. To secure after gathering, knot the top and bobbin threads together. Make stitching lines no longer than 36 inches (91.4 cm) to prevent the thread from breaking when it is gathered.

■ Wear bandages to keep the thread from cutting your fingers while gathering.

■ Start a new thread at the corner of right-angle designs to lower the risk of breaking the thread when it is gathered.

■ Use a special smocking pleater machine for fine, regular pleats on thin, lightweight woven fabrics.

Above: 13.18 A stitch-resist example from Japan. Color was applied locally; the fabric was bound with thread, dyed in indigo, and unwrapped. The resulting fabric shows resisted local color in the bound areas. Photo by Joe Coca.
Right: 13.19 Stitch-resisted fabric from China (bottom) and Japan (top). Photo by Joe Coca.

13.20 Clamp resist and scoured silk organza. The folded black silk organza is clamped between acrylic shapes. The scarf was clamped as shown below and immersed in purple vat dye, which discharged the black, removed the sericin, and dyed the fabric in one step. 78" l × 29" w (198 cm × 73.5 cm). Photo by Tom Liden.

Resist-Scouring Silk

Silk fabric with sericin (the natural protein that coats the fiber and glues silk cocoons together) can be used for interesting effects. Sericin is left in many commercial fabrics to strengthen and stiffen them. These fabrics are often referred to as silk organza. Artists, including Ana Lisa Hedstrom (illustrations 13.22 and 13.25) and Yoshiko Wada, have developed techniques to remove sericin from specific areas of silk fabrics through scouring and shibori. Scouring removes the sericin, relaxing the fabric, making it soft, and giving it the appearance of being more tightly woven. The scouring agent is soda ash or sodium carbonate.

1. Weigh the dry *fabric.*
2. Measure *soda ash* at 6% to 8% WOF.
3. Measure *water* at a water/fiber ratio of 40:1.
4. Mix soda ash in water; the resulting solution should be about pH 10.
5. Fabric should be soaked and thoroughly wetted for a good resist, especially if pleats have been made with a smocking pleater.
6. Simmer the silk at 185° (85° C) in the soda ash solution for about 30 minutes. For softer silk, simmer longer. The alkali can dull the luster and destroy silk, so take it out as soon as it's done. To monitor the progress of the scouring, tie one end of a piece of scrap fabric onto the handle of the pot and check it periodically.
7. Rinse fabric well, then neutralize in an acidic solution of ¼ cup (59 ml) *vinegar* in 1 gallon (3.8 l) of *water.* Soak for 10 minutes.

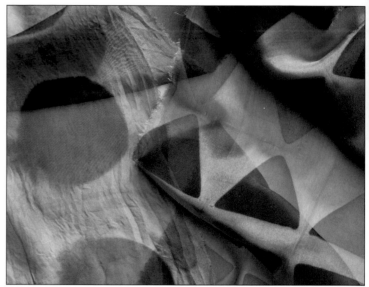

13.21 Scouring sericin silk with soda ash. Both fabrics began as white silk organza, which was clamped and scoured in soda ash to remove the sericin. Unscoured areas take up more Procion MX dye, resulting in darker colors. The red/pink piece was dyed in a single dyebath, and the unscoured shapes dyed a darker red than the scoured pink areas. 39" l × 12½" w (99 cm × 31.5 cm). The same effect is evident in the turquoise fabric. 71" l × 11" w (180.5 cm × 28 cm). Photo by Joe Coca.

13.22 Scarf by Ana Lisa Hedstrom. 78" l × 15" w (198 cm × 38 cm). Clamped Japanese Gunma silk, resist scoured, then acid dyed while clamped. After the clamps were removed, fiber-reactive dye was applied. Photo by Joe Coca.

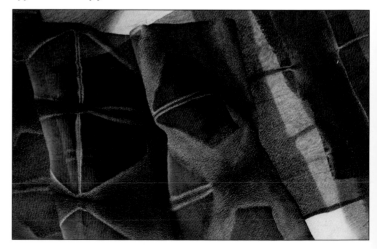

Clockwise from top left:

13.23 Silk Organza Netting *by Anita Sison. 19" h × 44" w (48.5 cm × 112 cm). Silk organza netting was tied with rubber bands, scoured in soda ash, immersed in vat dyes, and screen-printed with Procion MX dyes. The unscoured areas of silk take up more of the dye and are thus much darker than areas from which the sericin has been removed. Photo by Amy Melious.*

13.24 Organza Dress *dyed by Anita Sison and designed by Roxy Wells. Black silk organza was clamped between two squares of acrylic, scoured in soda ash, discharged with Thiox, dyed in Procion MX, and again discharged with Thiox. Photo by Amy Melious.*

13.25 Resist-Scoured Dress and Cloque Coat *by Ana Lisa Hedstrom. Japanese Gunma silk crepe dress resist-scoured and dyed in Procion MX. Coat with stitched organza and Gunma silk. Photo by Elaine Keenan.*

13.26 Scoured Silk Strip Studies *by Bren Ahearn. 7¾" h × 1¾" w each (19.5 cm × 4.5 cm). Plain-weave sericin silk, clamp resisted, scoured with soda ash, and acid dyed. These are color studies for a planned handwoven strip weaving exploring the juxtaposition of the stiff unscoured and the soft, luxurious scoured areas of silk. Photo by Joe Coca.*

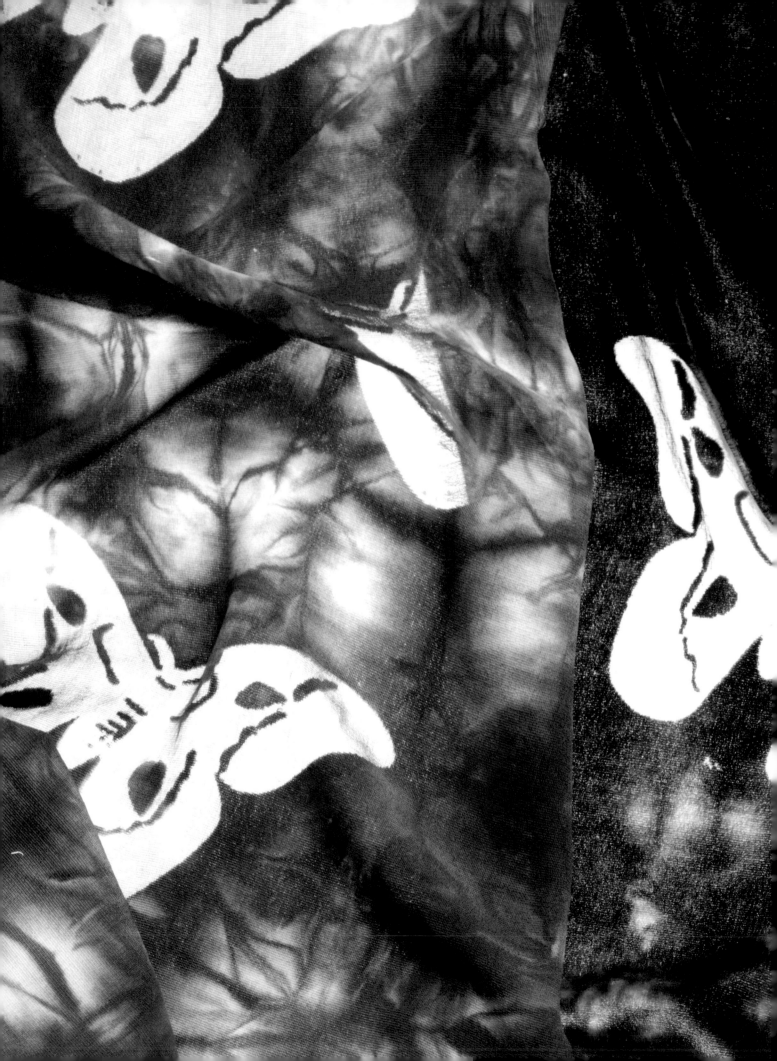

Chapter Fourteen
Dévoré

Dévoré ("devoured" or "destroyed" in French) is a process in which the cellulose part of a composite fabric is eaten away or burned out. A mild acid salt known as sodium bisulfate or sodium hydrogen sulfate is applied to the fabric; when heated, it becomes a mild sulfuric acid that burns out the cellulose. This technique, which has been used in industry since the nineteenth century, was introduced to artists in the United States in the 1990s by Joy Boutrup, a Danish textile chemist and teacher. Dévoré can be applied to fabrics by screen printing, stenciling, or painting on the burnout solution. It is easiest to use the process on white or light-colored fabrics.

The burnout technique works best on protein/cellulose or synthetic/cellulose composite (not blended) fabrics such as rayon/silk velvet or rayon/silk charmeuse, which have a silk (protein) backing with a face of rayon (cellulose) pile or satin weave, respectively. When you print with the solution on the flat, or back, side of the fabric, the rayon portion is burned out, leaving transparent silk areas (see illustrations 14.1, 14.2, and 14.14). Azeta, a fabric made of core-spun cotton/polyester (cotton wrapped around polyester) thread, burns out very cleanly, leaving sheer polyester (see "Resources" on page 136). By contrast, most cotton/polyester fabrics from fabric stores are blended fabrics, that is, the fibers are blended together before the yarn is spun and so they do not always burn out with a clean image.

Dévoré can also be used on pure cellulose fabrics by applying burnout solution to selected areas enclosed by machine satin stitches of polyester or nylon thread. The result resembles cutwork embroidery. Textile paints can be printed on cellulose fabric and followed by burnout paste. The paint will both add color and act as a resist when printed with larger burnout patterns.

Handwovens using fine cellulose yarns combined with silk, wool, nylon, or synthetics will yield good results with this technique. Core-spun cotton/polyester sewing and industrial threads also work well (see illustrations 14.10 and 14.13).

Pure rag watercolor paper can be printed or stamped with burnout solution (see illustration 14.5). After ironing and rinsing, the recessed design that results from the par-

14.2 Deco Evening Wrap *by Michael Kane and Steve Sells. Silk/rayon velvet resisted with masking tape, sprayed with dévoré solution, quickly dried, heated to activate the burnout, and washed to remove loose fibers. Dyed with Procion MX. Photo by John F. Cooper.*

Opposite: 14.1 Moth Shibori Silk/Rayon Velvet Scarf by Holly Brackmann. 69" l × 10¾" w (175.5 cm × 27.5 cm). Design was first burned out with dévoré, then soda soaked and dyed with Procion MX. Photo by Joe Coca.

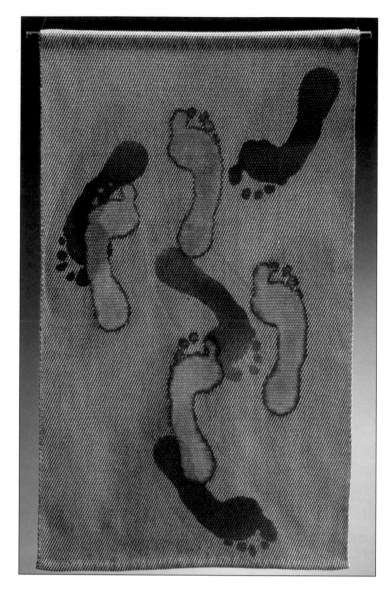

tially burned-out paper looks like a printing plate impression. If the paper is then dyed with fiber-reactive dyes, the burned-out area will take the dye differently from the rest.

Thickener

P4 thickener is an industrial gum thickener from the Silkpaint! Corporation (see "Resources" on page 136). The following mixture will last for months when stored in a cool, dark place.

1. Pour 2 cups (474 ml) *water* into a blender container.
2. Slowly add ¼ cup plus 2 teaspoons (48.8 g) *P4 thickener* and mix well.
3. Pour into a glass jar or plastic container, cover and allow the mixture to stand overnight; it will become clear, thick, and smooth.

Dévoré Paste

Dévoré paste will keep for months when covered and stored in the refrigerator. Crystals may form in it, but they should disappear when the paste is returned to room temperature.

1. Pour ¼ cup (59 ml) cold *water* into a blender container.
2. Blend in ⅓ cup (105 g) *sodium bisulfate*.
3. Blend in 4 teaspoons (20 ml) *glycerin*.
4. Blend in 1¼ cups (296 ml) *P4 thickener* mixture (see above).
5. Blend in 2 drops *food coloring* (optional, makes solution visible on fabric).
6. Thin with additional water as necessary.
7. Paint, print, or stencil the burnout paste on fabric or paper.

Note: Fiber Etch, made by the Silkpaint! Corporation is a ready-to-use substitute for the above dévoré paste.

14.3 The Path of Travel *by Holly Brackmann. 32" h × 18½" w × ½" d (81.5 cm × 47 cm × 1.3 cm). Handwoven polyester/cotton with dévoré and structural burnout (altering an eight-shaft crepe weave to twill weave). Disperse dye used in the burnout and transfer printing. Images are based on Holly's footprints.*
14.4 The Path of Travel *detail. Photos by Hap Sakwa.*

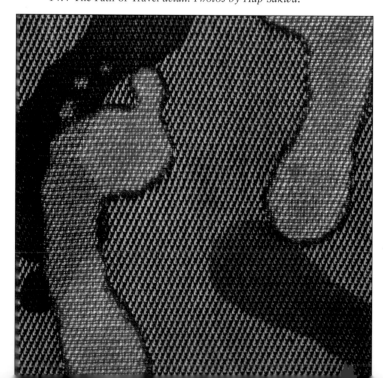

14.5 *Screen print of moth on cotton rag paper ironed to activate the dévoré paste, leaving a negative area where the paper was burned out. Dyed with Procion MX using the soda soak method. Photo by Joe Coca.*

Dévoré Screen Printing or Stenciling

Screen printing applies a thin, even layer of dévoré paste, which is especially important on rayon/silk velvet or charmeuse as uneven application on silk may cause holes in the fabric. A pattern with a strong negative/positive design and bold lines is best. Burn out the design first and then dye since it is hard to see burnout on colored fabric.

1. Pin or tape down *fabric* on a *padded surface* covered with plastic.
2. *Screen or stencil* the fabric with burnout paste or Fiber Etch.
3. Use a *hair dryer* or air-dry the burnout solution.
4. Immediately *iron* with dry heat on "wool" or "permanent press" until the dévoré paste turns a light brown. Be careful. Too much heat can melt synthetics or carbonize silk and make holes. You can also use a clothes dryer to activate burnout. If burning out rayon/silk velvet, scratch the pile after heating for a few moments; if it releases from the backing, it has been heated sufficiently.
5. Wash fabric gently by hand or in the washer for 2 minutes with *Synthrapol* to remove burnout paste and air-dry or use a clothes dryer. Too much agitation in washing or drying will remove fine design details.

Dévoré and Disperse Dyeing in One Step

Disperse dyes can be mixed with dévoré solution to color polyester and burn out at the same time.

1. Mix ½ cup (118 ml) boiling *water* and 3 teaspoons (20 g) *disperse dye*.
2. Stir until dissolved. Let cool. Stir again.
3. Add a small amount of the dye mixture to *thickened burnout paste* or Fiber Etch.
4. Cover the *printing surface* with stretched *plastic wrap* because the burnout solution will penetrate the fabric, especially Azeta. Discard the plastic after each print.
5. *Screen print* design.
6. Dry immediately with a *hair dryer* to prevent wicking of the burnout paste.
7. Iron immediately to burn out the cellulose, wearing a respirator with acid gas cartridges and providing good ventilation.
8. Gently wash and rinse the fabric.

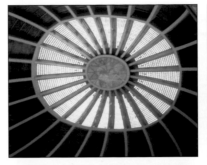
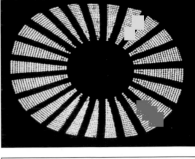
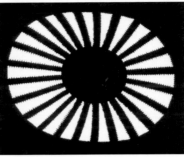
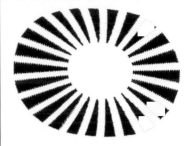

Top right: 14.6 Mexico Dome screen process by Holly Brackmann. Original photo taken in Mexico City, manipulated in Photoshop for a high-contrast black-and-white image. The detail in the photo was reduced, and the inverted image used to make a screen for printing. Bottom right: 14.7 Mexico Dome Scarf by Holly Brackmann. 69" l × 10¾" w (175.5 cm × 27.5 cm). Dévoré on rayon/silk velvet, dyed with Procion MX dyes. The silk side of the fabric is always lighter in color than the rayon pile side for two reasons: the silk has fewer molecular sites to absorb the dye, and the velvet absorbs light, giving the effect of a darker color. Photo by Joe Coca.

Clockwise from top right:

14.8 *Dévoré on polyester/cotton Azeta fabric. The fabric has been printed with Fiber Etch and is being ironed to activate the burnout solution. A piece of aluminum foil placed under the fabric protects the ironing surface, and a Teflon sheet placed on top protects the iron soleplate. On the lower left is a piece of Azeta that has been burned out, leaving a visible transparent design. The other three pieces of Azeta have been burned out and dyed in one step by combining disperse dye with dévoré paste. These pieces were samples for the Squiggles Scarf. Photo by Tom Liden.*

14.9 *Squiggles Scarf by Holly Brackmann. 73" l × 8¼" w (185.5 cm × 21 cm). Handwoven of plied polyester and cotton industrial sewing thread in both warp and weft in plain weave. First, several colors of disperse dye were mixed separately with the dévoré paste to burn out and dye in one step, leaving colored sheer areas. Next, areas were transfer-printed with paper painted with disperse dyes, leaving color but no holes. Finally, the whole scarf was soda soaked and dyed with purple Procion MX. Because polyester does not absorb fiber-reactive dyes, the MX dyed only the cotton, leaving the purple areas heathery, and the polyester in the burned-out designs has not absorbed the Procion MX. The transfer-printed fabric, however, which still contains both polyester and cotton, is affected by both Procion MX and disperse dyes. Photo by Tom Liden.*

14.10 *Memories of Montreal by Holly Brackmann. 17¾" h × 13¾" w (45 cm × 35 cm) fabric; 29¼" h × 23¼" w × ⅜" d (74.5 × 60.5 × 1 cm) mounted. Handwoven polyester/cotton plain weave. Image for the print screen based on maples leaves collected while teaching in Montreal. Dévoré with disperse and Procion MX dyes. Mounted on fiberglass screening. Photo by Hap Sakwa.*

14.11 *Japan Comma Kahma by Holly Brackmann. 11¾" h × 8¼" w fabric (30 cm × 21 cm); 18¾" h × 14⅜" w × ¼" d (47.5 cm × 36.5 cm × 6 mm) mounted. Dévoré on handwoven plain weave polyester/cotton fabric. The same screen was used for dévoré and transfer printing. Procion MX and disperse dye, cotton and nylon thread. Mounted on fiberglass screening. Photo by Hap Sakwa.*

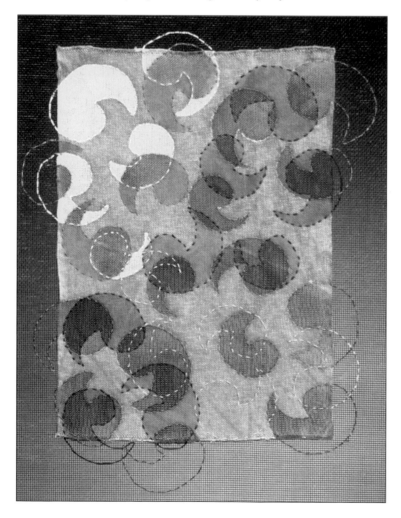

Hints for Dévoré

■ Synthetic/cellulose composite fabrics can be transfer-printed; the synthetic component will accept the disperse dyes (see Illustrations 14.10 and 14.11 and "Transfer Printing" on page 51).

■ Fiber-reactive dyes will color the cellulose components of composite fabrics. Dévoré areas of polyester colored with disperse dyes will not be affected by the fiber-reactive dyes, but transfer-printed areas will be because cotton still remains in those areas (see illustration 14.9).

■ Use a Teflon sheet (available at fabric stores) on top of the fabric when ironing to protect the iron soleplate.

■ Use aluminum foil to protect the ironing board, catch burned-out fibers, and reflect heat up into the fabric.

■ Burn out fabric immediately after the solution has been applied and dried on silk. Prolonged exposure to burn-out solution will cause silk to deteriorate.

■ If you blur a print, immediately wash the dévoré paste out of the fabric, dry, and start over. The fabric will not be affected.

■ Sample commercial fabric to see if sufficient woven structure remains after burning out. In composite fabrics with a polyester warp and cellulose weft, only the loose polyester warp yarns will be left after burning out (this may be a desired effect).

14.12 Petroglyphs *by Cassie Gibson. 58" l × 14" w (147.5 cm × 35.5 cm). Dévoré on silk/rayon velvet. Procion MX dyes thickened with sodium alginate and painted for an ombré effect. Scarf lined with silk crepe. 14.13* Petroglyphs *detail. Photos by Tom Liden.*

Chapter Fifteen
Textile Paints

Textile paints consist of finely ground pigment or color particles suspended in a polymer resin binder. While dyes color the entire fiber, paints cover only the surface. Think of dye as a beet: red permeates the fabric through and through. Think of paint as a radish: red sits on the surface of the fabric. Textile paints can be transparent, semitransparent, opaque, metallic, pearlescent, fluorescent, or interference. Paints can be used with almost any fabric except those with a finish that interferes with the binder.

Textile paints are easy to use and long lasting. Water is sufficient to clean screens, brushes, mixing containers, and equipment. As long as the paint is wet, it is water soluble. During drying, as the water evaporates, a polymer bond is formed. The paints are no longer water soluble and have become affixed to the fabric. The colors are very fast and resistant to fading from ultraviolet light; however, repeated washings or rubbing on painted areas can break down the binder, gradually wearing it off. This is not a problem with a wall hanging but could be with upholstery. To minimize color loss, always turn painted garments inside out and wash by hand or machine wash on a gentle cycle. Dry cleaning is acceptable.

Textile paints vary from thin to thick. When deciding which type to use, consider the technique and the fabric. Thin paints, the consistency of water, are suitable for all weights of fabric and may be applied with a brush or by spraying. Like dyes, they bleed and spread, are transparent, and barely change the hand of the fabric. Thick paints have more binder and can be used for screen printing, stenciling, brushing, monoprinting, or stamping. They stay in place but will alter the feel of the fabric to stiff, soft, rubbery, or puffy, and so are not appropriate for very finely woven, delicate fabrics. Decorations such as beads, glitter, or sequins can be sprinkled in wet paint. Thick paint can be thinned up to 50% with water; however, too much water will cause the fine color particles to no longer be held in suspension, which will produce a dark-edged halo effect on drying. Excessive water also lessens the amount of binder, keeping colors from adhering properly and causing them to fade with washing or abrasion. A better way to thin paint is with an extender, which thins the paint without breaking down the binder or yielding a paler color.

Textile paints also vary from transparent to opaque. Apply transparent paints to white or light-colored fabric because the background color will mix visually with the paint color. A blue paint on top of a yellow background will result in a green design. When applied to black, transparent colors simply disappear (see illustration 15.8). Just because paint is thick does not mean that it will necessarily

15.2 Tree Park *by Linda MacDonald. 48" h × 36" w × ¼" d (122 cm × 91.5 cm × 6 mm). Cotton broadcloth airbrushed and handpainted with textile paint. Hand-quilted with cotton batting. Environmental issues are often a topic for Linda's art. Photo by Hap Sakwa.*

Opposite: 15.1 Celebration Vest by Linda Cannefax. Cotton painted with Procion MX, stamped with textile paints, stitched with metallic thread, and hand-beaded. Photo by Joe Coca.

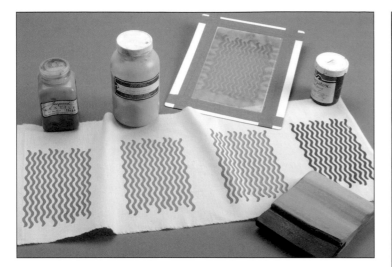

Clockwise from top left:

15.3 Screen printing and mixing textile paint colors during printing on cotton muslin. The first print was done with blue. Adding yellow to the screen produced a turquoise. Adding more yellow resulted in a yellow/green. Finally, adding fuchsia (red being the complement of green) yielded a neutral brown.

15.4 Shirt by Anita Sison. Screen-printed with thickened Procion MX dye and textile paints. Photo by Amy Melious.

15.5 Decay III by Lynn Harris. 72" h × 48" w (183 cm × 122 cm). Cotton fabric was rusted over several weeks in a wet, rusty wheelbarrow, then covered with rusted metal from a Mendocino coast beach dump to form a background fabric texture. The fabric was then resisted, dyed with Procion MX, screen-printed with textile paints, and foiled. 15.6 Decay III detail. Photos by Jane Dunnewold.

15.7 Turn, Turn, Turn by Dede Ledford. 50" h × 50" w × ¼" d (127 cm × 127 cm × 6 mm). Cotton fabric random dyed with Procion MX. Trucks polychromatic-screen prints, painted with textile paints, watercolor, and fabric pens, and embellished with mica and copper metal. Fabric for the vineyard dyed in a rusty wheelbarrow with other rusty objects. Some fabric discharged with dishwasher gel. Machine appliqué, thread painting, embroidery, and quilting. Photo by Roger W. Foote.

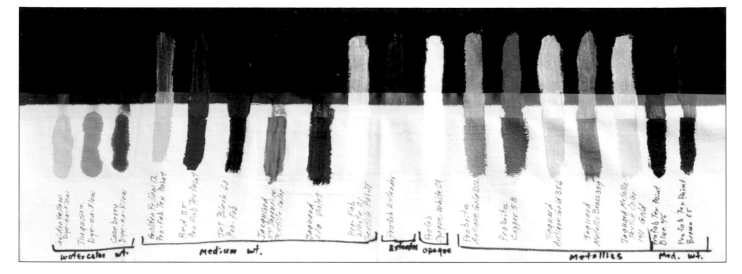

Clockwise from top:

15.8 Opaque and transparent textile paint samples. Pieces of black and white cotton fabric were taped together. Stripes of different types of textile paint, including thin, medium-weight, extender, opaque, and metallics, were applied. The thin and medium-weight paints disappear on black fabric, leaving only the metallics and opaque white clearly visible. Photo by Joe Coca.

15.9 Tribes by Cassie Gibson. 60" l × 22" w (152.4 cm × 55.9 cm). Silk scarf printed with thickened Procion MX, discharged by Thermofax printing with Jacquard Discharge Paste, and printed with metallic textile paint. 15.10 Tribes detail. Photos by Tom Liden.

15.11 Shrouded by Pavlos Mayakis. 30" h × 32" w (76 cm × 81.5 cm). Handwoven using natural cotton. Dyed as a flat fabric with Procion MX, then woven shibori pulled tight and dyed again with Procion MX. Next, vat dye discharged and textile paints applied. Photo by Joe Coca.

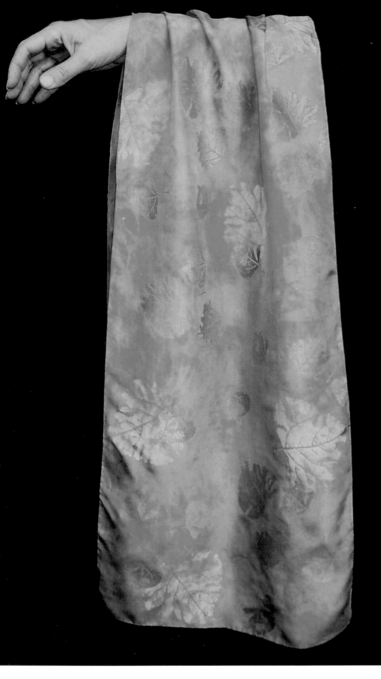

Hints for Textile Paints

■ Wash fabrics before applying paint.

■ Smooth, ironed, dry fabrics will produce the clearest images, regardless of how the paint is applied.

■ Openings in the mesh can be permanently clogged if paint dries in a screen. Many manufacturers sell a retarder, which slows the drying of the paint to prevent screen damage.

■ An antiwick or antibleed additive may be needed on polyester or polyester blends to keep the paint from spreading.

■ Fabrics treated with a combination of thickened dye and paints must be heat-set before steam fixing and washing out dye.

■ If a transparent paint is applied to white fabric that is subsequently dyed, the dye will show through the paint. Overall, it is better to dye fabric first and paint second because dye may erode the paint.

■ Thin, transparent textile paints are suitable for star-burst effects. Sprinkle wet fabric with coarse table, kosher, or rock salt. The salt will produce small halos of color for a mottled effect. After drying, fix by heating.

Safety Alert

Water-based textile paints are generally considered to be non-toxic and safe, but they contain additives that may be harmful. When spraying, wear eye protection and a respirator to avoid inhaling the fine mist. Also wear a respirator and provide ventilation when heat-setting, since acrylic binders may release small amounts of ammonia or toxic gases, which can cause respiratory irritation and allergies.

15.12 Leaves Scarf by Leila Kazimi. 54" l × 9" w (137 cm × 23 cm). Silk dyed with random and soda soak techniques in Procion MX. Thermofax screen-printed with Jacquard Discharge Paste and transparent and metallic textile paints.
15.13 Leaves Scarf detail. Photos by Neal Mettler.

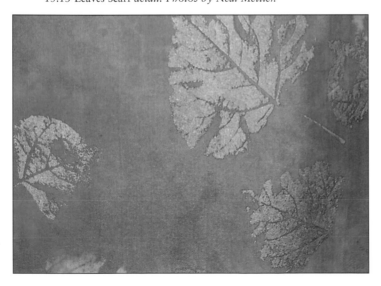

15.14 Wildlife Sanctuaries by Linda MacDonald. 35" h × 45" w × ¼" d (89 cm × 114.5 cm × 6 mm). Textile paint applied by airbrushing and handpainting on cotton. Hand-quilting with cotton batting. Photo by Hap Sakwa.

Left: 15.15 A Walk in the Forest by Gail Mackenzie. 37½" h × 18½" w (95 cm × 47 cm). Traditional marbling techniques using plastic bottles to drip acrylic pigments on the size of water thickened with caragheenan. Marbling pigments manipulated with wooden hibachi sticks and combs made from stickpins to form the "thistle" pattern. Screen-printed bamboo imagery with textile paints on douppioni raw silk. Photo by Joe Coca.
Above: 15.16 Aztek and Hilo Neckties by Gail Mackenzie. Aztek has a step and striped design underneath the French curl marbling pattern on silk crepe. Hilo's silk jacquard fabric was first screen-printed, then marbled with a thistle pattern. Both ties use traditional marbling techniques and acrylic pigments. Photo by Joe Coca.

dry opaque. (Consider white glue, which is opaque and then dries clear.) True opaque paints do not allow the background color to show through; therefore an opaque white paint can be applied to black fabric (see illustration 15.8). Opaque paints are usually thick and stiff; they affect the fabric hand but are excellent for stamping, printing, and stenciling. They can be thinned up to 50% with water, but thinning reduces their opacity and lightens the color. Transparent paints are made opaque by mixing in an opaque color, such as white. Unless a paint is clearly labeled opaque, it will be transparent.

Luster can be added to fabric with metallic, pearlescent, and interference textile paints, all of which contain minuscule bits of Mylar or mica but which, unfortunately, will clog a printing screen with mesh finer than 12xx. Pearlescent paints shimmer most successfully on light-colored fabrics. For a hint of shimmer, blend pearlescent paints with

another color of textile paints. Interference paints reflect their complementary color and work best on dark or black fabrics.

You may find textile paints labeled as textile inks for screen printing, textile pigments, fabric paints, fabric colors, fabric inks, or airbrush inks. Even within a single brand of paint, colors can vary in transparency and opacity, regardless of what the label says. Alternatively, and at less cost than ready-to-use paints, you can purchase pigments separately and mix them with a transparent or opaque binder (also called a medium). Many brands, colors, and consistencies can be combined, but some may have incompatible binders. Always sample before undertaking a large project and allow one brand of paint to dry thoroughly before overlaying with another brand. Paints also vary in quality: in general, cheaper paints have less effective binders, are thicker, and stiffen the fabric more.

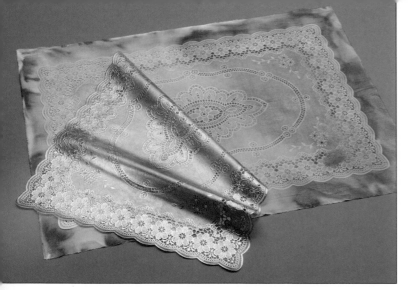

15.17 Heliographic or sun print made with wet transparent textile paints on cotton using a plastic doily for resist. Very detailed prints are possible with the heliographic technique. Photo by Tom Liden.

Heat Setting or Fixation

Most textile paints require heat setting to make them permanent although some will be fixed simply by air-curing for a week—check the manufacturer's instructions. In general, textile paints should be allowed to dry undisturbed for 24 hours, then set by heating.

1. Heating method (choose one).
A. Heat-set for 2 to 5 minutes with a *dry iron* at the setting appropriate for the fiber type, applying heat to the back of the fabric or to a *pressing cloth* laid over the printed area. Move the iron to avoid scorching. Do not use steam or the colors may bleed. A *heat press* can also be used.
B. Use a home (45 to 90 minutes) or commercial (20 to 60 minutes) *clothes dryer* at the hottest setting.
C. Roll fabric loosely in unprinted newsprint and bake in a dry *oven* for 2 to 10 minutes at 250° to 350° F (121° to 177° C).
2. Cool paint before washing. Letting the fabric sit for 7 to 14 days after heating and before washing may produce more permanent results.

Heliographic or Sun Printing

Heliographic printing uses transparent textile paint. Areas exposed to sunlight dry sooner and wick wet paint from underneath opaque objects lying on the wet fabric. Covered areas become pale negative designs. In cloudy weather, or at night, an infrared heat lamp, plant grow light, halogen bulb, or sun lamp with an ultraviolet bulb may be used as a light source. Finer-weave fabrics will produce more distinct images than coarser ones.

1. Wash, dry, and iron *fabric* (see "Preparing Fabric for Dyeing" on page 120).
2. Place fabric on a smooth, stiff, *waterproof surface* such as sheet acrylic, heavy cardboard, or plywood covered with plastic.
3. Stretch fabric and secure with *pins or tape,* especially on a windy day. The fabric must remain flat and still during exposure.
4. Gather *objects for designs* such as leaves, feathers, wooden shapes, lace doilies, paper cutouts, plastic washers, buttons, coins, keys, tools, pasta, seashells, rocks, yarn, paper clips, scissors, or metal screening.
5. Mix 1 part *paint* to 2 parts *water.* The paint can be diluted up to 1 part paint to 8 parts water. The more diluted the paint, the less contrast there will be between background and design. If mixing colors, first mix the paint and then dilute with water. Mix enough paint for the entire project.
6. Working in subdued light, use a *foam brush* or *spray bottle* of paint solution to thoroughly wet the fabric, which should stick to the plastic or acrylic sheet.
7. Quickly position shapes on the damp fabric.
8. Move the fabric board with the objects into the sun or under a light source. Be careful not to move the objects.
9. Leave fabric in bright sunlight for 15 minutes to 1 hour or until dry. Other light sources will take longer.
10. Remove objects and fabric from the work surface.
11. Follow the instructions for "Heat Setting or Fixation of Textile Paints" above.

Hints for Heliographic Printing
■ Pure cotton, silk, and linen yield the best results.
■ Use white, dyed, or commercially printed fabric—just be sure to wash it before sun printing.
■ Two or three colors per piece work best. Too many colors may look muddy and overly busy.
■ Objects lying flat against the fabric will give the most distinct designs.
■ A second design layer can be applied to previously sun-printed fabric that has dried for at least 24 hours.
■ Rather than laying objects on the wet fabric, try wadding it up or applying rubber bands for a tie-dye effect.

Chapter Sixteen
Embellishments

The creative process of dyeing and surface design culminates with embellishments such as foiling, embroidery, beadwork, or collage. Embellishments may be added randomly or placed intentionally, as on garments.

Foiling

Foiling adds a glimmer, richness, and sheen not possible with paints or dyes alone. For some it is too flashy, for others it adds welcome complexity. Foils are composed of thin metallic sheets, usually colored aluminum, fused to a plastic backing. Heating bonds the foil to fabric with adhesive glue or fusible web. It should be the last surface technique used on a piece because some chemicals and further ironing will remove the sheen. Wash foiled fabric in cool water; do not dry-clean as solvents may remove the metallic color. Screen-Trans and Jones Tones are two brands with foils available in many colors.

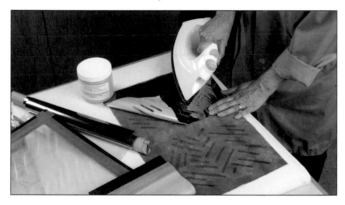

Clockwise from top left:
16.1 Foiling on fabric with Screen Trans adhesive and foil. Foil adhesive has been screen-printed on dyed fabric. The foil is placed against the fabric with the metallic side up. The edge of a hot iron is stroked across the foil to transfer the metallic copper to the fabric. Photo by Tom Liden.
16.2 Polyester fabric by Anita Sison. 118" l × 45" w (299.5 cm × 114.5 cm). Disperse dyes painted and Thermofax-printed on paper, then transfer-printed on sheer fabric. Foil imagery applied last. Photo by Amy Melious.
16.3 Discharged black cotton screen-printed with textile paint, sprinkled with powdered fusible glue, and foil applied to produce small blue metallic dots. Photo by Joe Coca.

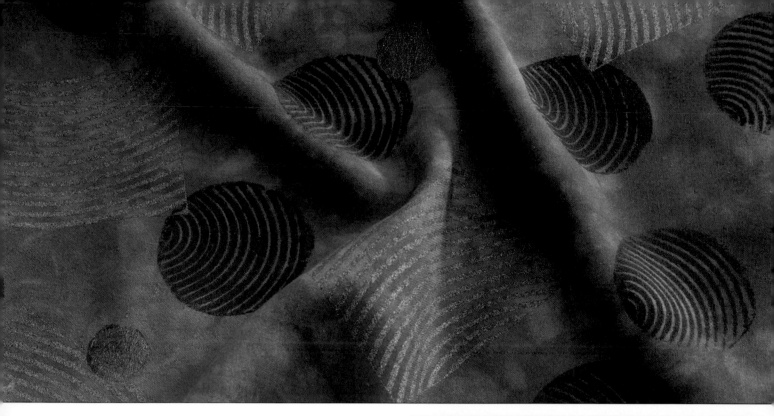

Clockwise from top:
16.4 Fabric dyed with Procion MX, screen-printed with textile paints, and red foil dots applied. Photo by Joe Coca.
16.5 My Own Berkeley Telephone Pole by Lynn Harris. 80" h ×
57" w (203 cm × 145 cm). Hemp fabric stapled, rusted, dyed with Procion MX, discharged, and dyed again with Procion MX, then screen-printed with textile paints and foiled.
16.6 My Own Berkeley Telephone Pole detail. Photos by Jane Dunnewold.

Foiling with Adhesive Glue

1. Place clean, ironed, dry *fabric* on a *printing surface.*
2. Apply *adhesive* design with a *screen, brush, stencil, stamp, or sponge.*
3. Allow the adhesive to dry thoroughly; drying may take several hours.
4. Heat *iron* (Teflon plate preferred) set on "cotton."
5. Cut a piece of *foil* to cover the design area.
6. Place foil with the color side up on top of the design.
7. With the narrow edge of the iron, stroke three times across the foil.
8. Peel off the foil while it is still hot.
9. If the foil did not entirely cover the adhesive or glue, repeat Steps 6 through 8.

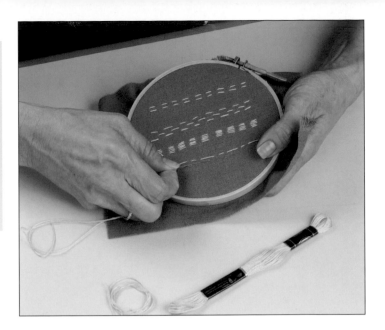

Embroidery

Embroidery adds a tactile surface dimension. Today, as throughout history, textile artists are free to embroider on top, around, or over areas of fabric (see illustration 16.8). Embroidery can be added at any step of the dyeing, printing, discharging, stamping, stenciling, or embellishment process. Think of embroidery as adding another layer of richness to dyed and decorated fabric. The variety of embroidery stitches is virtually endless, but the simple running stitch will go a long way to enhancing fabric (see illustration 16.7). This stitch can be worked evenly or in alternating long and short rows. Stitches can be grouped together or placed singly.

Threads for embroidery include six-strand embroidery floss, pearl cotton, metallic threads, small ribbons, and a host of newly developed yarns, including thermoplastic, light-emitting, and heat-sensitive yarns. Many yarns used by weavers are suitable for embroidery. It is important to use a thread that is in scale with the fabric. A fine cloth requires a thread that will not make large holes in the fabric. On the other hand, a fine thread can get lost on a heavy, textured fabric. Dye thread if the color you want is not available.

Embroidery needles should be the appropriate size and type for the thread and technique being used. Crewels (sizes 1 to 10) are sharp-pointed, medium-length needles with large eyes for easy threading; they are used with embroidery floss and other traditional threads. Chenilles (sizes 13 to 26) are sharp-pointed but are thicker and longer, have larger eyes, and are used for heavier threads. Tapestry needles (sizes 13 to 26) are similar in size to chenilles, but they have a blunt tip and are better for open weaves. As for needle sizes within each type, the larger the number, the shorter and finer the needle. The eye of the needle should be large enough for the thread to go through without splitting and fraying.

Whether you stretch fabric tight in an embroidery hoop for stitching is a matter of preference. Embroidery hoops are available in many sizes in both hand-held and floor models. Stitches made in an embroidery hoop will be more even and not distort the fabric, but some artists prefer the three-dimensional distortions created by not using a hoop.

16.7 *Running stitch worked on linen fabric being held tight in an embroidery hoop. Three strands of embroidery floss were used at once. Photo by Tom Liden.*
16.8 Textile Jumble *by Holly Brackmann. 15¾" h × 9" w (40 cm × 23 cm). Running-stitch embroidery on linen, silk, cotton, polyester, rayon, and nylon fabrics. Photo by Joe Coca.*

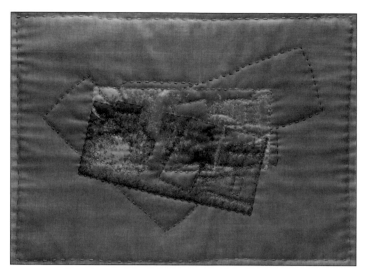

Clockwise from top left:
16.9 Vitra Museum #1 *by Holly Brackmann.* 11" *h* × 14¼" *w fabric*
(28 cm × 37.5 cm); 19" h × 22¾" w × ¼" d (48.5 cm × 58 cm × 6 mm)
mounted. Running stitches with embroidery floss mimic the lines in
the prints on two layers of fabric. Dévoré on commercial polyester/
cotton fabric with disperse dye in the burn-out solution. Colored
with Procion MX and textile paint. Digital image for screen print
based on photo taken in Weil am Rhein, Germany. Cotton batting
between layers and mounted on fiberglass screening. Photo by Hap
Sakwa.
16.10 *Samples of embroidery stitches to create layers of texture,*
transparency, and depth. Photo by Tom Liden.
16.11 A Figure of Stitching No. 14 *detail.*
16.12 A Figure of Stitching No. 14 *by Misao Tsubaki.* 15¾" *h* × 12" *w*
× 1¼" *d (40 cm × 30.5 cm × 3.2 cm). Cotton, silk, and synthetic fab-*
rics, pieced with thread, and handstitching. Photos by Joe Coca.

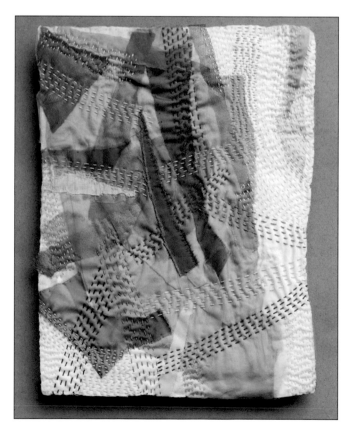

Clockwise from top left:
16.13 Creative Chick Self-Portrait by Susan Sorrell. 17" h × 19" w (43 cm × 48.5 cm). Wall hanging stitched with embroidery thread, embellished with glass and plastic beads, button, and old jewelry. Cotton fabric colored with fabric paints, color pencils, and watercolor crayons. Collage assembled with polyester batting and cotton backing. Photo by Rodney Sorrell.
16.14 Dragonfly Vest by Linda Cannefax. Cotton warp painted with Cibacron F dye, handwoven, discharged with Jacquard Discharge Paste, and hand-beaded. Photo by Joe Coca.
16.15 Louie's Dog-Jazz by Susan Sorrell. 15" h × 15" w (38 cm × 38 cm). Wall hanging handpainted with textile paints, color pencils, and watercolor crayons on cotton fabric; stitched with embroidery thread, decorated with glass beads and sequins. Polyester batting and cotton backing. Photo by Rodney Sorrell.

Beadwork

Beading adds texture and color to fabric. Beads can create a focal point or be scattered across a wall hanging, garment, or quilt. Beads are available in a wide array of materials including glass, metal, stone, and plastic. You can make your own polymer clay beads in your studio. Beads can be sewn on by hand or with a sewing machine. For handsewing, long, thin beading needles are available. Other needles can also be used as long as the threaded eye of the needle will go through the hole in the bead. Beading thread is available, but any thread can be used as long as it does not break or shred easily.

Beaded fabrics need special care. Avoid placing beads in areas of heavy friction, such as under the arms on garment sleeves. Heavily beaded fabrics tend to shrink as beads are applied so allow for this shrinkage if specific dimensions are required. Wash beaded fabrics by hand and lay flat to dry. Dry cleaning may discolor or destroy beads.

16.16 Falling Leaves Vest by Mollie Freeman. Cotton and rayon warp painted with Cibacron F, handwoven, discharged with Thiox, stamped and stenciled with textile paints. Embellishments include kumihimo, appliqué, polymer clay buttons, machine couching and stitching, free-motion stitching. 16.17 Falling Leaves Vest detail. Photos by Mollie Freeman.

Collage

Collage brings together many of the techniques described in this book to create layers of imagery on fabric. Fabrics can be created specifically for collage, or you can use fabrics that you otherwise considered samples or failures. Do not throw your rejects away—they may become the germ of an idea or provide just the scrap you need to complete a project. Look at a piece of fabric and ask yourself what would happen if you added paint, overdyed it, cut it up, combined it with other materials, layered it, or stitched over it? Try to look at samples and scraps of fabric with this new perspective and continually ask yourself, What if?

Appendices

Appendix A: Dye Worksheet

Date ___________

Title of project___________________________

Fabric type and source___________________________

Dry weight (WOF)___________________________

Fabric preparation and scouring___________________________

Dye type___________________________ Dye brand and source___________________________

Colors of dye	DOS (% Depth of Shade)	Amount of dye or stock solution	Water/fiber ratio	Amount of water in dye solution	Water temperature	Time in dye

Additives (salt, soda, lye, acid)	Weight of additives	Percentage WOF
1.		
2.		
3.		
4.		

Attach undyed and dyed fabric sample:

Dye procedure

Rinsing, washing, and drying

Rinse water temperature_______________ Number of rinses___________________________

Hand or machine wash

Wash water temperature_____ Detergent/soap_____ Agitation time_____ Cycle___________________________

Machine or line dry________ Heat or no heat___________ Time___________________________

Cost analysis

Fabric_______________ Supplies _______________ Labor cost__________ Selling price_______________

All fabric, even fabric labeled as "prepared for dyeing" (PFD), needs to be scoured before dyeing to remove any impurities such as natural waxes, spinning oil, sizing, or dirt. If in doubt as to whether a fabric is ready for dyeing, perform a Water-Drop Test (illustration 2.3 on page 10) to see how readily it absorbs liquids. Wash fabrics by hand or by machine, but do not add fabric softener or dryer sheets as they will interfere with the uptake of dyes or dye chemicals. Weigh dry fabric and record the weight of fabric (WOF) on "Dye Worksheet" on page 119 for later dyebath calculations.

Cotton and Cellulose

Cotton fabrics often contain sizing made from cellulose starches. Since fiber-reactive dyes bind to cellulose, they will react with the sizing before they can react with the fabric. This results in a lighter color and loss of dye. Other impurities, such as natural waxes, are often present in cotton, linen, hemp, and especially unbleached muslin or canvas, so an extra scouring in boiling soda ash solution may be necessary.

Machine-Scouring Cotton and Cellulose

1. Set the machine on "large load" and "hot wash/warm rinse." Use water at 140° F (60° C). You may need to add boiling water to achieve this temperature.
2. Add ¼ teaspoon (1.3 g) soda ash and ¼ teaspoon (1.25 ml) Synthrapol per gallon (3.8 l) of water (see owner's manual for machine capacity). Agitate to dissolve chemicals.
3. Distribute the fabric evenly around the agitator.
4. Run the machine through a complete cycle; remove the fabric.
5. Use the fabric wet if dyeing immediately or dry by line or machine.
6. Iron flat if a smooth surface is required.

Hand-Scouring Cotton and Cellulose

1. Measure 1 gallon (3.8 l) water at 140° F (60° C) into a bucket.
2. Stir in ¼ teaspoon (1.3 g) soda ash.
3. Stir in ¼ teaspoon (1.25 ml) Synthrapol.
4. Immerse fabric and agitate continuously for 10 minutes with a stir stick or gloved hands.
5. Rinse thoroughly. If soda ash remains in the fabric, spotty dyeing will result.
6. Use the fabric wet if dyeing immediately or dry by line or machine.
7. Iron flat for processes requiring a smooth surface.

Scouring Unbleached Muslin or Cotton Canvas

These fabrics have a lot of natural plant wax, necessitating two scourings.

1. Measure 1 gallon (3.8 l) or more of water into a nonreactive pot.
2. Stir in 1¼ teaspoons (6.3 g) soda ash per gallon (3.8 l) of water.
3. Bring water to a boil, immerse fabric, and simmer for 30 minutes. The water will turn brown from resins, waxes, and sizing.
4. Rinse thoroughly.
5. For the second scouring, use the instructions above for machine- or hand-scouring cotton.

Scouring PFD Fabrics, Nylon, Rayon, and Polyester

PFD fabrics, viscose rayon, nylon, and polyester may contain spinning oils, sizing, or soil from shipping and handling. A hand or machine washing in Synthrapol or other neutral detergent is usually sufficient preparation for dyeing. Nylon and polyester tend to float and do not absorb water quickly. For handwashing, place a heavy plate on the fabric to keep it submerged. Viscose rayon can be 30% to 50% weaker when wet so handle it carefully. To scour PFD fabrics, nylon, viscose rayon, or polyester more vigorously, follow the instructions above for machine- or hand-scouring cotton.

Scouring Silk

Spun silk is usually fairly clean from the manufacturing process, but it may still contain some of the natural gum, or sericin, from the cocoons, which will affect the dyeing. Handle silk carefully when wet. Harsh treatment of silk during scouring can cause the fibers to rupture and fibrils to project from the surface, which is irreversible. A clean, smooth, lustrous spun silk can be simply soaked overnight in warm water and a neutral detergent and rinsed before dyeing. Avoid alkaline laundry detergents. Raw silk or silk noil can be handwashed using the instructions above for scouring cotton but omitting the soda ash. The following recipe is for scouring spun silk containing impurities in a washing machine.

1. Set the machine on "delicate" and "warm wash/cool rinse" to minimize wrinkles.
2. Add ¼ teaspoon (1.25 ml) Synthrapol per gallon (3.8 l) of water (see owner's manual for machine capacity). Agitate briefly.
3. Place fabric in the machine and distribute evenly around the agitator.

4. Run the machine through a complete cycle; remove the fabric.

5. Use the fabric wet if dyeing immediately, iron it dry, line-dry away from sunlight, or machine-dry.

Hand-Scouring Wool and Hair Fabrics

Wool and hair fabrics contain lanolin and spinning oils, which must be removed for complete dye absorption. Gentle washing with a neutral detergent (alkalis are harmful to wool) and water that is not too hot are important to prevent felting.

1. Measure 1 gallon (3.8 l) water at 104° F (40° C) into a bucket.

2. Stir in ½ teaspoon (2.5 g) Orvus Paste.

3. Immerse the fabric in the bucket.

4. Gently wash for about 10 minutes, occasionally agitating.

5. Rinse thoroughly in water at the same temperature as the wash water to avoid shocking the fiber and minimize felting.

6. Use the fabric wet if dyeing immediately or line-dry away from sunlight, which yellows wool.

Most fabrics should be thoroughly rinsed and washed after all dyeing procedures. Unfixed dye must be removed to prevent bleeding and crocking. Many dyes exhaust during the dye process, and unfixed dyes easily rinse away, but fiber-reactive dyes, mainly Procion MX, need especially thorough rinsing and washing. I prefer to use Synthrapol detergent because it was formulated to remove unfixed dye. Some artists prefer to use Orvus Paste by Procter & Gamble (available from farm and tack suppliers) for washing silk because it leaves a softer hand. Neither contains perfumes or optical whiteners that are found in many commercial laundry detergents and interfere with further dye processes. See page 128 for water temperatures used in this book, which can be critical in removing unfixed dye. When washing and drying, do not add fabric softener or dryer sheets—they will interfere with any additional dyeing.

Fiber-Reactive Dyes

Procion MX requires more care and attention to temperature than Cibacron F or Procion H. First, rinse the dyed fabric in cool water to remove the salt and make the unfixed dye more soluble, then wash it in hot, soapy water and rinse thoroughly in hot water.

Handwashing. Rinse in cool running water or in a bucket until very little color runs out. Wash in a bucket of hot water with ½ teaspoon (2.5 ml) Synthrapol per yard (meter) of fabric. Wash thoroughly for 10 minutes (5 minutes for Cibacron F). Rinse in warm water. Black and very dark colors may need several rinses in warm water. Continue rinsing until the water is clear.

Machine washing. Set the machine on "warm wash/warm rinse." Immerse fabric after the machine fills and begins to agitate. Run the machine through a complete cycle with water alone. Reset the machine on "hot wash/warm rinse." Add 1 teaspoon (5 ml) Synthrapol for a small load or up to 2 tablespoons (30 ml) for a large load. Run the machine through a complete cycle. Check during the last rinse whether the water is still colored: dark colors may require additional rinse cycles.

Dry on a clothesline or in a dryer.

Acid Dyes

Handwashing. Rinse fabric under cool running water or in a bucket until very little color runs out. Wash in a bucket of cool water with ½ teaspoon (2.5 ml) Synthrapol per yard (meter) of fabric. Rinse in warm water. The last rinse should be clear. When washing wool, use either cool or warm water for both washing and rinsing as drastically changing the temperature promotes felting.

Machine washing. Set the machine on "warm wash/warm rinse." Add fabric after the machine fills and begins to agitate. Run the machine through a complete cycle. Reset the machine on "hot wash/warm rinse." Add 1 teaspoon (5 ml) Synthrapol for a small load or up to 2 tablespoons (30 ml) for a large load. Run the machine through a complete cycle. Do not machine wash wool unless felting is desired.

Dry on a clothesline away from sunlight, which yellows wool, or in a dryer.

Vat Dyes

Handwashing. Wash fabric thoroughly in a bucket of hot water with ½ teaspoon (2.5 ml) Synthrapol per yard (meter) of fabric. Rinse in warm water until the water is clear.

Machine washing. Set the machine on "hot wash/warm rinse." Add 1 teaspoon (5 ml) Synthrapol for a small load or up to 2 tablespoons (30 ml) for a large load after the machine fills. Immerse the fabric and run the machine through a complete cycle.

Dry on a clothesline or in a dryer.

Indigo on Cotton and Silk

Handwashing. Place fabric in a bucket of hot water with ½ teaspoon (2.5 ml) Synthrapol per yard (meter) or shave a small amount of Ivory bar soap into the water. Add sodium hexametaphosphate if using soap with hard water. Wash thoroughly. Rinse in warm water until the water is clear.

Machine washing. Set the machine on "hot wash/warm rinse." Add shaved Ivory bar soap or 1 teaspoon (5 ml) Synthrapol for a small load or up to 2 tablespoons (30 ml) Synthrapol for a large load. Add sodium hexametaphosphate if using soap with hard water. Add fabric and run the machine through a complete cycle.

Dry on a clothesline or in a dryer.

Indigo on Wool

Wash the fabric by hand in a bucket of warm water with ½ teaspoon (2.5 ml) Synthrapol or shave a small amount of Ivory bar soap into the water. Add sodium hexametaphosphate if using soap with hard water. Wash thoroughly, agitating gently. Rinse in warm water until it is clear. Drastically changing the water temperature will promote felting. Machine washing is not recommended because agitation causes felting.

Neutralize the fabric by soaking in a solution of 2 tablespoons (30 ml) plain distilled vinegar in 1 gallon (3.8 l) water the temperature of the wash and rinse water, then rinse again in plain water.

Dry on a clothesline away from sunlight, which causes wool to yellow.

Inkodyes

Handwashing. Rinse fabric under cool running water or in a bucket until very little color runs out. Wash in a bucket of hot water combined with ½ teaspoon (2.5 ml) Synthrapol per yard (meter) of fabric. Rinse in warm water until the water is clear.

Machine washing. Set the machine on "warm wash/warm rinse." Add fabric after the machine fills and begins to agitate. Run the machine through a complete cycle. Reset the machine on "hot wash/warm rinse." Add 1 teaspoon (5 ml) Synthrapol for a small load or up to 2 tablespoons (30 ml) for a large load. Dark colors may need additional rinse cycles.

Dry on a clothesline or in a dryer.

Disperse Dyes

Handwashing. Rinse fabric under cool running water or in a bucket until very little color runs out. Wash fabric in a bucket of cool water with ½ teaspoon (2.5 ml) Synthrapol per yard (meter). Rinse in warm water until the water is clear.

Machine washing. Set the machine on "warm wash/warm rinse." Add fabric after the machine fills and begins to agitate. Run the machine through a complete cycle. Reset the machine on "hot wash/warm rinse." Add 1 teaspoon (5 ml) Synthrapol for a small load or up to 2 tablespoons (30 ml) for a large load. Run the machine through a complete cycle.

Dry on a clothesline or in a dryer.

Discharging with Thiourea Dioxide, Jacquard Discharge Paste, Sodium Hydrosulfite, Color Remover, or Chlorine Bleach

Handwashing. Rinse fabric thoroughly, then wash in a bucket of warm water with ½ teaspoon (2.5 ml) Synthrapol per yard (meter) of fabric. Rinse in warm water.

Machine washing. Set the machine on "warm wash/warm rinse." Add 1 teaspoon (5 ml) Synthrapol for a small load or up to 2 tablespoons (30 ml) for a large load. Add fabric after the machine fills and begins to agitate. Run the machine through a complete cycle.

Dry on a clothesline or in a dryer.

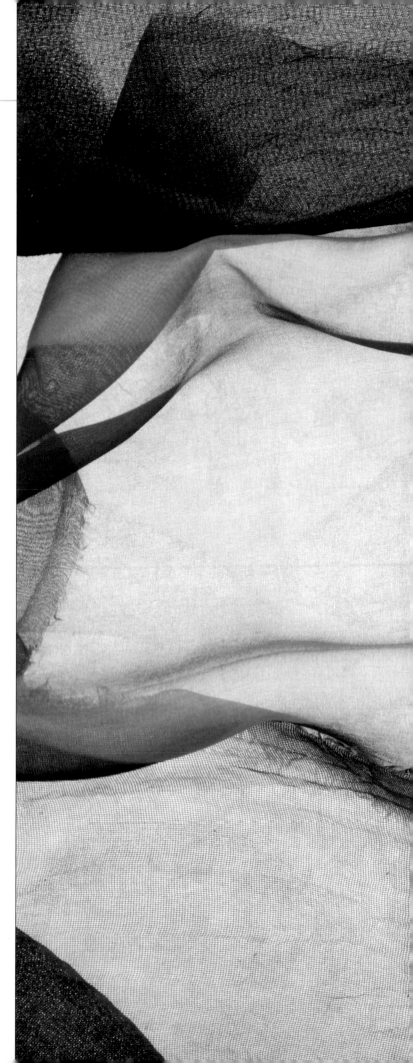

You can use either dye powders or stock solutions for mixing dye colors. Except for the very reactive Procion MX dye, I recommend using stock solutions as small amounts of liquid are easier to measure and there is less chance of inhaling dye powder.

Stock Solutions

Cibracron F, Procion H, Kiton, 1:2 Metal Complex (Lanaset), WashFast acid (with some exceptions) and disperse dyes mix easily with water for stock solutions. A 2% stock solution of fiber-reactive dyes produces a medium depth of shade (DOS) while a 1% stock solution gives the same depth of shade for disperse and acid dyes, except acid black, which requires a 6% solution. The following recipe makes 500 ml of a medium DOS with dye quantities calculated for each of these three classes of dye.

1. Weigh dye powder very accurately on a piece of waxed paper and slide the dye off the paper into a nonreactive pan. Save the paper for Step 2.
   Fiber-reactive (Cibracron F, Procion H): 10.0 g
   Acid (Lanaset, WashFast, Kiton): 5.0 g
   Disperse: 5.0 g

2. Fill a graduated cylinder with 200 ml warm water. Holding the waxed paper on a slant over the pan, pour the water over it to wash any remaining dye particles into the pan.

3. Add one drop Synthrapol.

4. Stir to thoroughly dissolve the dye. No dye particles should be visible in the container.

5. For disperse dyes, heat and stir the mixture for 3 to 4 minutes, but DO NOT BOIL. You may need to heat Washfast acid dyes to 185° to 195° F (85 to 91° C) to dissolve them.

6. Pour the solution into a graduated cylinder that holds at least 500 ml.

7. Pour a little warm water into the empty pan. Swirl it around the pan to dissolve any dye remaining on the sides of the pan. Add this to the solution in the graduated cylinder.

8. Repeat Step 7 until the pan is clean and the solution is at the 500 ml mark. Do not go over this mark.

9. Transfer the dye solution to a covered glass jar or plastic container for storage. Label container with dye type, dye color, and date.

10. Store stock solutions in a dark, cool place. If refrigerated, return to room temperature before using.

Calculating Dye Quantities

Record your calculations on the "Dye Worksheet" on page 119. WOF stands for weight of fiber or fabric, DOS is depth of shade, and DSS is dye stock solution.

Stock Solution Hints

- Shelf life of stock solutions: Cibracron F, 2 weeks at room temperature or 2 months refrigerated; Procion H, 2 months at room temperature or 1 year refrigerated; Lanaset and Washfast acid, 6 months to a year at room temperature; Disperse, 2 to 3 years at room temperature.
- If yellow Kiton acid dye crystallizes during storage, shake the dye container thoroughly, pour into a pan, and stir and heat until dissolved.
- Red WashFast acid dye is difficult to dissolve. Add 2 g urea per 200 ml stock solution as a wetting agent to help prevent clotting and thickening.
- Color changes or thickening in Lanaset stock solutions will not affect the final color.
- If mold forms on stored acid solutions, skim it from the surface and filter the solution through layers of cheesecloth or pantyhose. Heat the solution to kill the remaining spores. It is now ready to use.
- For paler colors, use ½ the amount of stock solution, and for darker colors, use twice as much stock solution as for a medium shade.
- For a 6% acid black, use 6 times as much 1% stock solution.
- Stock solutions of disperse dyes look opaque and chalky because they are actually suspensions of dye particles, not solutions. The particles will settle on standing. Shake or stir well before using.
- Stock solutions are easily measured with a syringe or graduated cylinder.

Dry dye powder: WOF x % DOS = total dye needed (by weight)

Example: 900 g x 2% = 18 g

Stock solution: $\dfrac{\text{WOF x \% DOS}}{\text{\% DSS}}$ = total DSS needed (by volume)

Example: $\dfrac{900 \text{ g x 2\%}}{1\% \text{ DSS}}$ = 1800 ml

Calculating Quantities for Color Mixing

To mix colors, you must calculate the quantity of each color in the blend. Always add the amounts after calculating to make sure that the total dye amount is correct.

Dry dye powder: WOF x % DOS = total dye needed (by weight)

Example: 900 g x 2% = 18 g

Example for a red-orange using 85% yellow and 15% red dyes:

18 g x 85% yellow = 15.3 g
18 g x 15% red = 2.7 g
Total = 18 g

Stock solution: $\dfrac{\text{WOF x \% DOS}}{\text{\% DSS}}$ = total DSS needed (by volume)

Example: $\dfrac{900 \text{ g x 2\%}}{1\% \text{ DSS}}$ = 1800 ml

Example for a red-orange using 85% yellow and 15% red dyes:

1800 ml x 85% yellow = 1530 ml
1800 ml x 15% red = 270 ml
Total = 1800 ml

Screen printing, stamping, and stenciling dyes on fabric require a thickener to keep the dye in specified areas. The thickener must allow the dye to go into the fabric without bleeding, remain stable during dye fixation, and wash out without leaving a residue. A paste that is too thin may migrate beyond the design area; one that is too thick may not fix to the fabric and/or clog the mesh of a screen. In general, a thin, lightweight fabric needs a thicker paste and a textured, coarser fabric needs a thinner paste to penetrate the weave structure. The thickness or consistency of the printing solution is a matter of preference and printing technique.

The most common thickener used with fiber-reactive, acid, union, and other dyes is sodium alginate. Early dye thickeners were starches, which bonded preferentially with fiber-reactive dyes and thus not with the fabric. Sodium alginate, a protein made from seaweed, does not bond with these dyes, allowing the dye to go into the fabric. Sodium alginate has an indefinite shelf life in dry form; even after mixing with water, it can be stored for months in a cool place or refrigerator. Discard it when it begins to smell like ammonia. When dried on fabric, sodium alginate remains flexible and does not split delicate fabrics. It does not brown when heated or steamed but does break down, which allows easier washout. One disadvantage is that it releases less color than Monagum when used with disperse dyes. Grades available in the United States include high viscosity, low solids and low viscosity, high solids. For general printing, use high-viscosity, low-solids sodium alginate because it yields more thickener and therefore costs less. But for printing fine details or lines, especially on silk, or for printing one color on top of another, high solids, low viscosity gives better results. Sodium alginate is manufactured from different types of algae; it is sold under various names, including Manutex, Keltex, and Lamitex, and simply as alginate together with the name of the distributor.

Other thickeners used for textile techniques include Monagum, a modified starch gum. It allows for finer details when printing with disperse dyes and can be used to thicken bleach. P4 is a thickener especially suited to mixing with sodium bisulfate in the dévoré process.

Steaming is required to fix some dyes permanently to fabric. This procedure is used with thickened Procion MX, Cibacron F, Procion H, Lanaset, WashFast acid, and disperse dyes, as well as thickened Thiox discharge. The moisture from steaming swells the fibers of the dyed or printed fabric, making them receptive to the transfer of dyestuff or chemical from the thickener. It is imperative that the thickener absorbs enough water to dissolve the dye or chemical but not so much that it spreads out. Heat accelerates fixing. Steaming times vary depending on the fabric, dye, process, chemical, and type of steamer. Water drops must not touch the fabric during steaming, or dyes may bleed. Low-tech methods are appropriate for small quantities, but professional steamers are best for production.

Low-Tech Methods

You can use an oven, canning kettle, pressure cooker or canner. Roll dry fabric in unprinted newsprint, steaming paper, an old sheet, or nonwoven synthetic interfacing; all these wrappers should be wider than the fabric. The fabric must not have pleats or folds or touch the sides of the container. Fold the bundle back on itself or coil to fit the kettle and secure with cotton string (see illustration below).

Oven method. Place a flat pan containing 1 inch (2.5 cm) of water on the lowest rack of an oven preheated to the temperature specified below for the dye you are using. Place the rolled fabric on a rack just above the pan. For Procion MX and Cibacron F, steam 30 minutes at 285° F (141° C), then reroll the fabric in the opposite direction and steam 30 minutes longer. For Procion H, steam 5 to 15 minutes at 300° F (149° C), reroll, and steam 5 to 15 minutes longer. For Lanaset, steam 15 minutes at 285° F (141° C), reroll, and steam 15 minutes longer. Steam thickened Thiox 10 to 20 minutes at 285° F (141° C), reroll, and steam 10 to 20 minutes longer. Add more water to the pan as necessary to keep steam coming.

Canning kettle with rack method. Place the rack upside down in a canning kettle. Add water to within ¾ inch (1.9 cm) of the rack and heat to boiling. Place a firm

layer of felt or quilted fabric or a circle of upholstery foam on top of the rack. Place two circles of unprinted newsprint on top of the padding. Put in the rolled fabric, keeping it away from the sides of the kettle to prevent bleeding of the dyes. Add another set of newsprint circles, then a final layer of padding. Finally, wrap the lid with a towel to catch condensation, place the lid on the kettle, and heat until steam escapes from under the lid. Begin timing. Steam thickened Procion MX, Cibacron F, or Lanaset 15 to 30 minutes; Procion H, 30 to 45 minutes; WashFast acid, 30 to 60 minutes; disperse dye, 30 minutes; and thickened Thiox, 10 to 20 minutes. Heavier fabric may need to be unrolled and rerolled during steaming. Wear oven mitts and open the pot very carefully. An electric rice cooker/steamer can also be used for small projects. Don't use either of these containers for food.

Pressure cooker or canner method. In the bottom of the pot, place an expandable vegetable steamer (or improvise a rack from 3 or 4 shallow cans from tuna or pet food with one or both ends removed) and 2 inches (5 cm) of water. Place a firm layer of felt, quilted fabric, or upholstery foam or eight layers of circles cut from unprinted newsprint on top of the rack. Put the fabric bundle in the pressure cooker, keeping it away from the sides of the kettle to prevent bleeding of the dyes. Add more padding, then put on the lid and pressure gauge. Heat the pressure cooker until the pressure regulator begins to rock slowly. Adjust heat to maintain a slow, steady rocking motion, and begin timing. Steam thickened Procion MX, Cibacron F, or Procion H for 5 to 10 minutes. Do not exceed the manufacturer's pressure limits. Cool the cooker to reduce pressure before opening the lid.

Steam iron method. Pieces of fabric with an area of up to 12 by 18 inches (30.5 by 45.5 cm) can be steamed with an iron. In a room with good ventilation, steam at the setting for the fiber for 5 minutes with Procion MX and Cibacron F or 10 minutes with Procion H. If the iron spits water, colors may bleed.

Professional Steamers

Professional artists' steamers are of two main types. The vertical steamer has an electric element built into the base while the horizontal version is placed on a stove. Regardless of the steamer's orientation, the fabric is rolled around a core of cardboard or metal mesh.

1. Lay fabric to be dyed on a flat surface. Make sure there are no folds or pleats in the fabric, which could become permanent during steaming. Place a layer of unprinted newsprint, steaming paper, lightweight synthetic interfacing, or an old sheet on top of the fabric. (All coverings should be slightly wider than the fabric.) The covering will keep the dye from transferring during steaming. Lay the cardboard or mesh tube at the edge of the fabric and covering and roll up. When one piece of covering ends, add another, overlapping ends.

2. One long or several shorter lengths of fabric or many small pieces such as scarves can be rolled (without touching) onto the tube.

3. After all the fabric pieces are on the tube, roll on three more layers of covering. Tape or bind the outermost layer with cotton string. The rolled bundle can be as wide as 8 inches (20 cm) in diameter.

4. Fill the bottom of the steamer with water. If using a vertical steamer, cover the heating element with at least 2 inches (5 cm) of water.

5. Place the rolled tube in the steamer rack.

6. Heat and begin timing when you see steam escaping from the vent. The more fabric there is on the tube, the longer it will need to steam. Make sure that the steamer does not boil dry. Steam Procion MX, Cibacron F, or Lanaset 15 to 30 minutes; Procion H, 30 to 45 minutes; WashFast acid, 30 to 60 minutes; and thickened Thiox, 10 to 20 minutes.

7. Turn off the steamer. Be careful, it will be very hot! Wearing oven mitts or other hand protection, remove the roll of fabric.

8. Remove the string or tape and unroll.

Opposite: Canning kettle method of steaming. Although not visible, the canning kettle rack has been turned upside down and a round piece of upholstery foam placed on top of it. The dyed fabric has been rolled in a piece of sheeting fabric and secured with string so that it does not touch the side of the pot. A round of upholstery foam will next be placed on top of the fabric roll. An old towel has been clipped over the lid of the kettle to collect condensation during steaming. Photo by Tom Liden.

U.S./Metric Conversions and Measure Equivalents

Volume/Fluid Measurements

Cup	Fluid Ounce	Tablespoon	Teaspoon	Milliliters
			¼ tsp	1.25 ml
			½ tsp	2.5 ml
			¾ tsp	3.7 ml
			1 tsp	5 ml
	0.5 fluid oz	1 tbl	3 tsp	15 ml
⅛ cup	1 fluid oz	2 tbl	6 tsp	30 ml
¼ cup	2 fluid oz	4 tbl	12 tsp	59 ml
⅓ cup	2⅔ fluid oz	5⅓ tbl	16 tsp	79 ml
½ cup	4 fluid oz	8 tbl	24 tsp	118 ml
⅔ cup	5⅓ fluid oz	10⅔ tbl	32 tsp	158 ml
¾ cup	6 fluid oz	12 tbl	36 tsp	177 ml
1 cup	8 fluid oz	16 tbl	48 tsp	237 ml
2 cups	16 fluid oz	32 tbl	96 tsp	474 ml
4 cups	32 fluid oz	(1 quart)		946 ml
16 cups	128 fluid oz	(1 gallon)		3,800 ml
				(= 3.8 liters)

Volume

1 gram water occupies 1 milliliter = 1 cubic centimeter
1000 ml = 1 liter

Length

1 inch = 2.54 centimeters (cm)
36 inches = 1 yard = 0.9 meter (m)
100 cm = 1 m = 39.4 inches

Weight

1 ounce (oz) = 28.3 grams (g)
16 oz = 1 pound (lb) = 454 g
2.2 lb = 1 kilogram (kg) = 1000 g

Temperature

212° F = 100° C = boiling point of water at sea level
32° F = 0° C = freezing point of water at sea level

Water Temperatures

The following water temperatures are noted in recipes found in this book:
Cool, 65° to 75° F (18° to 24° C)
Room temperature, 75° to 90° F (24° to 32° C)
Warm, 95° to 115° F (35° to 46° C)
Hot, 120° to 140° F (49° to 60° C)

Glossary

Thanks to Doug Wilson of Calgary, Alberta, Canada, for his assistance with this glossary. Doug's complete Dyes and Dyeing Glossary can be found at http://list.emich.edu/~dyers/pdfs/dyeglossary.PDF

Acetic acid. An organic acid used in many dye processes. Vinegar is about 5% acid, requiring large amounts because it is so dilute. 56% and 28% acetic acid, available from photographic darkroom suppliers, is recommended for quantity dyeing. Glacial acetic acid, commonly sold for industrial purposes, is 95% to 99% pure acetic acid, pungent and flammable. It is called "glacial" because it crystallizes at about 62° F (17° C). Concentrated solutions of acetic acid are corrosive. Wear rubber gloves and a respirator with acid gas cartridges when using them.

Acid. A chemical having a pH of less than 7. The lower the pH value, the stronger the acid. *Always add acid to water:* some acids produce so much heat when mixed with water that they boil and spatter.

Acid dye. A large class of dyes used on protein fibers including wool, mohair, alpaca, angora, and cashmere; feathers; leather; and fur, as well as on silk, nylon, and some acrylics. They are applied in a bath that may range from strongly acid to neutral, at temperatures approaching boiling. Major subgroups include Wash-Fast acid, milling, supermilling, leveling acid, 1:1 metal-complex, and 2:1 metal-complex. The distinction between some of the groups is vague.

Albegal SET. Used with 1:2 metal-complex dyes such as Lanaset and Sabraset to promote level dyeing by retarding the rate at which the dye migrates into the fiber.

Alkali (base). A chemical having a pH greater than 7. The higher the pH value, the stronger the alkali.

Ammonium sulfate. A crystalline salt used most commonly with WashFast acid dyes. When ammonium sulfate is heated in a dyebath, the ammonia evaporates, leaving behind a sulfuric acid solution. As the dyebath slowly becomes more acidic, the dye molecules evenly attach to the fiber.

Antichlor. A reducing agent, such as sodium bisulfite, used to neutralize chlorine bleach used in discharging.

Baking soda. See sodium bicarbonate.

Batch curing. Fixing Procion MX and Cibacron F dyes by wrapping damp, dyed fiber in plastic and allowing it to sit for at least 24 to 48 hours at 70° F (21° C) to complete the reaction of the dye with the fiber.

Bast fibers. Cellulose fibers from plant stems, including flax, ramie, hemp, and jute.

Binder. A material used to attach a pigment to fabric. Binders in textile paints are acrylic polymers.

Bleach, chlorine. A 5% sodium hypochlorite solution, used for discharging dye colors by oxidation. See oxidizing agent.

Burn-out paste. See dévoré.

Buffer. A substance, such as sodium acetate, that helps to maintain the pH of a dyebath during the dye process.

Calgon T. Trade name for sodium hexametaphosphate without additives, a water softener. Water softeners sold in the grocery store usually contain additives.

Carrier. A chemical that aids disperse dyeing of polyester by swelling the fibers so that the dye can penetrate. Carriers are obsolescent in industry, partly because they are noxious and environmentally harmful.

Cellulose fibers. Fibers from plants, including cotton, linen, ramie, jute, and hemp. Viscose rayon and Tencel are man-made, regenerated cellulose fibers.

Cibacron F. A family of fiber-reactive dyes that are less reactive than Procion MX and intended for application between 113° and 150° F (45° and 65° C).

Citric acid. An acid sometimes used in dyeing as an alternative to acetic acid. It can act as a sequestering agent for some metals, so it may be inappropriate for some metal-containing dyes such as complex metal dyes (Lanaset and Sabraset).

Covalent bond. A strong chemical bond in which electrons are shared between atoms in a molecule. Covalent bonds formed between fibers and fiber-reactive dyes make the resulting colors very washfast.

Crocking. The transfer of color from dyed or pigmented fabric by rubbing.

Depth of shade (DOS). The ratio of the weight of dye to the weight of goods dyed, usually expressed as a percentage. The greater the percentage, the deeper the color.

Dévoré. A burn-out technique in which patterns made by a substance on fabric destroy some of the fibers. Dévoré on cellulose fabric uses sodium bisulfate to eat away the fibers.

Discharge. Stripping of color from fabric, leaving white or different color behind. Dyes vary in how easily they can be discharged. The most common discharge agents for studio dyers are thiourea dioxide, Jacquard discharge paste, sodium hydrosulfite, and chlorine bleach.

Disperse dye. A dye that is almost totally insoluble in water and exists in the dyebath as a suspension of minute particles. It is effective on polyester, nylon, and acetate. Disperse dyes are also used for sublimation printing of synthetic fibers and are the colorants used in crayons and inks sold for making iron-on transfers.

DOS. See depth of shade.

Dye. A usually soluble colorant whose molecules attach to fiber molecules. By contrast, a pigment sits on the surface and is attached to the fiber with a binder.

Dye sublimation. See sublimation.

Exhaust. The transfer of dye from the dyebath to the fiber. An ideal dye would exhaust totally, that is, all the dye in the dyebath would end up in the fiber. Whereas many acid dyes exhaust to the point where the dye liquor is nearly colorless, exhaustion of fiber-reactive dyes generally is moderate.

Fastness. The resistance of a fabric to change color from exposure to light, washing, or rubbing.

Fiber. The raw material from which yarns and fabrics are created. Fibers may be natural (from plants or animals) or manufactured.

Fiber-reactive dye. A dye, such as Procion MX, Procion H, or Cibacron F, that attaches to fiber molecules by forming covalent bonds. Most are intended for cellulose fibers but can also be used on protein fibers. These dyes are known for their bright colors and easy mixing to produce a wide range of colors. They are lightfast and washfast.

Fugitive. Fading, bleeding, changing, or disappearing on exposure to light or washing.

Glauber's salt (sodium sulfate). Often used instead of table salt (sodium chloride) in dyeing as a leveling agent or to promote exhaustion of the dyebath.

Hand. The feel of a fabric or yarn. Unlike dyes, many textile paints change the hand of a fabric.

Hue. A color name, such as red or purple. Also, a pure form of a color.

Hydro (hydros in Britain). See sodium hydrosulfite.

Hydrolysis. The decomposition of a chemical by reaction with water. In an MX dyebath, some of the dye bonds with the water (hydrolyzes) instead of with the fabric.

Hygroscopic. Readily taking up and retaining moisture. The tendency of many dry chemicals to absorb moisture from the air makes it necessary to keep them in sealed containers.

Indigo. A vat dye that is probably one of the oldest colorants used for textiles. Originally extracted from plants, indigo is now usually synthetic. Unlike other vat dyes, it has poor washfastness.

Immersion dyeing. A procedure in which the fabric is submerged in a dyebath to absorb color as opposed to direct application, in which the fabric is painted, stamped, or printed with dyes.

Intensity (chroma). The brightness, dullness, or saturation of a color.

Kiton dye. See leveling acid dye.

Leuco. Referring to the reduced, soluble form of a vat dye, converted from its original, insoluble form in an alkaline dyebath when oxygen is removed by a reducing agent. When the yarn or fabric is removed from the leuco dyebath, oxygen from the air changes the dye back to an insoluble compound, which is trapped in the fiber molecule.

Level dyeing. A uniform shade throughout a dyed fabric or yarn.

Leveling acid dye. A class of acid dyes noted for bright colors and ease of leveling but less washfast than other acid dyes.

Leveling agent. A substance added to a dyebath to promote even coloration.

Lightfast. Resistance of a dye to fading on exposure to light. Colors blended from dyes with different degrees of lightfastness may change color over time as the component dyes fade at different rates.

Ludigol. Trade name for sodium m-nitrobenzene sulfonic acid, an oxidizing agent that protects dyes and prevents reduction or changes in color that could occur at high pH and high temperature, such as during steaming of Procion H dyes. Because it is a benzene derivative, it is a health hazard. Wear a dust mask when working with the dry powder.

Lye (sodium hydroxide, caustic soda). A strong alkali used in dye recipes requiring a high pH, including vat dyes. It can cause severe skin burns and must be used with great care, including wearing eye protection and rubber gloves. Never use aluminum vessels or tools with lye, since they will corrode, generating explosive hydrogen.

Material Safety Data Sheet (MSDS). Technical information about a product, prepared by the manufacturer, including possible safety hazards and available online, with other safety information, at www.hazard.com/msds.

Mercerization. Treatment of cotton thread with a caustic soda (lye) solution. The process rounds the fibers, producing a slight sheen and making mercerized fabrics look about 25% darker when dyed than comparable nonmercerized fabrics.

Metal-complex (metallized) dye. A dye in which one or two dye molecules form a close permanent association with a metal atom. Lanaset and Sabraset are brands of 1:2 metal-complex dyes, which have two dye molecules per metal atom to help the dye attach to the fiber. These dyes have excellent washfastness but can be difficult to level.

Migration. Spreading of color through the fabric.

Monagum. A trade name for carboxymethyl starch, used to thicken bleach for discharge.

MSDS. See Material Safety Data Sheet.

MX dye. A family of fiber-reactive dyes popular with textile artists working with cellulose fibers. They can also be used for wool and other protein fibers in acid solutions.

Nylon (polyamide). The oldest synthetic polymer used for textiles. It is usually dyed with acid dyes but can also be dyed with disperse dyes.

Overdyeing. Dyeing over a previously dyed color or area of fabric, yarn, or fiber. The overdyed area is always darker than the original color.

Oxidizing agent. A chemical that causes another chemical to lose electrons. When fabric is removed from an indigo dyebath, oxgen reacts with the dye, changing the color. Chlorine bleach is a strong oxidizing agent. See also reducing agent.

pH. The pH is a measurement of the acidity or alkalinity of a solution. On a scale of 0 to 14, a pH of 7 is considered neutral, neither alkaline nor acid; distilled water has a pH of 7. A pH level below 7 is acid and above 7 is alkaline. As the pH value increases, the alkalinity of the solution increases and vice versa. Different dyeing processes require specific pH levels.

To measure the pH of a dyebath, use a pH meter or pH paper. The latter is readily available from dye suppliers. Dip the tip of one end of a piece of pH paper in the bath, allowing the moisture to wick up on the paper so that the dye won't mask caused by the pH of the solution. When a color change occurs, compare the new color to the reference color on the packaging, which will indicate the pH of the bath, and thus its acidity or alkalinity.

Pigment. A colored substance, usually in the form of a fine powder, that is relatively insoluble in water. Textile paints comprise pigment (color) and a binder, which adheres them to the fabric.

Polyester. A variety of synthetic polymers used both for solid plastics and for fibers. It is dyed almost exclusively with disperse dyes. Polyesters are very washfast because they are nearly impervious to water.

"Prepared for dyeing" (PFD). Designating a fabric that has been desized, scoured, and fully bleached, and that has not been treated with substances, such as optical brighteners or softeners, that will interfere with dyeing. Nevertheless, even PFD fabrics should still be washed before dyeing (see "Preparing Fabric for Dyeing " on page 120).

Primary color. One of the set of colors from which all other colors are derived.

Procion. A trade name, originally belonging to Imperial Chemical Industries of Britain. Procion MX and H are fiber-reactive dyes.

Protein fibers. Fibers from animals, including wool, mohair, alpaca, cashmere, and silk.

Reducing agent. A chemical that causes another chemical to gain electrons. Reducing agents used in dye processes include thiourea dioxide, sodium bisulfite, and sodium hydrosulfite. Reducing agents are used to discharge color and to convert an insoluble vat dye to its soluble form. See also oxidizing agent.

Resist. A substance or treatment applied to fabric to prevent penetration of dyes, paints, or chemicals. Mechanical resists include wax, starch, and glue. Physical resists include binding, clamping, wrapping, stitching, knotting, and folding the fabric.

Salt. See sodium chloride.

Scouring. Removal of contaminants and impurities from the fiber or fabric that can interfere with dyeing (see "Preparing Fabric for Dyeing " on page 120).

Secondary color. A color resulting from mixing two primary colors.

Shade. A color with added black.

Shelf life. The period of time that a product can be stored and remain usable. Shelf life can generally be maximized by storage at low temperature and away from bright light. Store dry chemicals in tightly closed, moisture-proof containers.

Shibori. Japanese term describing bound, stitched, folded, twisted, or knotted resist techniques to form a diffused edge pattern in the dyed cloth.

Soda ash. See sodium carbonate.

Sodium acetate. See buffer.

Sodium alginate. An extract of seaweed used to thicken dyes for direct application (see "Thickeners and Printing" on page 125).

Sodium bicarbonate (bicarbonate of soda, baking soda). A weak alkali often used when printing with thickened fiber-reactive dyes. It decomposes to sodium carbonate (soda ash) at high temperatures with steam, aiding in the reaction of Procion MX dye with the fabric.

Sodium bisulfate. The active ingredient in the burn-out solution for dévoré on cellulose fibers. Do not confuse this with sodium bisulfite.

Sodium bisulfite. A mild reducing agent, used in dyeing as an antichlor. Do not confuse this with sodium bisulfate.

Sodium carbonate (soda ash, sal soda). A weak base or alkali used in fiber-reactive dyeing to promote attachment of the dye to fiber molecules. Soda ash is hygroscopic, so it must be stored in a sealed container.

Sodium chloride (table salt). In fiber-reactive dyeing, salt promotes even absorption of the dye by the fiber. The darker the color of dye, the more salt is required.

Sodium hexametaphosphate. Water softener, used to keep calcium, magnesium, and other metal ions in hard water from interfering with the dye process. Also sold as Metaphos or Calgon T. The Calgon sold in grocery stores contains additives and therefore should not be used for dyeing.

Sodium hydrosulfite. A reducing agent used in discharge techniques and in vat dyeing and the active ingredient in household color removers. It produces a strong sulfurous smell, is flammable, and must be handled with care.

Sodium hydroxide. See lye.

Sodium hypochlorite. See bleach, chlorine.

Sodium sulfate. See Glauber's salt.

Stock solution. A concentrated solution of dye dissolved in water. A 1% stock solution is composed of 1 g dye powder dissolved in 100 ml water.

Strike-off. A sample print taken to make sure that a screen is ready to print.

Sublimation. The conversion of a solid directly to a gas without passing through a liquid phase. Sublimation occurs when a pattern is printed on paper with disperse dyes and the dried pattern is heat-transferred to polyester, nylon, acrylic, or acetate rayon fabric. The dye gas becomes trapped in the fabric as it solidifies.

Supermilling. A class of acid dye used on wool and nylon. There is no clear distinction between milling and supermilling acid dyes. See WashFast acid dye.

Synthrapol. A detergent, originally formulated to remove unfixed fiber reactive dyes, used to wash fabric before and after dyeing.

Table salt. See sodium chloride.

Tencel. Trade name for lyocell, a modern regenerated cellulose fiber with much higher wet strength than viscose rayon. Tencel is dyed like other cellulose fibers.

Tertiary color (intermediate color). A color made by mixing a primary and a secondary color.

Thermoplastic. Softening when heated and rehardening when cooled. Polyester can be permanently formed or pleated by heating because of thermoplastic properties.

Thiourea dioxide (Thiox, Spectralite). A reducing agent used in vat dyeing and discharging. Monagum is used as a thickener for Thiox. Wear a respirator to keep from inhaling powder and vapors.

Tint. A paler color made by the addition of white.

Transfer printing. See sublimation.

Trisodium phosphate (TSP). Cleanser used to remove residual spinning oils from new printing screens. Wear rubber gloves to protect skin from strong solutions.

Union dye. A mixture of two or more classes of dye, typically used to dye blends of fibers. The household dyes sold in grocery stores are usually union dyes that contain a direct dye, which will work on cellulose fibers, and an acid dye, which will work on wool or nylon.

Urea. An organic ammonia compound used in dye printing to keep moisture from migrating outside the print area during steaming and in batch curing to keep fabric damp long enough that a dye reaction can occur.

Value. The lightness or darkness of a color.

Vat dye. A class of dyes, insoluble in water, that are converted to a soluble leuco form by a reducing agent. After the fabric has absorbed the leuco dye, it is removed from the dyebath; the dye is converted back to the insoluble form by oxidation and is trapped in the fiber. Indigo is a common vat dye. Inkodyes are vat dyes in a reduced soluble form.

Vinegar. See acetic acid.

Warp. Yarns running lengthwise in a fabric, parallel to the selvedge.

WashFast acid dye. A group of acid dyes selected by dye suppliers as being especially washfast. Dyes designated as washfast may come from a variety of dye classes.

Washfastness. Resistance of a dyed fabric to fading from washing.

Washing soda. See sodium carbonate.

Water/fiber ratio. The ratio between the volume of water in the dyebath and the weight of fabric or fiber being dyed. If you want to dye 100 g of fabric at a water/fiber ratio of 20:1, the amount of water that you need is 20 ml/g × 100 g fabric = 2000 ml water.

Water softener. See sodium hexametaphosphate.

Weft. Yarns running crosswise in a fabric, perpendicular to the selvedge.

Weight of fiber or fabric (WOF). Also called weight of goods (WOG). The dry weight of the fabric or yarn in a dye calculation.

Wetting out. Thorough dampening of the fabric before dyeing to ensure even dye penetration.

Bibliography

Balfour-Paul, Jenny. *Indigo*. London: British Museum Press, 2000.

Beevers, Sue. *Off-the-Shelf Fabric Painting: 30 Simple Recipes for Gourmet Results*. Lafayette, California: C&T, 2004.

Biegeleisen, J. I. *The Complete Book of Silk Screen Printing Production*. New York: Dover, 1963.

Birren, Faber. *Creative Color*. New York: Van Nostrand Reinhold, 1961.

Blumenthal, Betsy, and Kathryn Kreider. *Hands On Dyeing*. Loveland, Colorado: Interweave Press, 1988.

Brackmann, Holly. "Dévoré." *Surface Design Newsletter* 18, 1 (Winter 2004), 8–11.

____. "Shibori Meets Dévoré in a Handwoven Scarf." *Handwoven* 121 (September/October 2004), 52–55.

____. "More Than Plain Weave: Handwoven Dévoré." *Handwoven* 113 (January/February 2003), 48–52.

____. "Cloqué & Deflected Double Weave." In *The Best of Weaver's: Fabrics That Go Bump*. Souix Falls, South Dakota: XRX, 2002.

Brito, Karren K. *Shibori: Creating Color and Texture on Silk*. New York: Watson-Guptill, 2002.

____. "Designing for Discharge." *Surface Design Journal* 28, 2 (Spring 2004), 8–15.

____. "Dyeing with Indigo." *Surface Design Newsletter* 17, 4 (Fall 2004), 8–10.

____. "A Dye by Any Other Name." *Surface Design Newsletter* 16, 4 (Fall 2003), 8–10.

____. "Dye Hazards; Myths and Facts." Seattle: *Color Trends*, 1990.

____. "Honorable Discharge: Decolorization of Natural Fabrics, Part I." *Surface Design Newsletter* 15, 1 (Winter 2001), 8–10.

____. "Honorable Discharge: Decolorization of Natural Fabrics, Part II." *Surface Design Newsletter* 15, 2 (Spring 2002), 8–10.

Burch, Paula. "Lightfastness of Different Types of Dyes." www.pburch.net/dyeing.

____. "Which Procion MX Colors are Pure and Which Mixtures?" www.pburch.net/dyeing/FAQ/pureMXcolors.shtml.

____. "Which Washfast Acid Colors are Pure and Not Mixtures?" www.pburch.net/dyeing.

Color and Design on Fabric. Minneapolis, Minnesota: Creative Publishing International, 2000.

Colton, Virginia, ed. *Complete Guide to Needlework*. Pleasantville, New York: Reader's Digest Association, 2002.

Dahl, Carolyn. *Transforming Fabric: Color on Fabric and Life*. Paducah, Kentucky: American Quilter's Society, 1987.

Delamare, François, and Bernard Guineau. *Colors: The Story of Dyes and Pigments*. Translated by Sophie Hawkes. New York: Harry N. Abrams, 2000.

Druding, Susan. "Instructions for Use of Acid Levelling Dyes (Kiton Type) for dyeing yarn or fiber." www.straw.com/sig/kiton.html.

____. "Synthetic Dyestuffs: Fiber Structure." *Straw Into Gold Newsletter* 1, 2 (Summer 1978), 1, 14.

____. "Synthetic Dyestuffs: Acid Dyes." *Textile Artists' Newsletter* 1, 3 (Fall 1978), 3–4.

____. "Synthetic Dyestuffs: Fiber Reactive Dyes." *Textile Artists' Newsletter* 1, 4 (Winter 1978), 4–6, 20.

____. "Disperse Dyes." *Textile Artists' Newsletter* 2, 1 (Spring 1979), 1, 18–19.

____. "Thickeners." *Textile Artists' Newsletter* 2, 2 (Summer 1979), 1, 15–16.

____. "Stock Solution Method of Dyeing." *Textile Artists' Newsletter* 2, 3 (Fall–Winter 1979), 3, 17.

____. "Fiber Reactive Additions Enrich Artists' Palette." *Textile Artists' Newsletter* 3, 3 (1982), 1, 6.

____. "Cibacron F: Careful Planning Leads to Better Dyeing." *Textile Artists' Newsletter* 3, 3 (1982), 4, 6.

Dryden, Deborah M. *Fabric Painting and Dyeing for the Theatre*. Portsmouth, New Hampshire: Heinemann, 1983.

Dunnewold, Jane. *Complex Cloth: A Comprehensive Guide to Surface Design*. Bothell, Washington: That Patchwork Place, 1996.

____. *Improvisational Screen Printing*. San Antonio, Texas: Jane Dunnewold, 2003.

Hedley, Gwen. *Surfaces for Stitch*. Chicago: Quilters' Resource, 2000.

Hodges, Susie. "Dyes and Dyeing: A Survey of Methods and Products." *Textile Artists' Newsletter* 4, 1 (1984), 5–7.

Hudson, Marj. "Solutions: Acids and Alkalis." *Color Trends* 4, 1 (Winter 1987 and 1988), 22–23.

Issett, Ruth. *Color on Paper and Fabric*. Madison, Wisconsin: Hand Books Press, 1998.

Johnston, Ann. *Dye Painting!* Paducah, Kentucky: American Quilter's Society, 1992.

____. *Color by Accident: Low Water Immersion Dyeing*. Lake Oswego, Oregon: Ann Johnston, 1997.

____. *Color by Design: Paint and Print with Dye*. Lake Oswego, Oregon: Ann Johnston, 2001.

Johnston, Meda Parker, and Glen Kaufman. *Design on Fabrics*, 2d ed. New York: Van Nostrand Reinhold, 1981.

Kahn, Sherrill. *Creating with Paint: New Ways, New Materials*. Bothell, Washington: Martingale, 2001.

Kemshall, Linda. *Color Moves: Transfer Paints on Fabric.* Woodinville, Washington: Martingale, 2001.

Kendall, Tracy. *The Fabric and Yarn Dyer's Handbook.* London: Collins and Brown, 2001.

Klos, Dagmar. *The Dyer's Companion.* Loveland, Colorado: Interweave Press, 2004.

Knutson, Linda. *Synthetic Dyes for Natural Fibers.* Seattle, Washington: Madrona, 1982.

Lambert, Patricia, Barbara Staepelaere, and Mary G. Fry. *Color and Fiber.* West Chester, Pennsylvania: Schiffer, 1986.

Larson, Jack Lenor. *The Dyer's Art: Ikat, Batik, Plangi.* New York: Van Nostrand Reinhold, 1976.

Laury, Jean Ray. *The Fabric Stamping Handbook.* Lafayette, California: C&T, 2002.

____. *Imagery on Fabric: a Complete Surface Design Handbook*, 2d ed. Lafayette, California: C&T, 1997.

____. *The Photo Transfer Handbook.* Lafayette, California: C&T, 1999.

Leitch, Christopher, and Jason Pollen. "Shop Talk: Polyester." *Surface Design Newsletter* 11, 3 (Summer 1998), 11–12.

____. "Shop Talk: Synthetics." *Surface Design Newsletter* 10, 2 (Spring 1997), 9–10.

____. "Shop Talk: Discharge Processes: Part 1." *Surface Design Newsletter* 9, 4 (Summer 1996), 9–10.

____. "Shop Talk: Discharge Processes: Part 2." *Surface Design Newsletter* 10, 1 (Winter 1996), 9–10.

____. "Shop Talk: Discharge Processes: Part 3: Pigment Illuminated Discharge." *Surface Design Newsletter* 10, 3 (Summer 1997), 9–10.

McNamara, Andrea, and Patrick Snelling. *Design and Practice for Printed Textiles.* Melbourne, Australia: Oxford University Press, 1995.

Miller, Dorothy. *Indigo: From Seed to Dye.* Santa Cruz, California: Indigo Press, 1993.

Moyer, Susan Louise. *Silk Painting: The Artist's Guide to Gutta and Wax Resist Techniques.* New York: Watson-Guptill, 1991.

____. *Silk Painting for Fashion and Fine Art.* New York: Watson-Guptill, 1995.

Newman, Michelle, and Margaret Allyson. *Handpainting Fabric: Easy, Elegant Techniques.* New York: Watson-Guptill, 2003.

Noble, Elin. *Dyes and Paints: A Hands-On Guide to Coloring Fabric.* Bothell, Washington: Martingale, 1998.

Phillips, Marilyn V. *Ginny's Color System for Dyes for Home and Studio Use.* Los Alamos, New Mexico: Marilyn V. (Ginny) Phillips, 1999.

Prideaux, Vivien. *A Handbook of Indigo Dyeing.* Tunbridge Wells, Kent, England: Search Press, 2003.

Proctor, Richard M., and Jennifer Lew. *Surface Design for Fabric*, rev. ed. Seattle, Washington: University of Washington Press, 1995.

Rex, Susan. *Dyeing Wool and Other Protein Fibers: An Introduction to Acid Dyes.* Susan Rex, 2004. Self-published.

Sandberg, Gösta. *Indigo Textiles: Technique and History.* Asheville, North Carolina: Lark Books, 1989.

Schwalbach, Mathilda V., and James A. Schwalbach. *Silk-Screen Printing for Artists and Craftsmen.* New York: Dover, 1970.

Scrivano, Sandy. *Creative Surface Design: Painting, Stamping, Stenciling and Embossing Fabric & More.* Newtown, Connecticut: Taunton Press, 2002.

Simons, Max. *Dyes and Dyeing.* New York: Van Nostrand Reinhold, 1978.

Stocksdale, Joy. *Polychromatic Screen Printing.* Berkeley, California: Oregon Street Press, 1984.

Valentino, Richard, and Phyllis Mufson. *Fabric Printing: Screen Method.* San Francisco, California, 1975.

Vinroot, Sally, and Jennie Crowder. *The New Dyer.* Loveland, Colorado: Intereave Press, 1981.

Wada, Yoshiko. *Memory on Cloth: Shibori Now.* New York: Kodansha International, 2002.

Wada, Yoshiko, Mary Kellogg Rice, and Jane Barton. *Shibori: The Inventive Art of Japanese Resist Dyeing.* New York: Kodansha International, 1999.

Walter, Judy Anne. *Creating Color; A Dyer's Handbook.* Evanston, Illinois: Cooler By The Lake, 1989.

Wells, Kate. *Fabric Dyeing and Printing.* Loveland, Colorado: Interweave Press, 1997.

Widger, Katy J. *Color Wheel Fabric Dyeing.* Edgewood, New Mexico: Katy J. Widger, 1991.

Wipplinger, Michele. "Lanaset: Protein Fiber Dye." *Color Trends* 2, 1 (Fall 1985), 4–9.

____. "Cibacron F for Cellulose Fibers and Silk." *Color Trends* 2, 2 (Spring 1986), 3–6.

____. "Variegated Silks: Fiber Reactive Dyes, Discharge and Vat Dyes." *Color Trends* 2, 2 (Spring 1986), 13–15.

____. "Vat Dyes and Discharge for Fabrics." *Color Trends* 3, 2 (Summer 1987), 8–10.

Aljo Manufacturing Co., 81-83 Franklin St., New York, NY 10013; (866) 293-8913, (212) 226-2878; www.aljodye.com. Dyes and auxiliaries.

Batik Oetoro, 203 Avoca St., Randwick, NSW 2031, Australia; (61) 2 9398-6201; www.dyeman.com. Dyes, pigments, auxiliaries.

Carolina Biological Supply Co., 2700 York Rd., Burlington, NC 27215-3398; (800) 334-5551; www.carolina.com. Safety and lab equipment.

Clotilde LLC, PO Box 7500, Big Sandy, TX 75755-7500; (800) 772-2891; www.clotilde.com. Teflon sheets, sewing notions, unusual stuff.

Dharma Trading Co., PO Box 150916, San Rafael, CA 94915; (415) 456-7657, (800) 542-5227; www.dharmatrading.com. Store address: 1604 Fourth St., San Rafael, CA 94901. Synthetic and natural dyes, paints, auxiliaries, PFD fabric and clothing.

Dick Blick, PO Box 1267, Galesburg, IL 61402-1267; (800) 828-4548; www.dickblick.com. Art, screen printing, and Thermofax supplies.

Dover Publications Inc., 31 E. 2nd St., Mineola, NY 11501-3852; (516) 294-7000; www.doverpublications.com. Copyright-free images in books.

Earth Guild, 33 Haywood St., Asheville, NC 28801; (800) 327-8448, (828) 255-7818; www.earthguild.com. Synthetic and natural dyes, auxiliaries, PFD fabric.

Earthues, A Natural Color Company, 5129 Ballard Ave. NW, Seattle, WA 98107; (206) 789-1065; www.earthues.com. Natural dyes, auxiliaries, instant indigo.

EZ Screen Print, 2160 N. Wildflower Ln., Casa Grande, AZ 85222; (520) 423-0409; www.photoez.us. PhotoEZ light-sensitive emulsion precoated on nylon screen.

George Weil/Fibrecrafts, Old Portsmouth Rd., Peasmarsh, Guildford, Surrey GU3 1LZ, England; (44) 1 483-565800; www.fibrecrafts.com. Synthetic and natural dyes, paints, auxiliaries, PFD fabric.

Ginny Eckley, 2423 Kings Forest Dr., Kingwood, TX 77339; (281)358-2951; www.photoezsilkscreen.com. PhotoEZ light-sensitive emulsion precoated on nylon screen.

Habu Textiles, 135 West 29th St., Ste. 804, New York, NY 10001; (212) 239-3546; www.habutextiles.com. Natural-fiber yarns, including silk.

Lab Safety Supply Inc. PO Box 1368, Janesville, WI 53547-1368; (800) 356-0783; www.labsafety.com. Safety and lab equipment.

Maiwa Handprints Ltd., #6-1666 Johnston St., Granville Island, Vancouver, BC, Canada V6H 3S2; (604) 669-3939; www.maiwa.com. Synthetic and natural dyes, paints, PFD fabric and clothing.

Nasco, 4825 Stoddard Rd., PO Box 3837, Modesto, CA 95352-3837, or 901 Janesville Ave., PO Box 901, Fort Atkinson, WI 53538-0901; (800) 558-9595; www.enasco.com. Art and screen-printing supplies.

PRO Chemical & Dye, PO Box 14, Somerset, MA 02726; (800) 228-9393 (orders), (508) 676-3838 (technical assistance); www.prochemical.com. Synthetic dyes, auxiliaries, paints, PFD fabric and clothing. Website has excellent reference materials.

Rupert, Gibbon & Spider (Jacquard products), PO Box 425, Healdsburg, CA 95448; (800) 442-0455, (707) 433-9577; www.jacquardproducts.com. Synthetic and natural dyes, auxiliaries, paints, PFD fabric, prereduced indigo.

Screen-Trans Development Co., 100 Grand St., Moonachie, NJ 07074; (201) 933-7800; www.screentrans.com. Foil in many colors and adhesive. Starter kit.

Silkpaint! Corp., PO Box 18 INT, 18220 Waldron Dr., Waldron, MO 64092; (800) 563-0074, (816) 891-7774; www.silkpaint.com. P4 thickener, Fiber-Etch, Azeta poly/cotton.

Testfabrics Inc., PO Box 26, 415 Delaware Ave., West Pittiston, PA 18643; (570) 603-0432; www.testfabrics.com. PFD fabrics.

Textura Trading Co., 116 Pleasant St., Ste. 343, Easthampton, MA 01027; (877) 839-8872, (413) 282-0071; www.textura trading.com. Corespun cotton/poly yarn for dévoré.

Thai Silks, 252 State St., Los Altos, CA 94022; (650) 948-8611, (800) 722-7455 (outside CA), (800) 221-7455 (in CA); www.thaisilks.com. Rayon/silk velvet, silk fabrics and scarves.

Treenway Silks, 501 Musgrave Rd., Salt Spring Island, BC, Canada V8K 1V5; (888) 383-7455, (250) 653-2345; www.treenwaysilks.com. Silk yarns.

Vermont Country Store, PO Box 6999, Rutland, VT 05702-6999; (802) 362-8460; www.vermontcountrystore.com. Dry iron without steam vent holes.

Welsh Products, PO Box 845, 932 Grant St., Benicia, CA 94510; (800) 745-3255; www.welshproducts.com. Thermofax machines, screen and printing supplies, heat presses.

Whaleys (Bradford) Ltd., Harris Court, Great Horton, Bradford, West Yorkshire BD7 4EQ, England; 44 (0) 01274 576718; www.whaleys-bradford.ltd.uk. Azeta poly/cotton for dévoré.

Index to Fiber Artists
Page numbers in bold type indicate photographs.